The Novels of Arun Joshi

THE NOVELS OF ARUN JOSHI

Ed.

R.K. DHAWAN

PRESTIGE

Published by
Prestige Books
3/28, East Patel Nagar, New Delhi 110 008
in association with
Indian Society for Commonwealth Studies
New Delhi

ISBN: 81-85218-62-5

Phototypesetting by
Laser Impressions
New Delhi 110 028
Ph. 537756, 537296

Printed at
Mehra Offset Press
New Delhi 110 002

Contents

The Fictional World of Arun Joshi

R.K. DHAWAN

I

In an essay entitled "Bc oks," Joseph Conrad discusses the novelist's craft. While recognizing that the genesis of the creative process is inseparable from the artist's initial perception, he cautions the artist not to restrict himself to the experience of his own imagination in violation of the actuality of human experience:

> In truth every novelist must begin by creating for himself a world, great or little, in which he can honestly believe. This world cannot be made otherwise than in his own image: it is fated to remain individual and a little mysterious, and yet it must resemble something already familiar to the experience, the thoughts and the sensations of his readers.[1]

The artist, while creating his own world, must be cautious, lest he force his own sensations into some too-convenient a pattern. That is, he might not project mere reality. Conrad recognizes a reality beyond the phenomenal world, a reality which the artist could imagine and capture by giving a consistent form to the shapeless facts of actual human existence.

Arun Joshi's fiction conforms to Conrad's conception of the novel. Joshi recognizes a reality beyond the mere phenomenal world, a reality which the artist could imagine and capture by giving a consistent form to the shapeless facts of human existence. The source of most of Joshi's novels is actual experience. Joshi the artist, however, is not content merely to restate experience in a coldly scientific manner. He feels a need to shape it, a need to discover the reality which lies hidden in the actuality of his own life.

For Joshi, the fiction is neither a source of entertainment nor an instrument of publicizing some sets of ideas. Unlike Mulk Raj Anand, he does not use his genius for propagating any political or social creed, nor does he escape from the world of human struggle and seek aesthetic relief in an imaginary place as R.K. Narayan does. Joshi does not write fiction according to a formula, rather he grapples with the moments of acute trying situations in human life. He experiments with the medium of literature for studying man's predicament, particularly in the light of motives responsible for his action and the reaction of his action on his psyche. "My novels," says Joshi, "are essentially attempts towards a better understanding of the world and of myself. . . . If I did not write, I imagine I would use some other medium to carry on my exploration."[2]

Joshi's "fictional world" is revelation of a world where man is confronted by the self and the questions of his existence. His search is directed at the inscrutable region of uncertainty and inscrutability. This effort of his makes him a great artist of psychological insight. Reading Joshi's novels is not always a smooth experience; there are moments when one is assailed by doubts and questions. There is "something" that attracts one's attention and then grips. Joshi delves into the inner recesses of human psyche where he finds instincts and impulses at work; he seeks a process of the apprehension of reality which may lead him to the world of the core of the truth of man's life. He realizes man's uniqueness and loneliness in an indifferent and inscrutable universe.

II

Born in 1939, Joshi has had a brilliant academic career. He obtained an engineering degree from the University of Kansas and a degree of Industrial Management from M.I.T., Cambridge, Massachusets. For a brief period in 1957, he worked at a mental hospital in the United States. After returning to India in 1962, he joined DCM in a managerial capacity, on the recruitment and training side. At present, he is

Executive Director of Shri Ram Centre for Industrial Relations and Human Resources.

Joshi comes of an enlightened family. His father, an eminent botanist, was Vice-Chancellor of Panjab University and, later, of Banaras Hindu University. Joshi got married in 1964 and has three children – two girls and a boy. His wife Rukmani, an entrepreneur herself, "has a respect for writers and understands them."[3]

There are a number of literary influences that have worked on Arun Joshi. He has been influenced by Albert Camus and other existentialist writers. "I did read Camus and Sartre," admits Joshi, "I liked *The Plague* and read *The Outsider*. I might have been influenced by them. Sartre I did not understand clearly or like. As for existential philosophers like Kierkegaard, I have never understood anything except odd statements."[4] Joshi has also been influenced by Mahatma Gandhi and the *Bhagavad Gita*. He strongly believes that individual actions have effect on others and oneself. One cannot therefore afford to continue with an irresponsible existence but has to commit oneself at some point. Hinduism, believes Joshi, is highly existentialist-oriented philosophy since it attaches so much value to the right way to live (to exist).

III

Joshi came into limelight with the publication of his very first novel, *The Foreigner*, which appeared in 1968. Writing for him is not a conscious process: "some parts of *The Foreigner*, my first book, were written when I was a student in America. I gave it up then and completed it later in 1966."[5] The novel about a Kenyan-Indian is largely autobiographical. This was followed by the publication in 1971 of his second novel, a more imaginative one, *The Strange Case of Billy Biswas*. The book is about a mystical urge, a compulsion which makes Billy go away. Both these novels, Joshi says, "are primarily concerned with religious issues – the problems of an essentially Hindu mind."[6]

Joshi's third novel, *The Apprentice*, was published in 1974. It is different in tone from the earlier novels. Ratan Rathor, its hero, is Everyman – a contrast to other protagonists in so far his intellectual level is much lower. *The Last Labyrinth*, published in 1981, won Joshi the prestigious Sahitya Akademi award. Though basically a love story, it explores the hero's search for meaning of life. Like *The Foreigner* and *The Strange Case of Billy Biswas*, the novel is preoccupied with man's mystical urge.

It was in 1990, after a gap of ten years, that Arun Joshi published his next novel, entitled *The City and the River.* In terms of theme, the newly-published novel is different from his earlier writings. It is a socio-political novel. While the backdrop of the novel is political, Joshi still deals with the authenticity of the self and the existential crisis of the "City."

IV

Along with novels, Joshi has also published a collection of short stories entitled *The Survivor*. Though he has excelled in longer fiction and his novels have been more popular, it does not mean that his short stories are, by any means, inferior. In fact, there is more force and more precision in some of them. The short story, for Joshi, is as effective a literary form as the novel:

> Each has its own place. In my case it is the theme which determines whether it would be a short story or a novel. For example, I wrote a short story called "The Gherao" which was about students gheraoing a principal. Thematically I would not like to handle a novel about the academic world which I don't know about; so a short story. The world which I know well is the industrial world which has not so far been handled in a novel.[7]

"The Gherao" is a story of a principal who having participated in the national movement of the country feels aghast at the deteriorating values of the modern students. He feels humiliated when gheraoed by his students; he takes leave and dies of heart attack.

Another story entitled "Harmik"[8] gives a picture of life in which men can thrive only by hypocrisy and deceit. It is a story of two friends who belong to the same village, are class-fellows in the college, and go to England one by one. Harmik is great with women; he offers them his body and his love. He believes that "once you have made friends with the women here they will do anything for you." (25) The story depicts a world of night clubs and sex: "Harmik watched, excited and avid as the woman stripped. Her breasts were large. When she was naked a man joined her. . . . The man and the woman embraced and kissed. . . They lay down, the man on top of the woman."(28)

"The Survivor"[9] once again uses first-person narration. After five years in America, the narrator-protagonist Kewal Kapur takes up a teaching job in the university. But the salary, he finds, is not enough to meet the demands of his wife who suddenly decides that they should have a five-room house instead of the three-room house that they have. His father-in-law uses his influence to get him a job in the public relations department of a drug company. His job there is to receive the complaints and then select one of the twenty form letters designed by some half-literate consultant, have it nicely typed and sign it: "I remain, Yours faithfully, Sir . . . or Madam." (20) Kewal gets fed up with the routine work in his office. One day he impulsively goes in for an Indian movie. Half-way through he starts enjoying the film and, like the taxi-drivers and the shoeshine boys in the stalls, he too starts laughing and singing with the hero. The experience proves a turning point in his life. He gets hooked up on the Indian films, viewing twenty movies a month.

"Another turning point in his life" (21) is buying a transistor which he does after seeing the pavement-sweeper working in front of his office carrying one. He listens to the film songs day and night – in office, at home. Since the films and film songs come in way of his work, Kewal Kapur starts destroying half his mail without admitting it. And then one day he goes out with a girl called Mary or Lucy or Daisy, working in the marketing section. They have tea at Chowpatty and, after viewing a movie, take dinner at a tenth-rate hotel. Under the false names of Mr and Mrs Vatsyayan, they hire a room which is quite dirty – with its threadbare carpet, stinking toilet and a creaky bed. But what puts Kewal off is the girl's underclothes: "her wretched bras that looked like they were made of sacking or something." (23)

Kewal's wife does not like his meandering ways, and his father-in-law tries to put him on a straight path. But Kewal revolts: "Before I knew what I was doing, I said: 'If I may say so, Sir, I can't stand your daughter." (25) The result: Kewal loses his job and the money in the bank where he has a joint account with his wife. He goes to his brother

Robu but leaves after a week as he cannot stand his hypochondriac wife Minna.

In a south-Indian hotel, Kewal shares a room with one Penalty Rao, called so because once he played for some football team in Telangana and had specialized in penalty corners. At present, Penalty Rao is a thief, a smuggler, a pickpocket, a politician and a pimp. Urged by a desire to see his daughter, Kewal plans to go to his father-in-law's house. Penalty Rao and his friend Ghorpade, a taxi-driver, join him. As Kewal goes up to see his daughter, the other two collect all the jewellery of the "whole ice-cream-gobbling, money-talking imbecile crowd" (27) in an Air-India bag. Later they drive to Marve Beach where the three of them have drinks and yell out prayers for "surviving" them that night. Kewal's prayer is a severe indictment of the materialism of the modern society: "I am a survivor, gentlemen, of card parties, of wedding receptions, of five-year plans! Of nosy neighbours, of conjugal bliss, of well-meaning friends and of bloody-minded bosses. I am a survivor of life insurance schemes, of stock exchanges and of family planning techniques. In brief, gentlemen, I am a survivor of that fantastic racket that passes for MODERN INDIAN SOCIETY. I am a survivor of mendacious mothers and of relentless fathers, of tuppenny politicians, of lawyers and of doctors. Above all I am the survivor of the greatest disaster of them all: THE MODERN INDIAN WOMAN." (27-28)

"The Only American from Our Village"[10] is unfolded from omniscient point of view. Dr. Khanna, the most outstanding immigrant physicist at the University of Wisconsin, is in India on a four-week trip. Dr. Khanna's lectures at various seminars and conferences are a roaring success. His wife and their two sons are worshipped by his relatives for whom they have brought Gilette razors, pop-records and neck-ties. All goes well till Dr Khanna meets an old man, Mr Radhey Mohan who sells court papers in front of the District Courts and belongs to the same village as Dr Khanna.

Radhey Mohan was a childhood friend of Dr Khanna's father Kundan Lal and the two had gone to the same school. They sat at the same desk on which the old man, when he was a child, had carved the two names on the two sides. Dr Khanna's father, a brilliant student, stood third in the state and had his name on the Honours Board. He did well in college too and took up a job. He came back to the village when he retired and was proud of his son who had settled abroad: "He said you were the only American from our village. I asked him once what was so great about being the only American from our village. He said it was an honour." (66)

The old man's talk is quite embarrassing to Dr Khanna, more so when he shatters Dr Khanna's belief that his life has been a great achievement: "What did we care for your achievements; what you did and what you did not do." (66-67) He tells Dr Khanna of the expectations his father had of his America-settled son, how frustrated he got when the long-awaited return ticket did not come. He further narrates how when he was ill and dying, Dr Khanna's father revisited the school and while coming back crossed the boiling sand of *cho* with *dhak* leaves on his naked feet – a repetition of what he, a poor boy with no shoes, used to do in his school days. By the time he reached home, Dr Khanna's father had a fever and died the next day.

Dr Khanna, with his perfect training in the new civilization, calmly tells the old man: "I am sorry to hear of his death." (70) But the knowledge of the way his father died shatters Dr Khanna's personality. To a psychiatrist he confides that he has periods of great burning in his feet. And to people all around, "he has generally come to be known as the man who does nothing but stare at his feet." (70)

V

The Foreigner,[11] Arun Joshi's first novel, is written in the form of things past. The narration keeps moving from the recent past in Boston to the present in Delhi. Joshi has a vast range and makes a novel out of the wide variety of scenes. During the course of the novel, he takes us to Nairobi where Sindi, the central character as well as the narrator of the story, was born; to London where he studied; to a night club in Soho where he worked as a dishwasher and barman; to Scotland where he worked at a small village library and discussed religion, God and mysticism with a Catholic priest; to Boston where he studied for six years and met June and Babu; and to Delhi where he ultimately settled down. Despite his disclaimer, "I am not very good at remembering events," (32) we find Sindi acquitting himself well as a narrator.

Born of an English mother and a Kenyan-Indian father, Sindi is a child of mixed parentage. Since both his parents died early in an air crash near Cairo, Sindi is brought up by an uncle settled in Kenya. Rootless as he is, Sindi's life takes him to London, Boston and New Delhi. He has his education in London where he meets Anna, a minor artist separated from her husband. He has an affair with this Soho artist who yearns neither for him nor anybody else, but "for her lost youth." (167) Later he is deeply involved with Kathy, an English housewife, who hungers for adulterous love. She leaves Sindi after carrying on with him for a few weeks and goes back to her husband because "she thought marriage was sacred and had to be maintained at all costs." (168)

The novel opens like a thriller with the scene set in a morgue where Sindi identifies the dead body of his friend Babu Rao Khemka who has been killed in a car accident on mass Turnpike. Subsequently he goes to June and, over a cup of coffee in a restaurant, breaks the news of Babu's death.

The very next chapter takes us to a new setting – Babu's house in New Delhi. When Sindi visits Babu's family, he is apprehensive of the reactions of his relations. Once there, he finds that Sheila and Mr Khemka – Babu's sister and father – have accepted Babu's death with a calm resignation. There is no violent show of grief; rather Sheila and her father keep insisting that he have a drink.

Sindi notices the kind of life the affluent in India are leading: "The house was old and single-storeyed with a magnificent lawn that contrasted beautifully with the red gravel of the drive"; (9) "I looked at. . . the richness of Mr Khemka's drawing room. . . . Plush carpets, low streamlined divans, invisible lighting, bell buttons in every corner, and sculpture." (11) Sindi realizes that Babu was brought up amid all these material luxuries. Later when he has lunch with the Khemkas, he finds the lunch room "furnished as luxuriously and tastefully as the drawing room."(13)

Contrasted with this is Sindi's visit to Muthu's family towards the end of the novel which makes him aware of the poverty amidst which these people live. On the one hand are Khemkas who have "three houses in Delhi and a villa in Mussoorie," (21) on the other is Muthu, a low-paid employee in Khemka's office, who lives in a one-room tenement with a dozen other people. This makes evident the population explosion and overcrowding in India amidst poverty and hunger and disease. The appalling living conditions of Muthu's large family make Sindi aware of "accumulated despair of their weary lives." (226) He is shocked to his very depths when Muthu gives an expression to the misery of his life: "it becomes difficult to remain calm when you find so many children going hungry most of the time. . . . I wouldn't worry so much if I could at least be sure of food for these people." (225) Sindi is deeply touched by the squalor of the place and the wretchedness of Muthu's lot. Earlier, he had sympathized with the labourers and indicted Mr Khemka for exploiting his workers:

> It is you who have swindled those miserable wretches in rags who push carts on your streets and die at twenty-five. It is you who have been telling lies and fabricating documents just so that you could air-condition this ostentatious house and throw gigantic parties for the horde of jackals who masquerade as your friends. (215)

The poverty, the deprivation and the helplessness of the workers make Sindi take cudgels for them. He is shocked to find the employees in mortal dread of Sheila and Mr Khemka. The workers cringe before them as if the two were malevolent spirits whose curse could be all-consuming. Sindi feels pained at man's exploitation of man, and denial of rights to people in spite of declared democratic and socialistic polity.

Sindi also notices the hypocrisy and artificiality of the modern society in America. Participants at the ball arranged by the International Students Association pretend to be courteous. Even the strangers at the time of parting promise to meet again, knowing full well that it would not be possible. That, comments Sindi, "was the American way." (25) Similar is his experience at the social parties at Mr Khemka's house. He finds these parties to be a bit of a hoax with people drinking, eating and talking of money—doing nothing worthwhile.

Sindi finds that Mr Khemka is obsessed with the unscrupulous accumulation of wealth. He had sent Babu to America for higher education in the hope that Babu, on his return, will be an asset to the family's social status. Babu, however, is unable to cope with the American system of education. As he writes to Sheila: "We had an exam this morning and I didn't do well. I never seem to do well in these exams. They are very strict here." (52) And he is thrown out of college when he fails all his courses the second time.

Babu considers America to be a dreamland where he can have free sex. "What is the good of coming to America," he asks Sindi, "if one is not to play around with girls?" (22) However, he gets stuck with June whom he meets soon after his arrival in America. Babu's emotional involvement with June leads to his death. He belongs to an orthodox Hindu family and his fastidious, strict and domineering father has a damaging influence on his character. His moral inhibitions and orthodox background restrain him from marrying June. Added to this is his father's threat to disown him if he married June. The father-fear and intellectual weakness of Babu drive June to despair. The Babu-June marriage does not come off when Babu realizes that June has been sleeping with Sindi and uses this as an excuse for driving himself to death.

Sheila too represents the tradition-bound society in India when she says that June "wasn't virtuous" because "she was not a virgin." (57) Sindi reacts strongly to this observation: "So you think one of these Marwari girls is really superior merely because of a silly membrane between her legs?" (57) It is clear that he still has a soft corner for his sweetheart June Blyth.

Sindi had met June, a beautiful, sensual, affectionate, feminine American at a foreign students's party. Their relationship grows gradually; they start living intimately. He loves her intensely and has sex with her but avoids getting married to her. The talk of detachment alienates June from him. She turns to Babu when Sindi does not respond to her insistent pleas to marry her. It is only when June leaves him for Babu that Sindi becomes aware of his strong love for June. He feels depressed and agonized when June refuses to meet him. Pressing his face against the cold, hard metal of the telephone, Sindi cries at June's refusal. He busies himself with his work at college but June remains in his thoughts. He visits the various places where he had been with June earlier:

> Occasionally I would run into an old landmark, a cafe or a theater or a stretch of the beach, and I would say to myself: Here is where

> we met, here I bought her a book, there she wanted me to kiss her, and my heart would sink with the burden of my memories and I couldn't help whispering to myself, "My darling! Oh, my darling!" (142)

Sindi's various experiences in life lead to his decision to leave America. A flip of the coin decides that he migrate to India, the land from where his forefathers had come. "Like many of my breed," says Sindi, "I believed *erroneously* that I could escape from a part of myself by hopping from one land mass to another." (176, Italics mine) Erroneous indeed his decision was, Sindi soon comes to realize: "In truth it had only been a change of theater from America: the show had remained unchanged." (207) Sindi drifts over the surface of earth because he feels himself to be a misfit in the ultra-modern society of Boston. But his foreign background makes him a misfit in the Indian society also.

Sindi is a humane person who sympathizes with Babu, June and Sheila when they are in trouble. As an employee of the foreign student centre, Sindi takes charge of Babu when he arrives in Boston to join college. When Babu fails in his exams, Sindi meets the Dean in order to save Babu from being thrown out of the college. Later, when June informs him that she is carrying Babu's child and seeks his help and advice, Sindi decides to marry June. In a bid to be away from her, he had left Boston and taken up a job in New York. But now he decides to give up his philosophy of detachment. He goes to Boston but only to learn that June has died in the course of an operation for abortion. June's death leads to his realization of the fallacy of detachment: "Detachment consisted of right action and not escape from it. The gods had set a heavy price to teach me just that." (193)

Sindi's involvement with Sheila and her father's business further reveals his humaneness. Sheila often asks Sindi to tell her about his relationship with his brother, to explain the cause of her brother's death. For her, Sindi recapitulates the events in Boston in which he, June and Babu were intricately involved. Though he assures Sheila that Babu died in a car accident, Sindi owns up that he was responsible for Babu's death. His painful realization that he had "driven a man [Babu] to his death" (174) reveals his humaneness.

When the dishonest business ethics of Mr Khemka lands him in the jail and his firm is sealed by the income tax people, Sindi works in the interest of the employees. Muthu persuades Sindi to take charge of Khemka's business and save them from starvation. A talk with Muthu makes Sindi realize that detachment means getting involved with the world. With courage and efficiency, he saves the various clerks from losing their livelihood. His secret love for Sheila is another ray of hope with which we put the novel down.

VI

The Strange Case of Billy Biswas,[12] like Conrad's *Lord Jim*, is narrated from the witness-narrator's point of view. The narrator in this novel is Romi (Romesh Sahai), a friend of the protagonist Billy (Bimal Biswas) whom he met as a student in New York. Like Marlow in *Lord Jim*, Romi performs the task as an involved friend and a detached narrator. Both become more and more involved as the novel progresses; both follow the tale to the end. And they have another feature in common. Throughout the narrative, Marlow repeatedly asserts that he was not able to comprehend Jim fully: "He [Jim] was not – if I may so – clear to me. He was not clear."[13] Similarly, Romi disclaims in the beginning of the narrative that he has understood Billy:

> As I grow old, I realize that the most futile cry of man is his impossible wish to be understood. The *attempt* to understand is even more futile. If in spite of this I propose to relate Billy's story, it is not so much because I claim to have understood him as it is on account of a deep and unrelieved sense of wonder that in the middle of the twentieth century, in the heart of Delhi's smart society, there should have lived a man of such extraordinary obsessions. (7)

Despite the disclaimer, Romi does have a sympathetic understanding of the enigmatic Billy. Later, he says: "I had neither the imagination nor the obsessive predilections of Billy Biswas." (152) The statement reminds one of Conrad's narrator in *Under Western Eyes* who begins by disclaiming "the possession of those high gifts of imagination and expression which would have enabled my pen to create for the reader the personality of the man who called himself . . . Razumov."[14]

Romi had met Billy while hunting for accommodation in New York. Billy offers to share with him his apartment in Harlem, the black ghetto of America. Billy has chosen to live there because, as he tells Romi, he finds it "the most human place." (9) Romi accepts Billy's offer and the sharing of the flat develops into an unusual friendship which lasts till the end.

Billy is a man of brilliant intellect, profound sensibility and extraordinary obsessions. He belongs to a rich respectable family, his father being a judge of India's Supreme Court. His father expects him to take up engineering as a career and Billy does go to America for a degree in engineering. However, he earns his Ph.D. in Anthropology because that is his first love. Billy is basically an anthropologist and studies deeply the tribal attitudes and customs. He feels deeply interested in the places described in the books he reads. In fact his whole life is organized "around his interest in the primitive man." (14)

On Romi's first day in his room, Billy talks of Avocambo, a play running off Broadway: "It is quite an odd play, really. This chap from New York, quite educated and all that, goes down to the Congo and is so incensed by the heat and the light and the primitive music that he just goes out with his shot-gun and starts killing everybody. What is fascinating, of course, are the workings of his deranged mind, what he says between each shot." (10-11) Billy has liked the play because "one can quite imagine something like that happening to oneself." (11) The statement gives Romi a glimpse of restlessness of Billy's soul and in a way anticipates Billy's disappearance in the *saal* forests.

The Bhubaneshwar episode makes evident how at the impressionable age of fourteen, Billy had experienced the urge to live like a primitive man in a primitive world. He had received the intimations of his primitive self from the moment he emerged from the railway station: "It was as though a slumbering part of me had suddenly come awake." (122) It had seemed to him that the sculptures at Konark can give him a solution to his questions about the problem of his identity. Who was I? Where had I come from? Where was I going?" (122) It had seemed to him that the sculptures at Konark can give him a solution to his questions about the problem of his identity: "If anyone had a clue to it, it was only the adivasis who carried about their knowledge in silence, locked behind their dark inscrutable faces." (124) Watching the tribal dance, the young Billy had felt: "Something has gone wrong with my life. This is where I belong. This is what I have always dreamt of." (125)

Romi has a glimpse of this urge for the primitive at a music party in George's apartment. As Billy plays a pair of bongo drums for nearly quarter of an hour, a hush descends on the scene. Romi and others feel the mesmeric pull of the music which holds everyone by its sheer vitality. Billy's Swedish friend, Tuula Lindgren, who has come to the United States for advance training in psychiatric social work, is "the second person who had any clue to what went on in the dark, unscrutable, unsmiling eyes of Bimal Biswas." (19) She understands Billy's interest in the primitive. As she tells Romi: "Billy feels something inside him, but he is not yet sure. . . . A great force, *urkraft*, a . . . a primitive force. He is afraid of it and tries to suppress it. . . . But it is very strong in him, much stronger than in you or me. It can explode any time." (23)

After his father's death, Romi returns to India and enters the Indian Administrative Service after passing the competitive examination. Billy also returns to India and starts teaching Anthropology at Delhi University. His interest in Anthropology continues and he undertakes numerous expeditions for investigations among primitive communities in hills and forests.

In order to cure his obsession for the primitive and to settle down in life, Billy decides to get married. He hopes that marriage would restrain him. However, his marriage to Meena, a sophisticated and most beautiful girl of his own Bengali community, is not a success. Meena tries her best to understand Billy but his interest in the wild exasperates her. As Billy himself says: "the more I tried to tell her what was corroding me, bringing me to the edge of despair so to speak, the more resentful she became." (185)

All of a sudden, Billy is seized by a phantom which makes him anxious to leave the so-called civilized world of greed, avarice, riches and hypocrisy. On one of his anthropological excursions to a hilly region of Madhya Pradesh, Billy mysteriously vanishes. His love for the primitive in life makes him leave his wife, his only child and his aged parents. Ignoring family responsibility, filial expectations and societal obligations, Billy disappears in the *saal* forests of the Maikala Hills.

His restless soul escapes from the civilization to the jungle. An enormous search is launched by the police and the entire tribal area is combed to find Billy out. When the search parties fail to locate him, it is presumed that Billy has been killed by a tiger prowling in the area.

Billy forsakes meaningless existence in civilized world because he feels choked by the phoney atmosphere of the modern society. He rejects the artificiality, hollowness and snobbery of the sophisticated people. As he analyzes it later:

> What got me was the superficiality, the sense of values. I don't think all city societies are as shallow as ours. I am, of course, talking mainly of the so-called upper classes. I didn't really get to know the others. I don't think I have ever met a more pompous, a more mixed-up lot of people. Artistically, they were dry as dust. Intellectually, they could no better than mechanically mouth ideas that the West abandoned a generation ago. Their idea of romance was to go and see an American movie or go to one of those wretched restaurants and dance with their wives to a thirty-year-old tune. Nobody remembered the old songs, or the meaning of the festivals. All the sensuality was gone. So was the poetry. All that was left was loud-mouthed women and men in three-piece suits dreaming their little adulteries. (178-79)

In a bid to seek communion with the primitive world, Billy opts out of the modern world. As Joshi puts it so succinctly, Billy rejects "the post-independence pseudo-Western values."[15]

Billy finds his fulfilment and the essence of human existence in the primitive tribal life. He likes living with the foresters because they are not materialistic: "Nobody here is interested in the prices of foodgrains or new seeds or roads or elections and stuff like that." (113) He likes the unrestrained life-style of the primitive people who go in for uninhibited drinking and dancing and open orgiastic love-making.

Billy explains his mysterious disappearance to Romi: "I had two clear choices: I could either follow this call, this vision, whatever the cost, or be condemned to total decay." (190) And he chooses to respond to the tribal girl Bilasia's call. He is madly in love with Bilasia who he feels is "the essence of that primitive force that had called me night after night, year after year." (142) Her sensuality lures Billy. The sexual union with Bilasia is the climactic moment of the forces of darkness claiming Billy:

> Her hair was loose. Just behind her left ear there was a red flower. The necklace of beads glowed a little in the darkness. Her enormous eyes, only a little foggier with drink, poured out a sexuality that was nearly as primeval as the forest that surrounded them. Come, come, come, she called, and Billy Biswas, son of a Supreme Court Justice, went. . . . It was closer to madness, the terrible madness of a man who after great sin and much suffering finally finds himself in the presence of his god. (141-42)

Billy's union with Bilasia makes him discover "that bit of himself that he has searched for all his life and without which his life is nothing more than the poor reflection of a million others." (142)

The mysterious glow of the Chandtola peak revives after the idealized union of Billy and Bilasia in the tribal world. This flame had glowed during moonlit nights when the King and queen happily lived: it was extinguished when the King was poisoned. Its revival leads to the primitive people's belief that Billy is the reincarnation of their King who was poisoned thousands of years ago. They believe that Billy is endowed with magical and supernatural powers. Dhunia claims that he has seen Billy send away a tiger who had been roaming the jungle for a week killing their cattle, and bring back his grandson to life who had been dead for two hours. He believes that Billy's return signifies the end of their evils and miseries. He tells Romi that Billy "is like rain on parched lands, like balm on a wound. These hills have not seen the like of him since the last of our kings passed away." (159-60)

In *The Foreigner*, Joshi had moved from Boston to New Delhi. In *The Strange Case of Billy Biswas*, he moves from New Delhi to Satpura Hills in Madhya Pradesh. The two geographic locations represent two different cultures – the sophisticated and the primitive. Billy's unconscious self drives him to renounce the monotonous respectability of his high middle-class society and seek his roots in the company of a primitive tribe. The sophisticated Meena represents New Delhi's anglicized ruling-class immersed in the phoney materialism whereas the primitive Bilasia represents the Satpura bhils.

Billy hears the voice of his soul and renounces the materialistic society. From his letters to Miss Tuula, we learn that he left this civilization to find an answer to the questions tormenting him: "Who am I? Who are my parents? My wife? My child? At times I look at them, sitting at the dinner table, and for a passing moment I cannot decide who they are or what accident of Creation has brought us together." (97) Haunted by nature, the primitive man in Billy yearns to lead a simple life. And Billy renounces a life of hypocrisy and deceit to take to a life of noble savageness. Like Kurtz in Conrad's *Heart of Darkness*, Billy forsakes civilized human society, adapts himself to the primitive, and even has a native mistress.

Ten years after his mysterious disappearance, Billy meets Romi in the jungle. Romi, now a District Collector, is on a tour of the Maikala Range and is startled at Billy's appearance. Wearing "a loincloth and nothing else," (102) Billy is completely tribalized. He is a tribal in dress and behaviour except that he speaks in his impeccable English accent. He knows the entire difficult and unapproachable terrain very well and claims to be in secret communion with the forces of nature. He reveals to Romi that he had been drawn by an irresistible urge towards the tribal people and had settled to a primitive existence.

Billy visits Romi again after a few days and cures his wife Situ's agonizing chronic migraine with some herb. Romi promises not to disclose his whereabouts to anybody but his nagging wife forces him to tell her about Billy. Much against her husband's warning, Situ lets Billy's wife and father know about Billy's being alive. Billy's father, a retired ambassador now, moves the higher authorities to retrieve Billy. Mr Rele, the Superintendent of Police, zealously carries out the search. During one of the raids on the tribal people, a constable is speared to death by Billy. The police party hunts Billy down to his hidden lair and despite Romi's best efforts, Billy is killed by the hasty bullet of a policeman. Romi feels "as though we had killed one of the numerous man-gods of the primitive pantheon." (236) The strange case of Billy Biswas is thus "disposed of in the only manner that a humdrum society knows of disposing its rebels, its seers, its true lovers." (240)

VII

Like that of Camus's *The Fall*, the story of *The Apprentice*[16] is cast in the form of a dramatic monologue. In his long confession Jean-Baptiste Clamence, the narrator in *The Fall*, discloses the secret of his clandestine existence, the reasons for his fall. Similarly, Ratan Rathor, the protagonist in *The Apprentice*, is the narrator who "must tell all. All or nothing. What use is a confession if not total." (118) Clamence tells his story to a Frenchman – the person sitting at the next table in the bar. He attempts to open up conversation thus: "May I, Monsieur, offer my services without running the risk of intruding ?"[17] Ratan also tells his lifetale to a silent listener – a young student who has come from Punjab to Delhi to rehearse for the N.C.C. parade on the Republic day. Replying to a probable query about the direction to reach the grounds, Ratan finds the young student to be a fit listener to his tale: "Or, if you could wait a little I shall drop you. I go the same way. Can you wait ? Good." (7) Like Coleridge's Ancient Mariner, Ratan insists that the listener hear him out. Ratan also reminds us of Marlow, the first-person narrator in Conrad's *Youth*, who tells in retrospect the tale of his youth to a group of listeners. *The Apprentice*, like *The Strange Case of Billy Biswas*, is rendered in chronological fashion, with sporadic flashbacks interspersing it.

The Apprentice is set in an india familiar to the urban middle-class. Ratan Rathor is both the hero as well as the anti-hero of the novel. Though he does not feel at home in society, he does not abandon it as Billy Biswas had done. Interestingly, he embodies the very world of material values which his predecessors Sindi Oberoi and Billy Biswas had rejected. He is neither a rebel nor a dissident; he is a victim. After feeling alienated from society, he adapts himself to the ways of the world. He has a powerful instinct for survival through defiance while others do through their ability. And there are still others who survive by sychophancy and by being servile to those in power. Ratan fully succumbs to the worldly pleasures. At every stage he puts up an initial resistance only to discover the futility of his endeavour like so many of his kind, for nobody seemed to know: "What was right? What was wrong? . . . That was where the rub lay." (64)

Ratan is a child of double inheritance; the idealism of his father is matched by the pragmatism of his mother. He is greatly inspired by his father's active participation in the country's freedom movement. He was only ten years old when his father, responding to the call of Mahatma Gandhi, abandoned his practice as a lawyer and gave away most of his wealth to join the revolutionaries. Once as he stood at the head of a procession of freedom fighters, he was gunned down by a British Sergeant. The incident which Ratan had witnessed, made an indelible impression on his mind.

While he studies in the college, Ratan is haunted by the memory of his father who had advised him to be good, to be respected and to be of use. He intends to make a mark on the world, a mark as visible and striking as his father's. He toys with the idea of following his father and even decides to join the clandestine army of Subhas Bose. His mother however vehemently dissuades him from taking such a step. She advises him not to befool himself because "man without money was a man without worth. Many things were great in life, but the greatest of them all was money." (20) She asserts that "money succeeded where all else failed. There were many laws . . . but money was law unto itself." (20) Margayya, the protagonist in R.K.Narayan's *The Financial Expert*, comes to the same realization: "Money alone is important in this world. Everything else will come to us naturally if we have money in our purse."[18] Money in both the novels strikes the keynote and introduces the real theme of the book.

Ratan leaves home to seek a career in the metropolis of Delhi, for it "was a city of opportunities. To fail in Delhi would have been the sign of the greatest incompetence." (31) Contrary to his expectations, Ratan fails to get help from his father's friends. Alone, disheartened, deflated, the world appears to him "as a bundle of mirrors, tempting and somehow held together, but on the brink always of falling apart." (18) He undergoes a humiliating experience while hunting for a job. Getting a job is by no means an easy task as no job could be had without manoeuvring. The novelist makes a dig at the way vacancies are filled in the offices: "it was expected that the jobs would be filled by people who had, in some manner, been pre-selected." (30)

With the help of a roommate at the inn, Ratan ultimately gets a job as a temporary clerk in a government office for war purchases. No matter if it is a temporary one, he looks forward to a rise: "educated, intelligent, cultured, and it was my right that I should rise in life, to levels higher than the others aspired for." (32) Henceforth his only aim in life is to make his career.

Quite often Ratan remembers his father's mocking reference to an average man's desire to prosper in life, to make a career, which his father derisively called "bourgeois filth." (33) The irony comes full swing when his son devotes himself whole-heartedly to building his career by fair or foul means. He is in fact shattered by the breakdown of faith:

> What hurts is the collapse of the faith that they destroy. You believe there is justice in the world. You go about the world for fifty years, this belief sitting in your heart. Then something happens and you go seeking justice. And justice is just not there. Or, you assume your wife is faithful, your children love you, your boss fair, or that God exists. And, then, some day proof comes along that nothing is so. This is what hurts. (24)

In order to get confirmation of his job, Ratan has to agree to marry the boss's niece. By now he knows only too well that the world runs on the basis of deals, and "if men forgot how to make deals the world would come to a stop. . . . It is not the atom or the sun or God or sex that lies at the heart of the universe: it is deals." (51)

Though Ratan progresses upward in rank, he becomes increasingly fraudulent and unscrupulous: "The more money I accumulated, the more I was dissatisfied and the more I was determined to 'enjoy' life." (89) He confesses that he has become a "master faker." (28) He has added a new dimension to his life, and he has become, at the age of twenty-one, a hypocrite and a liar. He acquires a sense of docility and obedience. He readily accepts bribes and now owns a car, a flat, a refrigerator and also has twenty thousand rupees in the bank.

At the time of Indo-China War, Ratan feels strongly for his country which "had come to such a sorry pass."(57) He wonders who should be held responsible for the debacle in war: the ill-equipped military or the incompetence of the politicians. And he comes to conclude that "what was at the root of our downfall was not the military, nor the politicians, nor yet the treacheries of the weather but the INDIAN CHARAC-

TER." (57) In his essay on "Crisis of Character," he hits at the corruption in society and describes the Indian people as "a glorious monument in ruin." (59)

Ratan doggedly struggles through the political and ethical questions involved when making war purchases until one day he comes in contact with Himmat Singh, popularly known as Sheikh, and accepts a bribe from him. He becomes a whore in pursuit of his career and ends up by accepting a bribe when he least needs money. Ratan attributes this to the prevailing degenerated atmosphere. He finds himself trapped in the corrupt system where "men were weighed in Money or Power," (65) he had no other option. He wonders how he can be his own master when a system is his master. He is only a weather-vane or blotting paper.

Ratan derives solace from the annals of corruption which is rampant in society. Justifying his action, he gives a cross-section of Indian society:

> If I had taken a bribe I belonged rather to the rule than the exception. Peons were frequently taking bribes. So were government officials and traffic policemen and railway conductors. A bribe could get you a bed in a hospital, a place to burn your dead. Doctors had a fee to give false certificates, magistrates for false judgements. For a sum of money politicians changed sides. For a larger sum they declared wars. Bribery was accepted by factory inspectors, bank agents and college professors; by nurses, priests and chartered accountants; by all those who acted in the public interest. Men took the bribes to facilitate the seduction of their wives; women for seduction of other women. All this I knew and had known for twenty years. (112)

At Bombay, Ratan signs a deal with the Sheikh and takes a bribe for the supply of substandard war material. He derives satisfaction from the fact that everyone is busy amassing wealth by exploiting the opportunities provided by the war. Some had started hoarding commodities such as baby food and antibiotics, in which there was bound to be black market. Even a Member of Parliament, "a trustee of the Republic," feels unconcerned about the war: "Nobody lost a war these days, the M.P.

said. There were always compromises. To be candid, he whispered, *who* cared for wilderness that we were quarrelling over." (86)

It is the Sheikh perhaps who has penetrated the Indian reality more than anybody else: "This country had two kinds of people. . . . The rulers and the ruled. The rulers were a fraud . . . phoney people who knew only how to make speeches, be cruel, and feather their nests. . . . The ruled were brainless." (84) He despises either category. When Ratan, before entering the deal, shows some reluctance for the fear "that people would come to know," (75) the Sheikh admonishes him by telling that only fools like him believe that there is a law laid down by God which they must follow: "There was no such law book, Rathor, he said. What existed, he said, was not written by God but by a silly society that would do anything for money." (76)

The most striking change in Ratan is his sudden interest in wine and women. So far he had lacked the courage to give vent to his desires. But now he ogles at the women around: "I felt bold, unfettered. I stared at them, the women. Openly. Wilfully." (77) Not only this, he visits prostitutes. In short, Ratan is "at the peak of the dung heap that I had been climbing all my life." (85)

The war is allowed to be lost and the Brigadier, upon his return home from the battlefront, has a nervous breakdown. The Brigadier during the war had deserted his post, and this desertion was due to the fact that he had been supplied with defective war materials which had been approved by none other than Ratan. Significantly, once during Ratan's boyhood days, the Brigadier, himself a teenager then, had saved the former's life when he was attacked by a band of hooligans. The Brigadier, yelling and swearing, had leapt across the fallen bicycles to "fight for me, *me* who no one had ever fought for." (17) It is a strange irony of fate that the same Ratan becomes responsible for the Brigadier's death. The situation reminds one of Arthur Miller's *All My Sons* where Joe Keller's supply of defective gas-cylinders leads to the death of his own son, Larry.

Shocked and shaken by this tragedy, Ratan resolves to revenge upon the Sheikh. To his utter disappointment, he learns from him that he alone has not been responsible for the deal: the Secretary and the Minister have also been a party to it. Ratan has been made a scapegoat because he is "a spineless flunkey." (136) He is merely a tool in the hands of high-ups. The Sheikh makes a shocking and candid observation of Ratan's character:

> You are bogus, Ratan Rathor, he drawled in a voice that had begun to go out again. Bogus. From top to bottom. Your work, your religion, your friendships, your honour, nothing but a pile of dung. Nothing, he said, but poses, a bundle of shams. (137)

The Sheikh reveals to him that it is the callous and corrupt society that has made his mother a whore and his sister a vagrant, and that he has been driven to sell his soul to the Devil.

Ratan's morality is so completely eroded that he cannot bring himself to confess before the authorities. He visits the temple to seek peace and courage but he meets a priest who is ready to grease his palm to save the skin of his son, a contractor who having used substandard material in the construction resulting in the collapse of many roofs was facing punishment. He concludes that even religion is not free from corruption and no succour can be drawn from it. The novelist presents an India riddled with corruption. God can be propitiated by gifts in black money to his temples, where the priests themselves are as corrupt as the narrator.

Ratan realizes the futility and hollowness of his whole life. Having lived for two decades, as he says, "in smog: confused, exploited, exploiting, deceiving," (138) he is tired of body and spirit. He has neglected India's rich heritage and not created a new order he once envisaged. Penitent, especially after he learns that even the temple priest condones bribery, he takes to cleaning shoes of the congregation. Each morning before going to work, he goes to the temple and wipes the shoes of the people and then begs forgiveness of "my father, my mother, the Brigadier" and all those he has harmed "with deliberation and with cunning." (148-49) This symbolic act of penance, he thinks, will bring him humility.

Though the future of the country looks gloomy, yet the young, as Ratan tells the listener, "might yet hold back the tide." (150) The novelist pins his hopes on the new generation and ends the novel with a positive note of affirmation. There is hope as long as young men are willing to learn and ready to sacrifice, as they have done many a time before. Ratan exhorts the young to rise to the occasion and make a second start. It is never too late. And late is better than never.

VIII

The Last Labyrinth,[19] continues in the tradition of the first-person singular. The narrator-hero is Som Bhaskar, a wealthy young industrialist, who relates the events of his life in flashback. Like the heroes of *The Foreigner* and *The Strange Case of Billy Biswas*, Som belongs to the upper strata of society and his quest of life too, like theirs, is for the meaning of life.

Som becomes a millionaire by the time he is twenty-five. He has everything — an extraordinary wife, a fine education. He returns from Harvard to inherit an empire in plastics factory. His father has spent an immense fortune on his education by sending him to the world's most reputed universities. No wonder, he has learnt the way of life. He is a name to reckon with in the industrial world of Bombay, and his primary aspiration is to grab failing industries to add to his dominion.

Som's father was a scientist who delved deep into psychological truths and hungered to know what the First Cause was. At Harvard, Som completed a paper on Pascal. He knew of Krishna and the Buddha at Somnath. Though affluent, he knew that money was dirt, a whore. So were houses, cars, carpets.

Som flits from one pleasure to another; he becomes the incarnation of the quest for the joy of life. He therefore goes in search of new experiences whether they concern business or fornication. But ironically, far from attaining a sense of fulfilment, he has a terrible sense of emptiness of voids within and voids without: "It is the voids of the world, more than its objects, that bother me." (47) Everything in this mysterious world, he finds, is "a haze."

Som's cry of "I want, I want" (11) haunts him all the time. Knowing not what it is he desires, he is in some ways a facsimile of Saul Bellow's Henderson. But his search does not take him to a merely old Africa but to an infinitely mysterious Benaras. He gets fascinated by an obsolete world, decaying yet urbane — the world of Anuradha and Aftab — and by the labyrinth of the haveli they inhabit.

Som encounters Anuradha for the first time when he is already thirty-five in a Delhi hotel at a reception organized by Aftab Rai for the Plastic Manufacturers Association. He is irresistibly drawn towards her. He himself realizes that a demon has got hold of him but he feels helpless. The quaint house in which she lives with a lover strikes as being grotesquely labyrinthine. It is Aftab Rai who had invited him to Benaras and when Som visits him at his residence, Lal Haveli, he feels that "it was a maze that we were moving through. Perhaps, the entire haveli had been built as a maze." (34-35) The house was built either with no plan or with a most meticulous plan, though directed at an elusive objective: "it was a labyrinth." (35)

It is darkly alluring Anuradha who casts a spell on Som. He is bewildered by her charm: "She was not self-conscious about her body of whose grace and sensuousness she seemed unaware." (41) Indeed Anuradha, the haveli and its owner Aftab Rai represent antiquity and are a mystery, a labyrinth to the rational mind of Som. He wants to grab the plastics company of Aftab acquiring its shares as also Anuradha, Aftab's mistress.

Aftab Rai, also a plastic manufacturer, is Som's double. He is a man of culture and refinement, but more Oriental than Western. His conversations with Som invariably tend to be philosophical. He is not good at handling business but he has finer feelings of life. Though he loves Anuradha, he does not claim any ownership of her. His love for her is deep but not possessive. In fact, he respects her personality and would never imagine imposing himself on her.

Anuradha exercises such an overpowering fascination over Som that he neglects his business, his family and his health in an effort to win her. He makes frequent trips to Benaras and is determined to acquire her for himself, his soul and body. And Geeta, his own wife, is all that a wife could be – trusting, beautiful and well-bred. She shows tremendous loyalty and courage in standing by him despite his erratic conduct. And yet, Som is drawn into an aching, painful obsessive love for Anuradha.

In a way Som is similar to Billy because he too is in search of something. Says Joshi: "Yes, there is a similarity between the two. The faceless god is prominent in Billy Biswas's inner thoughts. One finds the same facelessness in Som Bhaskar."[20]

All his life Som seeks someone who has the capacity to resolve the contradictions of his life. He does not find it in his wife, nor in Leela Sabnis, the clever young professor who could readily quote from Freud or Descartes: "Oh yes, Leela Sabnis knew a lot." (79) She is a scholar, an "M.A. and Ph.D. from Michigan, something else from London." (75) She is married and divorced: "Her husband, she claimed proudly, divorced her for reading too much." (77)

Leela is an embodiment of reason and tries to explain Som's sickness through analysis: "You are much too high strung. Without reason. You are a neurotic. A compulsive fornicator." (80) Indeed while she offers Som the joy of her small and sweaty breasts, she analyzes all Som's problems. She tries to help him by prescribing Descartes's *cogi to ergo sum* without much success for the simple reason that one kept the two worlds – the world of matter and the world of spirit – separate. Says Som: "Maybe, *that* was why we fell apart. What I needed, perhaps, was something, somebody, somewhere in which the two worlds combined." (82)

Anuradha was an illegitimate child born of an insane mother. Her mother earned her livelihood by singing for strangers. She was taken away by one of her lovers who killed her with a broken whisky bottle. Anuradha, whose name was Meera then, was brought up by one of her aunts who gave her education. She was molested as a child and underwent many sufferings. She became a film star and was seduced by several producers. She left the profession with the help of Aftab. Now she had been living with him without any formal marriage. As she says: "You can't marry everyone you love. So, why marry anyone at all ?" (43) Som is amazed to learn that she wanted to be nobody's wife. When he asks her if she would like to be married to someone, she says: "I can imagine I am married to Aftab. I can imagine I am married to you. My mother used to imagine she was married to Krishna." (128)

Anuradha inherits from her mother a belief in faith; Som, son of a scientist, is a rationalist and a believer in intelligence and expediency. Though lowly born and scarcely educated, Anuradha has a wisdom higher than Som's. In her own way she is fond of Som and yields to him on many occasions: "I lived on nourishment of the shades thrown by her naked body under the chromatic shower." (121-22) But she has her own loyalties. Som wants to win her heart and not merely possess her body. At the height of their love affair, the enigmatic Anuradha disappears. She embodies the concept of sacrifice. Explaining this, Joshi says: "Anuradha's role in the novel is to lead Bhaskar through the subconscious. Then he loses her. I was hinting at the old classical dictum that you do not get anything without sacrificing something. So she is to be taken away from him."[21]

Though Som has sex with Anuradha, and earlier with Leela Sabnis, he is not happy because of his spiritual hollowness. He does not attempt to resolve the contradictions of life through faith. He fails to sublimate his desires from the animalistic to the spiritual; he becomes a spokesman for Westernized Indian aristocracy which has lost its spiritual roots. A more rational approach to life as represented by Western-educated and affluent Som, is not sufficient. The labyrinths of life can be resolved through intuition and faith rather than science and reason.

Som cannot achieve unwavering faith, for in order to do so one has to make a complete surrender of oneself, including one's intellectual rationalism. As Aftab tells Som: "You have to sacrifice before you are given. You can't have your cake and eat it too. . . . You want to have faith. But you also want to reserve the right to challenge your own faith when it suits you." (166) The novel fails to resolve Som's dilemma. He had always been vexed by the questions of life and death, his mystical craving remains unfulfilled and he continues to remain alienated.

All Joshi's heroes progress from alienation to existential affirmation. But *The Last Labyrinth* is an exception. In a letter to V. Gopal Reddy, dated January 8, 1981, Joshi confirms that "alienation of my novels which I have written so far ultimately leads them back to community. I realized that in my latest novel *The Last Labyrinth* for the first time it does not happen."[22] The novel ends with Som making a suicidal gesture by putting the revolver casually to his temple. As he tries to kill himself, he is stopped by Geeta who shakes him "gently as though rousing a man from sleep." (224)

IX

Arun Joshi's latest novel *The City and the River* is a parable. It is a commentary on the times, unfolding its story in the city by the river which is governed by the Grand Master, a benevolent patriarchal figure. The nature and content of the novel is explained in the blurb of the book which says that it "strikes an entirely different theme from Arun Joshi's earlier novels. At one level, it is a parable of the times; at another, it deals with how men, in essence entirely free to choose, create by their choice the circumstances in which they must live."

The theme of *The City and the River,* unlike Joshi's earlier works, does not have a streak of autobiography; nor is it a story of personal, private lives. The novel is an ample evidence of Joshi's "road not taken," for in this work he turns his focus from the private to the public. And in this, he is following the contemporary vogue of writing a political novel with a theme that holds good for all times.

In the recent times, a great body of politico-historical fiction has emerged on the literary scene. Many Indo-English novelists have turned to the past as much to trace the deepening mood of nationalism as to cherish the memories of the bygone days. A close study of the contemporary novel reveals writers's preoccupation with our historic past and the unabated interest of the readers in the novels that depict the past or that treat some event of national import that has had wide repercussions. As a critic I have always attached a great deal of importance to the impact on a writer of the historical milieu in which he lives and the historical periods of an earlier time with which the author wishes to associate himself by choice. Writers like Khushwant Singh, Manohar Malgonkar, Chaman Nahal, Shashi Tharoor, and Salman Rushdie amply illustrate this point of view.

A distinction must be made here between the conscious use of history and its sub-conscious presentation. The setting of most novels is in the context of some historical framework unless the novelist wilfully places his action in an imaginary locale hoping to highlight a special metaphysical or political point of view, e.g. William Golding's *Lord of the Files,* George Orwell's *Nineteen Eighty-Four,* and Arun Joshi's *The City and the River.* Sometimes, he creates the country, as does Joseph Conrad in *Nostromo.* It is my contention that whatever be the perfection of craftsmanship in this type of novel, such works are accepted by the public nothing more than utopias.

Modern deconstructionists would easily discuss them as exercises in self-deception. Utopias make fine reading; their relevance to the immediate problem is more of an escapist nature, suggesting remedies neither available nor practical. The historical novel represents no surface wave of escapism, but a deep, unconscious movement toward national homogeneity.

It is in the politico-historical novel only that the actual day-to-day problems of life can be encountered, examined, exposed, challenged and rectified. Entertainment and instruction are, by common consent, the most valued virtues of historical fiction. The factual and informational values of history illumine the subject and increasingly whet the readers's curiosity. In other words, for a true artist history is a handmaiden which helps him to achieve several purposes. How deft he is in the art of amalgamating the two must be judged only by the finished product. And herein the novelist who makes use of history by choice obviously must be held at a superior level than the one who consciously assimilates it.

In Arun Joshi's *The City and the River*, the story proper is prefixed with an impressive prologue, which introduces us to a devout disciple and his teacher, "the great Yogeshwara." The disciple, the Nameless-One, was of thirty years and all these years the Yogeshwara had taught him the ancient tongue that no one understood. The Yogeshwara had led the boy to the two kinds of thoughts. And he had taught him the secrets of the body and the secrets of the spirit. And then he had shown him how the spirits had gained control of the body. He had taught him several other things and finally he embarks on "a strange sorry tale." The ecstatic disciple sits at the feet of his master to listen to the story that follows.

The city-in-question is governed by the Grand Master, who is "the son and grandson of Grand Masters."[23] He has grown up in the palace where his family has lived for seventy years. He likes his people but, at times, he is not certain. Ever so often, it seems to him, the people lose faith in him, become unreasonable, turn mutinous. Of all the people, the Grand Master considers the boatmen to be most unreasonable. The brick-people can be persuaded, appeased, and, if necessary, threatened. Even the mud-people could be made to agree. But the boatmen were both incomprehensible and stubborn.

Things move smoothly, however, until one night the Grand Master has a dream that he becomes a king, sitting on top of a hill surrounded by the waters of a river. He seeks interpretation of the dream from the

Astrologer who predicts the crowning of a king in place of the Grand Master. He, egged on by his astrologer to be the king, finds in the rebelliousness of the boatmen an obvious threat: "their insolence, already great, has crossed all limits. At the slightest excuse they raise their rebellious standards and not a day passes when the streets are not filled with their vulgar din. . . . They are a disgrace." (16) And on the top of it, they are large in count. The danger posed by their numbers is not only to the city but also to the palace itself.

Some days later, on the banks of the river, the Astrologer declares to the populace: "My children, God has sent the Grand Master to be your servant. Looking after the city is like *yajna* for him, and his life the *ahuti*." (17) He carries the message of the Triple Way to the people and a new era called "the Era of Ultimate Greatness" is officially heralded. It enjoined the people to beware of the enemy within and the enemy without and reminded them of the Astrologer's Three Beatitudes. The new era was inaugurated with the arrest of a boatman and a clown. The boatman's wife had borne an illegal child, and the clown was arrested because he had been heard to laugh when the old boatman was being put in chains. In fact, the decree regarding the new era came as a surprise to the citizens and it filled them with fear and foreboding.

At a Festival of the River a *yajna* is performed by the Astrologer and the Grand Master's son is coronated as his successor. The Grand Master's plans however meet with stiff resistance from the boat people. Says the Headman: "We have no quarrel with the Grand Master and we have no quarrel with you [Astrologer]. If it is a matter of allegiance, our allegiance is only to the river and cannot be shared." (19) State terrorism is let loose and a large number of arrests are made.

As the New Era regulations required, Dharma next proceeded to arrest Bhumiputra's neighbour, an old man by the name of Patanjali. Handcuffs were put on Patanjali's hands but his wrists were too thin and they kept slipping off. Patanjali is told: "You have only to apologize and you will be set free." (26) Patanjali, a disciple of the Great Hermit of the Mountain, says: "Why should I apologize? I have done no wrong. Rather the Grand Master should apologize for making such absurd rules." (26) He is not scared of going to jail. He is concerned about the future of city, and warns Dharma that "when the Grand Master's jails are full," the city will seek its own protection.

The teachers and the students alike fall within the jurisdiction of the politically ambitious Education Adviser, but they owe their loyalty to Bhumiputra, alias Bhoma, a teacher of Mathematics, a "scrawny" boatman. Bhoma, we learn, is arrested in the general sweep on the boatmen for their resistance against the Grand Master's dream of becoming the king. Bhoma, however, manages to slip and abscond to the concentration of the commissioners and advisers.

Meanwhile, Bhoma's sister seeks the help of Dharma's father's brother, known in the city as the Professor. Incidentally, the Professor has not heard of the Astrologer's Three Truths. Nor is he fully aware that a new era has been launched to take the city to the heights of Ultimate Greatness. His time has mostly been spent in a cluster of brick buildings at one end of the city, where he has taught astronomy to anyone who wishes to learn it. Bhoma was one of those few city youths whom the Professor had taught astronomy. In fact, he was very bright and was always willing to teach others. He had been a favourite student of the Professor and the latter sets out to rescue and return Bhoma to the safety of his family. The Professor is in and out of the narrative searching for his disciple. Passionately pursuing this humanist quest, he is witness to the sordid underhandedness of the administrative machinery that the Grand Master oversees. The Professor who takes up the cause of Bhoma, like the Headman who earlier refuses to swear allegiance to the Great Master, is condemned to the Gold Mines. And the Gold Mines, the Commissioner explains, stand for the city jails.

At a deeper level, the novel is an allegory of Indian history and its mythic truth, but loses itself in over-literariness as when it tends to make an obvious allusion to the Emergency. The bulldozing of the mud-people's huts to widen a street is reminiscent of many such deeds in the mid-seventies in Delhi. Again, the Grand Master has sychophants like the Rallies Master who organizes rallies and mobs in the ruler's support to give an impression that he is popular and loved by his subjects.

Not only that, the power-structure in the city bears close similarity to the period-in-question in Indian history. We are told that the Grand Master has a self-contained oligarch paraphernalia: the Council of the Friends of the People – the Commissioner of Police, the Education Adviser, the Master of the Rallies. This principal trio formulates the strategy and the consequent machinations and schemings. The sole aim of this coterie of fawning councillors, surrounding the Grand Master, is to remain in the limelight and improve their hierarchial standing in the administrative ranking system.

The Grand Master and his syndicate adopt all kinds of methods to perpetuate their rule. All of them meet and mutually decide that it is in the interest of the people that the Grand Master be made the king. The Minister for Trade says: "For ninety-nine years at least all the functions of state represented here will continue to be represented by the male heirs of the present incumbents." (212) Very strategically, he puts forward certain criteria that the king of the city should meet: "First . . . he must be a wearer of the sacred thread. Second, he must come from a family which has already demonstrated its willingness to make sacrifice for this city. Third, he must command the affection of our masses and the trust of the armed forces and the business class. Fourth, he should be above the petty squabbles of the bazaar." (213) This is how these politicians manipulate various things in their favour. Not only that, the ruler adopts the malpractice of offering ministerial positions to persons for political reasons rather than on merit and talent. No wonder, the Education Adviser who enjoys the support of the students and the teachers makes his position indispensable.

The city as it is conceived in the novel bears a hierarchial structure, with Grand Master at the helm of affairs. It is divided into three parts – the Mud quarters inhabited by the nameless people, the Brick localities which produce administrators and intellectuals, and the Seven Hills, the real source of the State power. It is significant to note that the mud-people, called the boatmen, do not believe in personal possessions, and are product of primitive life-style. They are the main opposition group to the power and authority of the Grand Master. They rigidly insist on offering allegiance to the river alone; they are representative of their native rootedness. Arun Joshi has thus posited a contrast between natural life and sophisticated life; in the novel he gives us a parable about human choice between allegiance to God and allegiance to Man, between tradition and modernity. No wonder, in the novel we have a fine juxtaposition between the Grand Master and his police, his helicopters and videos on the one hand, and the dark, semi-naked boatmen with their *yajnas* and the religious faith on the other hand. We have Sanskritized names like Bhumiputra, Patanjali and Dharma Vira contrasting with laser weapons and gadgets of the contemporary times. Indeed the clash between the primitive and the modern civilization is a recurrent theme in Arun Joshi. The novelist is at his best in delineating this human predicament in all his writings; he dramatizes the conflict with a great deal of imagination. Interestingly, the Astrologer who guides the destinies of the City and the Hermit who identifies himself with the River are both disciples of Yogeshwara, but the choices they make turn them into opponents. In this novel, the city and the river are opposing symbols.

Systematic attempts are made to destroy the boatmen's way of life and the Grand Master who hates music even destroys their simple instruments. But creditably the mystic river washes away the intrigues and the turmoil of the preceding years. The sinful city is thus wiped out by the deluge. For seven days and seven nights it rained without a stop. On the eighth day the sun rose, and from a clear sky stared down at a vast sea of water. The river thus becomes a source of ultimate realization and the symbolic anchor of man's tranquillity. But the book is not a philosophical tract like Bunyan's *Pilgrim's Progress*. It is no mere story of an ambitious dictator desiring to be king in the face of opposition by the people. Written as a political allegory, the novel offers a rich commentary on the contemporary times. The use of allegoric mode and legend as a vehicle for social satire is highly rewarding, though a little intricate one.

At the end the Nameless-One asks the Great Yogeshwara as to what has happened. He wonders whether the ruins of the city are still there. He is told that "on the ruins of that city, as always happens, a new city has arisen. It is ruled by another Grand Master, which, of course, need not always happen. In the new city is another Professor, another Bhumiputra, another tribe of boatmen. There is also another Council and another set of Councillors. The men have other names but the forces they embody remain unchanged." (262) To someone, he says, this repetition of things might appear as a charade, a joke. But the tension is perennial and will also be the same: a matter of allegiance to God or to man." (262) If the city is not to dissolve again, it must purify itself: "The city must strive once again for purity. But purity can come only through sacrifice." (263) A new city springs up on the ruins of the old. The river flows on and the Seven Hills continue to rule. It is this unending cycle that imparts a new significance to life in *The City and the River.*

Arun Joshi has thus widened the canvas of his fiction by taking up issues that concern larger humanity rather than some individuals. His adept use of allegoric mode and the legend as a vehicle for political satire lend a new charm to the fictional mode. He imparts to the tale a universal and eternal significance. In fine in *The City and the River,* Joshi raises the political novel to the level of great literature which has an all-time appeal.

NOTES

1. Joseph Conrad, *Notes on Life and Letters* (New York: Doubleday, 1925), p. 6.
2. Reply to M.R. Dua, dated September 3, 1971.
3. Sujata Mathai, "I'm a Stranger to My Books," *The Times of India*, July 7, 1983, p. 8.
4. "A Winner's Secrets: An Interview with Purabi Bannerji," *The Sunday Statesman*, 27 February 1983.
5. *Loc. cit.*
6. Reply to M.R. Dua.
7. "A Winner's Secrets."
8. "Harmik" in *The Journal of Indian Writing in English*, II, 2 (July 1974), pp. 22-28.
9. "The Survivor" in *Modern Indian Short Stories*, ed. Suresh Kohli (New Delhi: Arnold Heinemann, 1974), pp. 19-28.
10. "The Only American from Our Village" in *Contemporary Indian-English Stories*, ed. Madhusudan Prasad (New Delhi: Sterling, 1984), pp. 64-70.
11. Arun Joshi, *The Foreigner* (Delhi: Hind, 1968).
12. Arun Joshi, *The Strange Case of Billy Biswas* (Delhi: Orient Paperbacks, 1971)
13. Joseph Conrad, *Lord Jim* (New York: Doubleday, 1925), p. 177.
14. Joseph Conrad, *Under Western Eyes* (New York: Doubleday, 1925), p. 3.
15. "A Winner's Secrets."

16. Arun Joshi, *The Apprentice* (New Delhi: Orient Paperbacks, 1974).
17. *The Collected Fiction of Albert Camus* (London: Hamish Hamilton, 1962), p. 253.
18. R.K. Narayan, *The Financial Expert* (Mysore: Indian Thought Publications, 1952), p. 21.
19. Arun Joshi, *The Last Labyrinth* (New Delhi: Vision, 1981).
20. "A Winner's Secrets."
21. *Loc. cit.*
22. Reply to V. Gopal Reddy, dated January 8, 1981.
23. Arun Joshi, *The City and the River* (New Delhi: Vision, 1990), p. 13.

Quest for Meaning in Arun Joshi's Novels

R.S. PATHAK

I

Arun Joshi is one of the very few Indian novelists in English who have successfully revealed subtleties and complexities of contemporary Indian life. He has produced very compelling works of fiction. Sensitively alive to the predicament of modern man, Joshi has ably delineated unfortunate consequences of the absence of values and faith in life. In fact, he has been rarely excelled in exemplifying the existential dilemma of the present-day world. He has also worked out various dimensions of pressures exerted by the complex character and demands of the society in which modern man is doomed to live. This awareness of man's rootlessness and the consequential anxiety is the keynote of Joshi's unique vision of the plight of modern man. His novels delineate human problems rather than issues arising out of ephemeral loyalties. Joshi marks a definite departure from the general run of Indian novelists in English and his experimentations in themes and technique have added new dimensions to the art of the novel.

Lionel Trilling is of the view that the novel is "a perpetual quest for reality" and that it is "the most effective agent of the moral imagination" in our time.[1] The Indian novel in English is now an integral part of Indian reality. Although it began as a "hot-house plant," it has "taken firm and deep roots in the Indian soil."[2] The development of the Indian novel in English can be traced from its experimental stage to realistic to psychological. Essentially realistic novels in English came to be written in India for the first time in 1920s, when with the surging nationalistic feelings the scene "shifted to contemporary battles and agitations."[3] The novels written between the two World Wars were chiefly concerned with exploration and interpretation of the social milieu, as is evident from representative works like Mulk Raj Anand's *Untouchable* (1935), R.K. Narayan's *Swami and Friends* (1935) and Raja Rao's *Kanthapura* (1938). These novels did not make any conscious attempts at dealing with the individual's personal predicament.

After 1950s, however, the novelists's interest shifted from the public to the private sphere. They began to delineate the individual's quest for the self in all its varied and complex forms and his problems and crises. Robin White maintains: "If anything is to distinguish Indian fiction . . . it would be varied literary attempt to portray the conflict of the contemporary Indian."[4]

Arun Joshi is one of those modern Indian novelists in English who have broken new grounds. In his search for new themes, he has "renounced the larger world in favour of the inner man" and has engaged himself in "a search for the essence of human living."[5] An outstanding novelist of human predicament, Joshi has chartered in all his five novels the inner crisis of the modern man.

The most besetting problem that man faces today is the problem of meaninglessness. As Edmund Fuller remarks in our age: "man suffers not only from war, persecution, famine and ruin, but from inner problem . . . a conviction of isolation, randomness, [and] meaninglessness in his way of existence."[6] The problem of meaninglessness is so pervasive that it threatens to corrode every sphere of human life. It has been treated in considerable detail in American and European literature. Its treatment by Indian novelists like Joshi is no less interesting.

Man fails to perceive today the very purpose behind life and the relevance of his existence in a hostile world. Notwithstanding unprecedented scientific and technological advancements, which have added immensely to his physical pleasures and comforts, the contemporary man is doomed to find himself in a tragic mess. The prevailing economic conditions culminating in the abject poverty of the masses and the economic squeeze of the middle class on the one hand, and the economic affluence of the newly rich on the other, the drag of social conventions and traditions, the fast-changing value system consequent upon the impact of rapid modernization accruing from industrialization and urbanization, the inter-generational tensions engendered with changing ethos—all these make increasing and often disturbing demands on the individual and contribute in their own ways to his sense of meaninglessness of life.

As it is, the contemporary man finds himself participating in a "rat race" and is estranged not only from his fellowmen but also from his innermost nature, having nothing within or without him to fall back upon in moments of crisis. The present century has seen the dissolution of old certainties and dogmas and, as Paul Brunton observes: "Never before were so many people plunged in so much uncertainty, so much perplexity and unsettlement."[7] Deprived of the succour of ancient wisdom, which provided the much-needed basis for value and meaningfulness in life, the modern man has no substitute for faith and religion except science and information. Thinkers like Aldous Huxley have aptly pointed out that "ours is a world in which knowledge accumulates and wisdom decays."[8]

The malaise of the contemporary man has been considerably aggravated by what Spengler calls "the crisis of the present." Today "everything conspires towards a philosophy of meaninglessness, boredom and the Absurd."[9] The twentieth century—especially the post-War period—has been an age of great spiritual stress and strain, and has rightly been regarded "The Age of Alienation."[10] It has shrunk in spirit languishing in confusion, frustration, disintegration, disillusionment and meaninglessness. As Rilke bewails in his first *Duino Elegy*, "we are not very reliably at home in the interpreted world." Our very notion of reality has been profoundly changed by Bergson's theory of *duree*, Freud's postulates about the subconscious, Einstein's concept of relativity and Heisenberg's uncertainty principle. We suffer from a gnawing sense of meaninglessness, which may be manifest in "the alienation from oneself, from one's fellow men and from nature; the awareness that life runs out of one's hand like sand, and that one will die without having lived; that one lives in the midst of plenty and joyless."[11]

The potential meaninglessness of human existence has corroded human life from various quarters. The existential "encounter with Nothingness" and the tenuousness of human existence are prototypical of modern life. The hiatus between what the individual aspires for and the hard reality of what he achieves, between what he professes and what he practises, and between what he really is and what he would like to appear, has mercilessly crumpled his life leaving an insidious effect on his inner being. The injuries inflicted and the scars left on his psyche generate a cynical attitude towards the established social norms and values and make him grope for life's relevance.

Man is shocked to find that he is no longer the master of his destiny and that there are forces which threaten to wither his life and all its joys and hopes. He "comes to feel helpless in the fundamental sense that he cannot control what he is able to foresee."[12] *Angst*-ridden and utterly hopeless, he finds quite a few mechanisms and processes beyond his understanding and, consequently, suffers from a deep sense of powerlessness and meaninglessness. Life has grown today "indefinitely vast" without any proper "interlinkage"[13] to hold it together from falling apart.

Painfully aware of his precarious position, man experiences severe limitations in today's set-up and an acute terror of the world augmented by its randomness. "Man," says Paul Tillich, "is drawn into the world of objects and has lost or is continuously losing."[14] The modern man's problems have been discussed variously. But, as Erich Fromm points out: "In the nineteenth century the problem is that man is dead. The danger of the past was that men became slaves. The danger of the future is that men may become robots," who "will destroy their world and themselves because they cannot stand . . . a meaningless life."[15] In fact, the absence of meaningful relations is the greatest curse of this age.

The pervasive sense of meaninglessness is thus the most dominant feature of the human condition in the contemporary epoch. It is the realization of what Frank Johnson calls "fractionated functions"[16] that is responsible for one's felt insignificance of life and its affairs. The plight of the modern man has been discussed by Seeman under a set of five inter-related operational conditions, viz. powerlessness, normlessness, isolation, self-estrangement and meaninglessness, which he considers to be different manifestations of alienation. He analyzes "the search for meaning" in terms of the increase of "functional rationality" and the concomitant decline of "substantial rationality."[17] As functional rationality increases, there is a parallel decline in the individual's "capacity to act intelligently in a given situation on the basis of one's own insight into the interrelations of events."[18] This state of affairs is most likely to generate feelings of inauthenticity and meaninglessness.

The existential states of disappointment, isolation and meaninglessness have received adequate attention in the West. All sensitive people feel concerned about the unfortunate spiritual predicament of the modern man. His inner problems have been treated in considerable detail in modern literature – particularly in the fiction. "Whatever the fiction may be said to deal with, it is surely safe to say that it deals, either manifestly or covertly, with our emotional problems."[19]

No emotional problem is more threatening today than the pervasive sense of meaninglessness. Conditions in India, though not so alarming as in the western world, have begun to take a dismal turn. Victor Anant has discussed the moral confusion of modern Indians who live on "an ad-hoc basis" in "a no-man's land of values." Heirs to two sets of customs and torn asunder by a dual code of behaviour, they live lazily "by opportunism, treachery, cowardice, hypocrisy and wit," and are, consequently, "sucked into a shuffling, sleep-walking mass," always dreaming of "walking up in some cloud-cuckoo land of bliss." This, according to Anant, is due to their "moral inertia and flabbiness," which has given them "all the grandeur and all the emptiness of a hypnotized people."[20]

Certain recent Indian novelists in English have made significant efforts to delineate the predicament of the modern man. The work of Arun Joshi in particular reads like the spiritual odyssey of the twentieth century man who has lost his spiritual moorings. Despite some differences in their approach, all of Joshi's heroes are "men engaged in the meaning of life."[21] The novelist has tried to project through their experiences the crisis of the urbanized and highly industrialized modern civilization along with its dehumanizing impact on the individual who is ever eager to find out and reaffirm the value of meaningful relatedness in life.

II

Arun Joshi's first novel, *The Foreigner* (1968), explores in depth the problems of Sindi Oberoi. It has been remarked: "A strange feeling of aloneness and aloofness . . . permeates the entire narrative and provides the necessary texture and structure to the novel."[22] In her review of the novel, Meenakshi Mukherjee describes the hero of *The Foreigner* as "a perennial outsider."[23] Sindi is always lonely and ill at ease in the world in which he has to live. He belongs to no country, no people and regards himself as "an uprooted young man living [aimlessly] in the latter half of the twentieth century." (195)[24]

Born in Kenya of an Indian father and a British mother, both of whom died early, Sindi is brought up by his uncle. He goes as an engineering student to Boston, where at a foreign students's party he meets June, an attractive American young woman, with whom he has a short-lived but passionate love-affair. His loneliness is apparent to anyone who meets and talks to him. In their very first encounter, June tells him:

> There is something strange about you, you know. Something distant. I'd guess that when people are with you they don't feel like they're with a human being. Maybe it's an Indian characteristic, but I have a feeling you'd be a foreigner everywhere. (33)

Sindi is trapped in his own loneliness, which is accentuated by his withdrawal from the society around him. He wonders:

> in what way, if any, did I belong to the world that roared beneath my apartment window. Somebody had begotten me without a purpose, and so far I had lived without a purpose. Perhaps I felt like that because I was a foreigner in America. But then, what difference would it have made if I had lived in Kenya or India or any other place for that matter! It seemed to me that I would still be a foreigner. (61)

At a deeper level, *The Foreigner* can be viewed as an attempt to plumb man's perennial dilemmas. It is about things that Sindi wants (and who doesn't!) – the courage to be and the capacity to love. His alienation is of the soul and not of geography. As he himself confides, his "foreignness" lies "within" him and drives him from crisis to crisis rendering it difficult for him to leave "himself" behind wherever he goes. (61) Right from the beginning, he is oppressed by a desire to find "the meaning of life." He himself wants "to do something meaningful." (14)

While gathering miscellaneous experiences in life, however, he becomes convinced of the impermanence of things. He says to June: "Nothing ever seems real to me, leave alone permanent. Nothing seems to be very important." (107) His entire life is geared around his quest for permanence in life. When they have been together for some time, June suggests that they get married. But he tells her: "We are alone, both you and I. That is the problem. And our aloneness must be resolved from within." (126) He argues with himself on the meaning of life and its affairs. Debating on the necessity of marriage, he comes to the conclusion:

> Marriage was more often a lust for possession than anything else. People got married just as they bought new cars. And then they gobbled each other up. (67)

All acts like marriage have no significance for him. He has a feeling that "even if he loved her [June] and she loved him it would mean nothing, nothing that one could depend on." His deep involvement in a married woman named Kathy, whom he loves with "the piercing, all-caressing love of an adolescent," (122) and the subsequent separation make him realize that "all love—whether of things or persons, or oneself—was illusion and all pain sprang from this illusion." (170)

In his eagerness to find out the meaning of life, Sindi lives "in a strange world of intense pleasure and almost equally intense pain." (82) But he fails to make a satisfactory progress and, as he himself tells us, his twenty-five years are "largely wasted in search of wrong things in wrong places." (92) His soul becomes "a battlefield where the child and the adult warred unceasingly." (130)

Sindi's sufferings are manifestations of a spiritual crisis which all sensitive people have to face today. His position is that of "the dull school boy who always gets stuck with the same unanswerable questions." (138) He wants peace, a capacity to love and the courage to live "without desire and attachment." (138) Above all, he wants "to conquer pain" and death, which "wipes out everything" leaving only "a big mocking zero." (107) His various experiences in life, however, leave him with unanswered questions "like swollen carcasses strewn on river banks after a flood." He is keen on knowing his "purpose" in life, a knowledge of which is essential before he can make earnest efforts to "fulfil" it. (138) All his attempts in this regard, however, fizzle out "like an ill-packed cracker." (139) He squanders away the meagre quota of happiness given to him. He feels always being pushed "on the giant wheel, going round and round, waiting for the fall." (85)

The "pathlessness" of the road to New York reminds Sindi of his own pathlessness. He also remembers the lines from a popular song which run: "Who knows where/ The road will lead?/ Only a fool can say." He becomes conscious of the fact that for no less than twenty years he himself "had moved whichever way life had led" him. (196) He compares his meaningless existence to that of "an idiot without a keeper." (163) Fully convinced of "the abominable absurdity of the world" (191) and "tired of living," he even contemplates suicide. (165) He does not "fit in" in the world and his way of life becomes intolerable. "In a way," says he, it has been "like a small death." (104) He becomes consequently "cynical and exhausted, grown old before [his] time, weary with [his] own loneliness." (152) He can compare his way of life only to walking "around the huge circle like a sleep-walker in an amphitheatre." (208) Of his condition after Babu's death, he remarks:

> it suddenly struck me that something had been knocked out of me. I was just not the same person any more. . . . I felt as if there was nothing left that I could depend upon. . . . I felt like a desert or like a vast field of naked oaks in winter time. I felt more alone and naked in the world than I had ever felt before. (174-75)

Sindi is critical of the ultra-modern, mechanized society in which he is "considered quite a misfit." (15) Before "the abominable wheel of industrialization," he feels driven "like torn bits of paper on a windy day." (43) The strain of adjustment on him proves intolerable. The emptiness that surrounds him leaves him "completely dazed" or in "just one long coma." "It was," he observes, "as if somebody had given me a big dose of anaesthesia." (141) The feeling of his nakedness in the hands of existence grew with every passing day. He felt some "abominable hands groping and probing" into his soul, "ripping dry scars open and dipping into old wounds." (48) He begins to question Mrs. Blyth: "And what use have you made of your extra height and extra years? You carry heavier guns and have a longer time to make each other unhappy, that's all. Can you call that an achievement?" (102)

He finds America "a place for well-fed automatons rushing about in automatic cars," (90) "much too sterilized" and "much too clean and optimistic and empty." (89) He develops an apathy for "grey, bedraggled and lonely people" like Mrs Blyth who realize pretty late in life that it has "left them by the wayside." (68)

Sindi wants to leave America to escape a bit of himself "that appeared the most decayed." Nigeria or India is the choice and a flip of the coin decides in favour of India. He comes to India hoping that it will provide him "a place to anchor on this lonely planet," (176) but his hopes are belied. He finds India no better than America: "In truth it had remained unchanged." (207) He only has to face here a different set of people with a different set of vanities and "different ways of squeezing happiness out of a mad world." (208) He is appalled by "the stagnant deadness" (207) of the Indian scene dominated by people like Mr Khemka, "man of the world . . . owner of a growing empire." (208)

Amongst young men there are Babu Khemkas who represent typical Indian fantasies and illusions about a glamourized foreign dreamland, where they go "to play around with [foreign] girls," (23) "to make American friends" and not "to mix with Indians all the time" because "Indians are so under-developed as compared to them," (91) and never to come back to India if they have the choice. (90) This life, Sindi himself is convinced, is not going to help him solve his problems. He finds the Hindu "nonsense about idols" (70) and their "mealy-mouthed philosophies" (75) thoroughly useless for his purpose. Explaining his "strangeness," he tells Mr Khemka: "My set of experiences has taught me a reality that is different from yours." (134) He further remarks:

> You had a clear-cut system of morality, a caste system that laid down all you had to do. You had a God; you had roots in the soil you lived upon. Look at me. I have no roots. I have no system of morality. (135-36)

It is this lack of a definite frame of reference and a system of values that is responsible for Sindi's problems. He feels himself stranger in India to both the corrupt rich man and the half-naked struggling labourer. The common people, he finds, "have the benefit of their delusions," which "protect them from the lonely meaninglessness" of life. (126) But Sindi has no delusions to bank upon. He is not "fortunate enough to have been born with their simpleness of mind" either. (43) His existential drifting over the surface of the earth and his experimentation with self (175) only intensify his dismal loneliness and acute sense of meaninglessness of life. He tries to seek, finally, in detachment a solution to his problems.

III

Joshi's another novel called *The Strange Case of Billy Biswas* (1971) also aims at delineating the human predicament. "Billy, like Sindi, is in search of a human world of emotional fullness – a world of meaningful relatedness."[25] Billy is aware of the deeper layers of his personality and feels totally alienated from the superficial reality of life. It is significant to note that Van Gogh's turbulent career "held considerable fascination for Billy at one time." (13) Billy's expression itself is symptomatic of "a mixture of nearly all those emotions that one tends to associate with a great predicament." (43-44) "No other man" than him, we are told, "so desperately pursued the tenuous thread of existence to its bitter end." (8) Renouncing his past, his family and the everyday world, the rich, sophisticated and U.S.-educated Billy goes in search of the meaning of life. The novel probes into his "dark mossy labyrinths of the soul that languish for ever, hidden from the dazzling light of the sun." (8)

As a student in America, Billy is less interested in books on anthropology than in the places described in them. He would like to learn with real interest and absorption about "the aboriginalness of the world" (14) and it is "around his interest in the primitive man that his entire life had been organized." (14) He has the first glimpse of "the other side" of his personality at a music "session," which keeps on exerting "a mesmeric pull" on him. (18, 21) Soon he finds himself "itching to be back" to a congenial atmosphere. (27) His itch for India is an itch for realization of the relevance of life.

On returning to India, however, he feels like a fish out of water and sees no other way out but to fly from the civilized, sophisticated modern society. He makes a trip to the tribal wilderness – "the vast emptiness of central India" (19) and vanishes into the *saal* forests of the Maikala

Hills with a view to leading the life of a tribal and carving for his soul an inner shrine of peace and happiness.

Romi Sahai meets Billy after a lapse of three years and is surprised to find him in a mental condition which is "closer to madness, the terrible madness of a man who after great sin and much suffering finally finds himself in the presence of his god." (142) Billy's behaviour makes him think "as though some part of him [Billy] had gone on strike." He ruminates:

> All my words simply sank upon his listless mind without so much as causing a ripple. Gone was the staggering intelligence, the spectroscopic interests, the sense of humour. . . . He was turned upon some obscure segment of himself, ferreting out a bitter secret. Whatever it might have been, the Billy Biswas I had known was finished, snuffled out like a candle left in the rain. (70)

Even before his physical disappearance into the jungles, Billy ceased to belong to the world. He felt being impelled by "a great force, *urkraft* . . . a primitive force." (23) His Swedish friend Tuula had long ago sensed this primitive force in him. Even at the age of fourteen, while staying in Bhubaneshwar, he received the intimations of his primitive self: "It was as though a slumbering part of me had suddenly come awake." (122) "Something has gone wrong with my life," he realized. "This is where I belong. This is what I have always dreamt of." (125) At that time, however, he was not able to understand the source and the precise nature of this call. He says:

> I could not figure out what excited or troubled me unless it was a sudden interest in my own identity. Who was I? Where had I come from? Where was I going? (122)

In America, too, at the age of twenty, he had visions "of being in a place other than where I was, in a place very, very old, at times a wilderness, at other times full of strange primitive people." (180) What makes the story of Billy fascinating and convincing is the wonderful coalescence of his rational outlook with his *urkraft* that triggers off the creative energy in him, prompting him to do what he does. The following extract from one of his letters to Tuula expresses his innermost feelings:

> When I return from an expedition, it is days before I can shake off the sounds and smells of the forest. The curious feeling trails me everywhere that I am a visitor from the wilderness to the marts of the Big City and not the other way round. (92)

Billy's experience just before he takes the momentous decision to make the final departure into the jungle on the second day of his expedition has mystic undertones and reminds us of Siddhartha's renunciation of his wife and child. Billy felt as if "the inheritors of the cosmic night" (121) were "waiting and walking and staring" at him and he was the "first man on earth facing the earth's first night." (119) His departure is for him a prelude to an arduous quest for something beyond himself. It is not an escape *from* life and its realities but an escape *into* what he considers to be the "real" life, far from the madding crowd and the sordid, meaningless existence in the civilized world. It is in the primitive tribal life that he finds his own fulfilment and the essence of human existence. When he comes into contact with Bilasia, who reflects, according to him, the very quintessence of the primitive force, he feels that he has "suddenly discovered that bit of himself that he has searched for all his life and without which his life is nothing more than a poor reflection of a million others." (142)

Billy does not find meaning of life either in white America or in the upper-class Indian society. He tells Romi that he decided to live in Harlem because "that was the most human place he could find" and that "white America was much too civilized for him." (9) He hates likewise "the upper crust of Indian society" (9) which he himself comes from, for he finds it swarming with pompous and mixed up people: "Artistically, they are as dry as dust. Intellectually they could do no better than mechanically mouth ideas that the West abandoned a generation ago." (197)

Billy never feels at home in the sophisticated world. He finds something basically wrong with it because it is "hung on this peg of money." (97) He has got boundless appreciation for Tuula for treating money for what it is worth: "a whole lot of paper." (177) In a place like Delhi he feels as if he is "pinned down . . . like a dead butterfly." (47) He often wonders "whether civilization is anything more than the making and spending of money." (96) He is terribly unhappy when he finds himself "tied up in a knot by a stifling system of expectations" of this mundane world, (127) squandering "the priceless treasure of his life on that heap of tinsel that passes for civilization." (141)

The ways of the upper class sophisticated society seem to Billy in no way different from those of kennelful of dogs "yawning or struggling against each other." He wonders "whether civilization is anything more than the making and spending of money. What else does the civilized man do?" (96) The "bizarre unintelligibility of Billy's world" (222) is pitted against "the bright glossy face of urban society" and its "tawdry nick-nacks of civilization." (217)

The ambition and superficiality of the modern phoney society are represented by Meena, Billy's wife. Meena and Billy are not made for each other. She is fully knowing that "things are falling apart" and that "Billy had gone through . . . [a] sea change." (74, 82) "All I know," says she, "is that Billy is getting stranger and stranger with every passing day." Billy's departure might have been avoided if only she had possessed "a rare degree of empathy or even a sufficient idea of human suffering." (185) It is her lack of understanding that lands Billy to the edge of despair culminating, subsequently, in the seduction of Rima Kaul:

> It gradually dawned on me that a tremendous corrupting force was working on me. It was as though my soul was taking revenge on me for having denied it for so long that Other Thing that it had been clamouring for. (189)

The terrible shock he feels at his degradation provokes his flight from meaningless civilized world. His alternatives are crystallized. He has two "clear choices"—either to "follow this call of the primitive, this vision, whatever the cost, or be condemned to total decay." (190) He decides to go in for the first option.

Billy is thus "a refugee from civilization." (140) The tenacity with which he pursues his quest in "an incoherent and meaningless world" (48) is really astounding. Billy withdraws from the civilized world because it begins to make inroads into his own character. He remembers that all his life he had been confusedly driving towards his real self. (116) He recapitulates: "I certainly underwent a deep metamorphosis that was, no doubt, responsible for all that I did subsequently. Layer upon layer was peeled off me until nothing but my primitive self was left trembling." (121)

Joshi's novel, incidentally, reminds us of D.H. Lawrence's *The Woman Who Rode Away* and Graham Greene's *A Burnt Out Case.* It has been remarked that Billy's strange case represents the "universal myth of the primitive in the heart of man ever alienating him from the superficial and polished banalities of modern civilization."[26] That the theme of the novel is nothing less than the search for meaning in life is evident from the following dialogue between Billy and Romi:

> "I don't want to sound too pompous, old chap. Becoming a primitive was only a first step, a means to an end. Of course, I realized it only *after* I ran away. I realized then that I was seeking something *else*. I am still seeking something else."
> "What is that?"
> He seemed to be thinking.
> "God?" [Romi] prompted.
> "There, there, old chap, that is too big a word."
> "Something like that?"
> "Yes, Something like that." (189)

Billy's search for meaning, however, is conducted in a very hostile atmosphere and he has to pay a heavy price for it. The sophisticated society, in its "middle-class mediocrity," makes it a point to bracket men like him with "irresponsible fools and common criminals" and does all that is possible to prevent them from "seeking such meagre fulfilment of their destiny as their tortured lives allowed." (231-32) Efforts to bring Billy back to civilization by capturing him by police force only lead to the final tragedy. He pays with his life for not conforming to the norms of the urban civilization – for daring "to step out of its stifling confines" and, as the novelist concludes, "the strange case of Billy Biswas had . . . been disposed of in the only manner that a humdrum society knows of disposing its rebels, its seers, its true lovers." (240)

IV

Joshi's another novel, *The Apprentice* (1974), also depicts, though less exhaustively, the plight of the contemporary man, who is "sailing about in a confused society without norms, without direction, without even, perhaps, a purpose." (74) The protagonist, Ratan Rathor, comes of an impoverished middle-class family. He has to find his own way and pay his own price in this world. He is the child of a double inheritance. His father was patriotic and courageous, but his mother was endowed with worldly wisdom. She often reminded Ratan that "it was not patriotism but money . . . that brought respect and bought security. Money made friends. Money succeeded where all else failed. There were many laws . . . but money was a law unto itself." (20)

Torn by these two conflicting philosophies of life, Ratan finds it extremely difficult from the very beginning to live smoothly in the "petrified and frozen" world of civilization. He has no other way but to keep up appearances and do away with the world of ordinary decencies. He, naturally, faces tension and resentment precisely because he has to put up with totally divergent social norms and expectations. He is convinced that life is characterized by chaos, absurdity, brutality, disorganization and insensitivity. Faced with the dehumanizing materialism of today, an unfortunately circumstanced person like Ratan, who is endowed with a heightened sensibility, feels crushed under the growing weight of meaninglessness and isolation from his innermost nature and surroundings.

Ratan's humiliating experiences of job-hunting make him realize the cruelty of the human lot. He himself becomes "at the age of twenty-one, a hypocrite and a liar; in short, a sham." (28) As a clerk he works "harder than almost anybody in the department except the Superintendent himself." (37) Ratan is nevertheless always haunted by the morbid fear of losing his job and suffers from a keen desire for getting promotion and an intense preoccupation with work. He is almost invariably in a high strung mental condition, which threatens to ravage his soul and deprive him of his personality and identity. Ultimately he succumbs inescapably to the needs of his job and, rewarded with security and promotion, ends up by accepting a bribe when he least needs money. (61)

Ratan undergoes thus a profound change. The man who grew violent and rebellious even at the thought of "careers and bourgeois filth," (41) becomes in due course "a thick-skin and washout." (41) While he tries to seek "solace from the annals of corruption," (112) his dying conscience keeps on pricking him. At every stage he puts up an initial resistance only to discover the futility of his efforts. He sums up the problem of people like him as follows:

> No one seemed to be sure whether what was right was practicable. That was where the rub lay. In the practicability of things. That was where I saw the best of them buckle. Because very often the best did not have the daring or the greed of the charlatans. Thus the charlatans won. And when they saw the charlatans winning the best became even less sure of themselves. And at times they turned charlatans. (64)

The whole business of living in a muddle confuses him all the more and he fails to differentiate between right and wrong:

> The feeling generated in me a great confusion. What had I done, what had I done which I should not have done? What was right, what was wrong? What was the measure for doing things or not doing them? (72-73)

Ratan's dilemma is typical of an average product of this highly sophisticated civilization. With a troubled conscience Ratan goes from place to place without finding any peace or solace. He confesses to Himmat Singh:

> That is a terrible sensation . . . the realization that one's life has been a total waste, a great mistake; without purpose, without results. There are many sorrows in the world, but there is nothing in the three worlds to match the sorrow of a wasted life. All else, thoughts of revenge, of pleasure, of pain, pale before it, are made pointless. (140)

Ratan is keen on finding out the "purpose" of life and all its activities. But he takes almost a life-time to free himself from the shackles of the valueless urban civilization. In his eagerness, he visits the temple to derive courage from the world of religion. To his horror, however, he discovers that even religion is not free from corruption; it is corrupt and can hardly be expected to provide any solutions to various problems of this meaningless world. He is shaken out of his moral inertia when he sees the faceless head of his friend, the Brigadier. He tries to restore his mental peace by undergoing, finally, the most difficult penance in the world; every morning on his way to the office, he wipes outside the temple the shoes of the congregation.

V

Joshi's Sahitya Akademi Award winner novel, *The Last Labyrinth* (1981), probes into the turbulent inner world of an industrialist, Som Bhaskar, who becomes a millionaire at the age of thirty. He is married to a woman of his choice, who has borne him two children and is "all that a wife could be," yet he "goofed it all up" (40) and is relentlessly driven by undefined hungers. Amidst intriguing juxtapositions, the novel plunges into a haunting world of life, love, God and Death, the greatest of all mysteries – "the last labyrinth." With its spiritual and sensuous dimensions interwoven, it is a story of deeper seekings through love. The novel raises some pertinent questions about life and its meaning and tries to unravel the still unresolved mysteries of God and Death.

Right from the beginning, Som realizes that he has "become a nuisance" and that he has been fooling around "like a clown performing before a looking glass." (10) He is constantly tormented by a great roaring hollowness inside his soul and "the boredom and the fed-up-ness" resulting from his variegated experiences. (21) His "orchestras of discontent" (12) are, in fact, so frighteningly ceaseless that at the age of thirty-five he becomes "a worn-out weary man incapable of spontaneous feeling." (14) He is always in a hurry "like a hare chased by unseen hounds." (12) In his own estimation, he is "wondering, curious, analyzing, correlating, [but] getting nowhere." (80) He once said to Anuradha:

> "I'll tell you what is wrong. . . . I am dislocated. My mind is out of focus. There is something sitting right in front of me and I cannot see it. (107)

He feels as though struck by thunder, he bled totally of all energy, and that inside him "there was nothing but an empty roaring, like the roar of the sea in a conch." (115) He is always "dizzy, off-balance" and suffers from vague fears which have nothing to do with his body or his nerves. (152) His inflictions plunge him into "a bottomless pit of despair, like a shipwrecked sailor sinking into the ocean." (144)

The root cause of Som's problems is that he is relentlessly chased by undefined hungers. He is always haunted by mysterious voices:

> audible only to my ears, a grey cry threshed the night air: I want. I want. Through the light of my days and the blackness of my nights and the disquiet of those sleepless hours . . . I had sung the same strident song: I want. I want. I want. I want. (11)

He tries to quench his ravaging desires by possession of an object, a business enterprise and a woman named Anuradha of indeterminate age and origin, tall, handsome and tender. His desires know no satisfaction. He remembers:

> for many years now, I have had this awful feeling that I wanted something. But the sad thing was it didn't make the slightest difference when I managed to get what I had wanted. My hunger was just as bad as ever. . . . Later, it became more confused. . . . A world spinning all by itself. (189)

Anuradha, who knew him so well, explains the reasons of his unhappiness and dissatisfaction. "You don't know what you want," says she. "You don't know what is wrong and you don't know what you want." (106) Leela Sabnis thinks that his troubles originate from his habit of "always playing games with the world." She tells him bluntly: "You are lonely on the one hand. On the other, you have built a shell around yourself. . . . You are bored, bored still in your little shell. That is the long and short of it." (80)

Som's troubles get multiplied not only because of "the terrible loneliness" of his heart (23) but also because of his awareness of the lack of relevance in life. He finds the world meaningless. As a student he was upset by futile activities of life and begged the Headmaster's wife "to explain the meaning of it all." (24) Later he becomes even more convinced that life is full of complications – "a labyrinth within the labyrinths" (29) like the lanes of Benaras. He calls life "vanity of vanities," (32) which could be compared only to "meaningless flights of stairs" (34) or "a fisherman's net." (37) Summarizing his opinion about life, Som remarks: "Nothing was straightforward. One was always running a hurdle race." (133) He would like to know whether there was a mystery about life into which everything fitted properly. (161)

As a consequence of his grim experiences in life, Som develops "a new loathing for the squalid world." (46) He is disgusted with the people and himself. He maintains: "It is the voids of the world, more than its objects, that bother me. The voids and the empty spaces, within and without." (47) And on Manikarnika in Benaras, he finds "voids with a bang. Both within and without. . . . Voids all." (48)

Som rushes about in search of happiness and meaningfulness in life. "How happy I must be," he exclaims, "to have no problems in life." (98) But life is teeming with troubles and pains, which are all the more keenly felt by sensitive people. The greatest dilemma of human life is its ultimate reality, i.e. death. Like his father, Som is vexed by the mere thought of it. He says: "There was nothing I loathed more than I loathed the sight of death." (15) He wants to know its secret "without nagging, enervating doubts." (53) If death is to wind up all, what is the point in running madly with outstretched arms in pursuit of "little pleasures" or "little vendettas" of life! (65)

Som is urged on by a keen desire to know the meaning of life. But he fails to make any headway in this regard. The world remains to him "a mysterious world, as pretentious and meaningless as the holy bulls of Benaras." (108) He tries his best to have a peep into its mystery. His interest in its secrets is genuine. As he himself says: "Nothing had interested me more than the secrets of the universe." (129) He continues:

> Why should there be this turn to evolution? Why should Man be equipped, burdened with this strange . . . this strange sensibility, or urge or drive? Is it by chance? Or, is there a meaning to it? (131)

The questions about life and death continue to haunt him throughout his life. "And always in various shades of coherence," he confides, "the spoken or unspoken question, like a vulture, circled the corpse of my life: what lay in the last labyrinth?" (122) Asked by him as to what lies in the last labyrinth in the Lal Haveli, Aftab replies: "Why, death, of course." (37) Som would also like to know where one went after this life:

> Was this it, then? The terminus? The last of the labyrinth? . . . Was it this that I had wanted all my life? Was this the answer to the relentless chant "I want, I want." Why was it so unsatisfying? Or, may be, the labyrinth hadn't ended. Something else lay ahead, something more fundamental than a miracle. (211)

Som could not find any satisfactory answer to his questions. Being a highly rational person, he would not accept any readymade solution to his problem, such as irrational belief in supernatural elements or blind adherence to fatalism or determinism. His father, a chemist-turned-businessman, emphasized "the fundamental unity in the construction of the universe" and maintained that "everything happens in cycles. Birth, Growth, Decline and Death." (27) He wondered if there could not possibly be a First Cause behind the creation of the universe, which he regarded to be "the expression of a will," though he had no evidence to believe that there was a divine will. (204) He was, subsequently, pushed off to the edge of melancholia by these "bigger interrogations" and "a knowledge of verities sparsely known among ordinary men." (156) Som's grandfather, on the contrary, was "reckless, happy, unburdened by philosophical speculation." (156) Som has no "explanation of life's problems and as an ardent believer in Darwin, feels bogged down when he finds that "Darwin didn't say how we are supposed to evolve further." (132)

Som's search for life's secrets becomes hopelessly complicated because of his yearning to have the best of both the worlds – the world of matter and of spirit. He maintains: "What I needed, perhaps, was something, somebody, somewhere in which the two worlds combined." (82) Such wishes are not normally granted and one is in for frustration and disillusionment. Som also suffers in life, as his friend K. puts it, on account of his proneness to "romanticizing . . . blowing things larger than life." (189) Speaking of the unfortunate situation he is trapped in, Som himself observes:

> But I was just not myself. That was where the rub lay. . . . I had sorrows that did not let me breathe. . . . Then, there was the greatest sorrow of them all – that no one even guessed: There was the sorrow of idleness. . . . But there was always this bit of me, a large bit, somewhere between the head and the chest, just idling about like a stationary engine, getting involved with nothing. It made me feel as though I was asleep. This was no joke. In fact it was one of the weirdest things to happen to anybody. . . . Had it always been like that? Had I always been half asleep? Or, could it be that I once had a stable, wakeful life but had gradually lost my bearings? . . . If I knew what had put me to sleep I could, perhaps, get rid of it like one got rid of a hangover. . . . Everything was a haze. Time itself seemed wiped off like the spools of a computer. (109-10)

Som is, naturally, unimpressed by what he calls Gargi's "mumbo-jumbo" (163) or the religious-minded people's "half-assed rigmarole." (208) His obstinate questionings, however, would not solve the riddle of life for him. There is no doubt about his eagerness to know the meaning of life. He says to Gargi: "I *want* to know. Probably, I *want* to believe. But one can't order belief. I must have evidence." (213) His approach is very close to the scientific methods of experimentation and validation. With this approach, however, he does not go an inch nearer the secret of life.

In his desperation, Som even plans to visit temples every evening. He begins, ultimately, to nurture self-pity and, like one who has been completely vanquished by life, utters the terrible death wish. "A peaceful death" – that is all he wants, for he is mercilessly torn apart by his doubts. (164) He is eaten up by his own "strange mad thoughts" (223) and is incapable of paying adequate heed to the world and its normal demands. His flourishing business is reduced to "a big mess." (223)

Finally, when he tries to kill himself, he is stopped by Geeta, who shakes him "gently as though rousing a man from sleep." (224) We are given to believe that the unquestioning trust of his intelligent and understanding wife will restore peace to his life.

VI

Joshi's latest novel called *The City and the River* (1990) continues to treat, in its own ironical manner, the predicament of his characters in a hostile world. The crisis of the individual, however, has been replaced by the socio-political crisis of the City, which is a conglomerate of individuals and can be said to represent the whole humanity. In this novel also, Joshi poses significant questions about identity, commitment and faith. But these questions are approached from the standpoint of politics. The novel also throws significant sidelights on the relevance of meaning in life.

The main plot of the novel revolves around the familiar theme of power struggle. The Grand Master, who rules the city by the river, is determined to become its unchallenged king. His intentions are reinforced by the existence of an old prophecy. The prophecy is, however, read differently by the palace Astrologer and the Hermit of the Mountain. The ensuing events are highly complicated by the Grand Master's overambitious councillors, the defiance of people like Bhumiputra (which literally means "the son of the soil"), and the rebellion of the boatmen, who owe their allegiance only to the great river and are willing to die for their allegiance. The river to them, as the Headman says, is highly sacred; it is "a symbol of the divine mother" – of God Himself. (22) The boatmen regard themselves as "children of the great river." "If it is a matter of allegiance," remarks the Headman, "our allegiance is only to the river and cannot be shared, that is all that I want to say." (19) This allegiance is the *summum bonum* of their life.

This simple tale is nevertheless imbued with universal and eternal significance. The action of the novel takes place in a Nowhere City. The two important characters in it, the ageless Yogeshwara and the Nameless-One, symbolize the processes of regeneration and decay. The Grand Master and the boatmen represent the urge to dominate and the desire to assert one's identity respectively. The novel's warp and woof hinges on an eternal conflict, which keeps on emerging again and again. The cyclic march of humanity continues; a new city is reborn like phoenix on the ruins of the old. The river of life flows on and a new King and the Hermit appear on the scene to play their roles. This is probably the most significant part of apparently irrelevant and meaningless life:

> On the ruins of that city, as always happens, a new city has arisen. It is ruled by another Grand Master, which, of course, need not always happen. In the new city is another Professor, another Bhumiputra, another tribe of boatmen. There is also another Council and another set of Councillors. The men have other names but the forces they embody remain unchanged. And into all this when you go you will, perhaps, be known as another Hermit of the Mountain. And it is possible you will have a disciple whose name will be Little Star. To someone this replay, this repetition of things, might appear as charade, a joke. But, then, whoever said the good Lord did not have humour. (263)

It is this 'repetition of things' which imparts meaning to life. Without this continuity all human activities would become futile.

Although the novel is a political allegory, it can be read as a commentary on life. For common people, life is merely "a strange story tale" (10) comprising "pointless episodes." (16) The novelist seems to suggest nevertheless that, with sincere efforts, one can make one's life meaningful. Interestingly enough, there are frequent references to life's meaning and its purpose. "What is the use, what is the use," says the Rallies Master, and this may be taken to be the refrain of the entire saga. Shailaja, though upset by the disappearance of her people, does not realize the real cause or secret of it; only "God knows for what purpose" (241) have they gone away. There is also a purpose, as Bhumiputra himself says, in his remaining free. This view is endorsed by the Grandfather also. (150) The great purpose reserved for the Professor's life is to feed the sacrificial fire with his life. (166) Most things, persons and acts in this apparently purposeless world are thus said to have a purpose of their own. This is indeed a great stride on the part of the novelist. The "Asthough attitude," in its base form, cannot provide any solution to the life's myriad problems. "No doubt there would be initial inconvenience but, in the long run, all was bound to work out for the best." (37)

The change in the novelist's attitude is also borne out by mentions of context and cosmic harmony and other such things. The celebrations held in connection with the Festival of the River fail to arouse the desired response because they "have cut their contextual roots," being "simply the outpourings of the heated imaginations of the Astrologer and the Grand Master." (231) On the contrary, the boatmen's rebellion itself has a meaning behind it: It is essential for the sacrifice that would purify the City. (263) Not only actions but also words are meaningful. Unlike other boatmen, the Headman perceives the deeper meaning which is "not apparent on the surface." (18) The meaning of words is a prelude to cosmic harmony. "A *nada* ... that is at the heart of all things," though "not everyone will hear it." (52) As Shailaja's brother in his meditation realizes, it is "played on a cosmic scale, as though the whole universe was a one-string and some forgotten god had returned and reclaimed it and had briefly toyed with it in the silent night." (205) This cosmic harmony underlies, like a hidden current, all things and phenomena in this world, despite all its discordances and dissonance. But only right kind of people can give a right response and meaning to it. As the novelist puts on the penultimate page of the novel, "How one read it was all that mattered" and "it is what you are inside that governs how your read the outside." (263) This is also the drift of the following dialogue between the Hermit and Shailaja's brother:

> "Was it you who made the prophecy?" [asked Shailaja's brother.]
>
> "No."
>
> "But you know its meaning?"
>
> "It is written in the horoscope of the city. I have seen the horoscope, yes."
>
> "There is one man in the city, it is said, who knows the meaning. Are you the man?"
>
> "There are two men in the city who have seen the horoscope. They give to it different meanings."
>
> "Who is the other?"
>
> "The court Astrologer."
>
> "And who are you, if I may ask?"
>
> "Some call me the Hermit of the Mountain."

> "And what is your meaning?"
>
> "I do not know the whole meaning. All I know is that a great deal still depends upon the men who rule the city. Only the great river knows the true meaning." (228)

Very few people, however, can perceive the deeper purpose in life in a God-forsaken place. The unnamed City in the present novel is, by all standards, a highly inconducive place for this purpose. Cities, said Yogeshwara, "make their own horoscopes." This City is immaculate white and abounds in "tall structures of steel and glass." (12) But it is "falling apart." (199) Thanks to maladministration of the Grand Master and his Advisory Council, it is "preparing to immolate itself." (75) So unnatural is the City's atmosphere that, despite the chief horticulturist's strenuous efforts, and to the Grand Master's great regret, neither grass nor flowers grow on the Seven Hills. (136) The palace lawns in this "city of wonders" are such that they "leave much to be desired. All brown and yellow. No trees. No flowers. Not a patch of green." (31) People here, except boatmen, are generally "subdued and not normal." (96) In it "nothing was moving in the right direction" and everyone "was waiting for something to happen." (55) Chaos "piled upon chaos" (180) is the final impression of the City.

It is but natural that even sensible people in a setting like this suffer from weariness and loneliness. The Master of Rallies, for example, is "an unhappy man" and the real cause of his unhappiness is rootlessness:

> His misfortune lay in the fact that instead of teaching him how to row a boat his parents had wanted him to join the ranks of the brick-people. . . . The boatmen did not have the money to hire him, the brick-people considered him an upstart. (71)

Notwithstanding his scholarship and equipoise, the Professor is "weary" and "tired" of the world. (87) His search for Bhumiputra eventually leads him on to seek something deeper and more meaningful; "his search had turned into a search for some lost bit of himself." (159) Crushed by solitude and burden of human misery, even Bhumiputra "felt very alone." (157) He was forced to roam in wilderness, often having the feeling of "wandering through a desert land." (176) "A sense of overwhelming futility filled him at such times, so much so that he saw no point in living." (174) The case of the Grand Master or Dharma's father is not very different. The Minister for Trade frankly tells the Grand Master that he is tired and that in his weariness he lets "his dark thoughts assail" him. (203) Dharma's father, a powerful profiteer, is doomed to suffer from "the Three Truths Syndrome, statis of the soul. Atrophy of the brain and locomotor functions." (135) The stiffness of his joints is symptomatic of the hardening of his soul. He himself admits: "My insides are rotting. I too am just vanishing." (133) His condition degenerates each day so much so that "his mind turned blank, [and] his will was reduced to zero." His doctor tells him in good faith that medical treatment will not definitely cure him: "Exercise your soul. Take it for walks. Let it speak when it wants to speak. Let it rip." (134) Various people thus suffer from alienation for different reasons. Those who are more sensitive and honest feel its impact more keenly. Like the Professor, they could bewail: "I have spent my life in sleep. My life has been a joke. . . . God gave me life that I might serve this earth. I have squandered it on bauble." (163) In a meaningless and sterile world, where people blatantly violate all natural laws and are grossly egoistic, such a feeling is not unexpected.

VII

Joshi has also tried to present in his novels solutions to problems arising out of one's awareness of the lack of the purpose or meaning of life. The most devastating effect that ubiquitous meaninglessness can have is the stifling of spontaneity of the individual's personality, which has been conceived in terms of the "spontaneous assertion of [one's] individual initiative, feelings, wishes, [and] opinions."[27] A realization of the meaninglessness in life is a prelude to its diagnosis and cure. As Knoff suggests, the process of creating meaninglessness itself becomes centrally meaningful. Becker, too, is of the opinion that various states of alienation, including meaninglessness, tend to become in proper hands quests for value, significance, meaning and transcendence.[28] It would therefore be worthwhile to evaluate in some detail the solutions suggested by Joshi in his novels.

The Foreigner presents detachment as a possible panacea for life's problems. Sindi's moral growth depends, in fact, upon his search for detachment. "I don't want to get involved," says he, though "everywhere

I turned I saw involvement." (70) He considers involvement to be the root cause of all problems. His own experiences in love were eye-openers. He remembers:

> After years of struggle I had almost achieved what I had always wanted to be; without desire. But I had bartered away the gains in an attempt to possess a woman. I had exchanged the steady tranquillity of my being for the excruciating moments of ecstasy in a woman's body. (117-18)

In due course of time he comes to the realization that "one should be able to detach oneself from the object of one's love." (67) He has to face, however, a prolonged conflict between the "saint" and "the lusty beast" in him. In the initial stage he becomes "detached from everything" except himself. (195) It is June's death which finally breaks his attachment to himself.

The detachment which Sindi so resolutely cultivates to overcome his painful memories and meaninglessness of life becomes a source of deeper agony to him. It is his detachment that is responsible for the tragedy of Babu and June. "All along," Sindi himself confesses, "I had acted out of lust and greed and selfishness, and they had applauded my wisdom. When I had sought only detachment I had driven a man to his death." (6) Sindi's detachment does not seem to be wise. Explaining the reluctant transfer of her love to Babu, June tells Sindi: "You are so tied up with your own detachment it makes little difference whether you love or you don't." She further protests: "I had wanted to belong to you, but you didn't want it. You are so self-sufficient there is hardly any place for me in your life – except perhaps as a mistress." (158)

Sindi's obsession with the notion of detachment makes him shirk his responsibility. Like Camus's Meursault, he is always bored with the world, and like Neil of Philip Roth's *Good Bye, Columbus* he does not want to shoulder even ordinary responsibilities. He muses if his detachment and objectivity have been of any value in life. He had all along tried "to speculate about these things objectively, not realizing that objectivity was just another form of vanity." (119) Detachment becomes a misty notion with him and is used to mean so many things including love in a detached manner: "Love without fooling yourself that the things you love are indispensable either to you or to the world." (170)

Originally Sindi mistook detachment to mean inaction, but now he begins to "see the fallacy in it. Detachment consisted of right action and not escape from it." (193) The neutrality between right and wrong, according to S. Radhakrishnan, is "a sign of moral perversity." An ordinary employee of the Khemka Industries named Muthu, who is better able to understand "the ultimate futility of human effort," (42) rightly maintains that "sometimes detachment lies in actually getting involved." (225)

The Foreigner reads like a bitter commentary on Somerset Maugham's *Razor's Edge*. Larry, the hero of Maugham's novel, keeps on asking himself "what life was for" and fails to understand properly the significance of its problems.[29] The novelist himself is not sure of the purpose of life. He thinks that "one has to make up one's mind what is the meaning and use of life. If death ends all . . . there is no reason for life and life has no meaning."[30] Larry is, however, a living example of detachment. He is without ambition and has no weakness for fame – that last infirmity of the noble mind; renounces all his worldly possessions except his taxi, which he regards as "the instrument" of his labour, like "the staff and the begging bowl of the wandering mendicant," (283) and would not mind where he sleeps and would be satisfied with one meal a day. He says: "It was hard for me to believe that God thought much of a man who tried to wangle salvation by fulsome flattery. I should have thought the worship most pleasing to Him was to do your best according to your lights." (254) It may be noted that the value of art, according to Maugham, is "not beauty, but right action."[31] Significantly enough, *The Summing Up* ends with a quotation from Luis de Leon: "The beauty of life . . . is nothing but this, that each should act in conformity with his nature and his business." This is what Larry precisely does. He practises the *Karmayoga* every moment in his life. "My mind is free," says he, "when I, washing a car or tinkering with a carburetor and when the job's done I have the pleasant sensation of having accomplished something." (282) Larry's detachment may appear "an ingenious notion" and not a "very satisfactory" way (279) of realizing one's possibilities, as it does to the narrator, but it helps him achieve what he wants, i.e. "happiness," and his life could not possibly have fallen into "a more perfect pattern." (295) Sindi's detachment, on the contrary, looks pale beside Larry's, which is born of his genuine conviction and "long quest."

In *The Foreigner* Joshi makes use of terms and concepts which evoke typically Indian philosophical thoughts in one's mind. For example, Sindi remarks:

> All love – whether of things, persons or oneself – is illusion and all pain springs from that.... Birth and death are constants. The rest is variable.... Each one of us lives in his own reality.... The wheel of Karma like the wheel of Industrialization never stops. To concentrate on the decisive action. The fruit of it was not my concern. (170)

The whole of this statement is a paraphrase of well-known Indian philosophical theories. The last line in particular translates the famous teaching of the *Geeta* (ii. 47): *karmanyevadhi-karaste ma phalesu kadacana*. Indian thoughts are used by the novelist mostly for explanation of attitudes and rationalization of happenings. But for its name, however, the Sindi Oberoi brand of detachment has no intrinsic relation with the Indian concept, and compared to it, appears rather superficial.[32] We find in *The Foreigner* Indian philosophical concepts grafted on the usual stuff of existential literature.[33] Detachment arising out of one's estrangement[34] and the genuine detachment characteristic of a *sthitiprajna* have very little in common. It is not surprising therefore that Sindi's problems are not satisfactorily solved by this veneer of metaphysical cover. Reckoning his final account towards the end of the novel, he remarks:

> In many ways the past had been a waste, but it had not been without its lessons. I had started adult life as a confused adolescent, awesomely engrossed with myself, searching for wisdom and the peace that comes with it. The journey had been long and tedious and still was not over.
>
> And the future? In an ultimate sense, I knew, it would be as meaningless as the past. But in a narrower sense, there would perhaps be useful tasks to be done; perhaps, if I were lucky, even a chance to redeem the past. (221)

The reason for Sindi's failures is not difficult to get. As he himself suggests: "Life is not a business account. . . . Once your soul goes bankrupt, no amount of plundering can enrich it again." (140)

The Strange Case and *The Apprentice* suggest different approaches to counteract life's meaninglessness. As Billy's example testifies, if one is able to establish a rapport with the primitive forces in the world of nature, one can get rid of all problems of life. Bilasia, it is held, symbolizes "the primitive culture, the untapped subterranean resources of psychic energy."[35] It would be better to regard her as the Matter (*Prakrti*), which according to the Sankhya system of Indian philosophy, is "one" and eternal, not an illusionary appearance but something real. Billy might be taken to represent the Soul (*Purusa*), which by its mere presence excites Matter and illumines the processes of the evolution of the universe. Bilasia, we are reminded, is "the embodiment of that primal and invulnerable force that had ruled these [Maikala] hills, perhaps this earth, since time began." (226) Her "enormous eyes," we are told, "poured out a sexuality that was nearly as primeval as the forest that surrounded them." (141) In the Sankhya philosophy the material universe is traced to a First Cause.

It is significant to note that in *The Last Labyrinth*, Joshi explicitly talks of the First Cause and hints at the Sankhya type of relationship. Gargi, asking Som not to quarrel with Anuradha, asks him to bear in mind that "she is your shakti." (121) The exposition of such a relation by the novelist is not mere conjecture. At the very first sight of the *Prakrti* (Bilasia), the *Purusa* (Billy) is confronted with a multitude of questions: "What was Bilasia? What is the playful effervescence of a mountain stream? What is sunlight filtering through a glade? What is the thunder of a volcano or the hardness of granite? What is the vengeance of a cobra whose mate has been killed?" (225) and so on. Once the *Purusa* comes into communion with the *Prakrti*, he is capable of realizing all his potentialities and, though remaining in the most complete passivity, of attaining godhood.

The Souls, it may be noted, are "many" and even in search of the Matter, though not many of them are able to maintain harmony with it. As Dhunia, the headman, explains, the Black Forest (representing the *Prakrti*) called Billy, as it does everyone else, "just so that he may know who he was." (163) Billy, as we know, is "seeking something *else*" (189) than merely a tribal way of living; it is "the search for truth" (177) and life's meaningfulness. When he comes into harmonious contact with the *Prakrti* (in the form of Bilasia and her world), he realizes the very essence of life and begins to behave "like rain on parched lands, like balm on a wound." (159-60) This is a sure, but difficult, way of solving the riddle of life, suggested by the oldest system of Indian philosophy. To quote H. Oldenberg: "The Soul . . . abides eternally released from delusion and suffering of this world, as a seer who no longer sees anything, a glass in which nothing is any longer reflected, as pure untroubled light by which nothing is illuminated."[36]

In *The Apprentice* Joshi has suggested another remedy to life's problems, which is within the easy reach of the common man. Ratan comes to realize – and rightly so – that life may well be a zero, but "it need not be negative." (148) He learns, ultimately, the lessons of humility and resignation to the Will of God, doing what he can "without vanity and without expectations and also without cleverness." (149) He becomes conscious of the folly of his earlier life and undergoes the most difficult penance for his earlier misdeeds. Every morning on his way to the office, he sits on the steps outside the temple and wipes the shoes of the congregation. He says:

> I never enter the temple. I am not concerned with what goes on in there. I stand at the doorstep and I fold my hands, my hands smelling of leather and I say things. Be good, I tell myself. Be good. Be decent. Be of use. (148)

Ratan's conversion may sound somewhat unnatural and rather extreme. But it is very much possible under the circumstances of his life, and has been found to take place more than once both in literature and actual life. An absolute humility and genial acceptance of life as it is can undoubtedly create an inner centre of peace and serenity for the individual.

The Last Labyrinth considers more pertinently the questions raised in the earlier novels. The protagonist, Som, is a modern millionaire who is guided by reason and not by faith. Pointing out his problem he says: "If I believed in God I could pray, maybe run a rosary through my fingers. But that's out. Sitting around, I get into arguments: with the living and with the dead, with myself. And I have had enough of the world's arguments." (10) He is, apparently, at war with himself.

Som's scepticism and highly rational approach only aggravate his problems as they did in the case of J.S. Mill. Som struggles hard to come to terms with life and find out its meaning, but to no avail. He can compare his struggling self only to "an ant threading through a maze, knocking about, against one wall, then another." (53) Curious to know the secret of life, he tries to probe into "that core of loneliness around which all of us are built." (54) He is fully convinced that all the problems can be solved if one has knowledge. He maintains:

> If only one knew! If only miracles were to take place, as of old, and one could suddenly, irrefutably, know. Without nagging, enervating doubts. I want, I want. If only one knew what one wanted. Or, maybe, to *know* was what I wanted. To know. Just that. No more. No less. (53)

Som's dilemma, however, is not solved by his thirst for knowledge. It was his father's knowledge, he knows, that pushed him over to melancholia. There is something wrong with the very means followed by Som to attain knowledge. Anuradha tells him: "You are wrong even about yourself. You think you know a lot, when, in fact, you don't." (61) Aftab also reminds him: "I told you, you are different. You don't understand us. You work by logic. By your brain. You are proud of your education or what you consider education. There is an understanding that only suffering and humiliation bring. . . . You are empty of that understanding." (217)

Life's riddles, it is suggested, can be solved by an unwavering "trust in the world's mechanisms, this faith that the engine shall not seize, or worse, explode." (63) But Som is not the type of the person who would readily trust. Not that he does not realize the value of genuine understanding and trust. He himself remarks:

> But I needed the trust—who doesn't? I needed it all the more because I did not trust myself, or my men, or my fate, or the ceaseless travel on the social wheel. Between the empty home and the cluttered offices . . . in this whore of a city what I needed most was to be reassured that all was well. (63)

He tries to assure Gargi that he is not vain or arrogant but curious – "may be over-curious." (214) He does not possess, however, a believing mind and is made of a sterner stuff. As he says in the beginning of the novel: "Above all, I have a score to settle, I forget nothing, forgive no one." (9) Having failed miserably to comprehend life and its dilemmas he cries (not unlike Marlowe's Doctor Faustus!) towards the end of the novel, requesting Anuradha to listen to him:

> Is there a God where you are? Have you met Him? Does He have a face? Does He speak? Does He hear? Does He understand the language we speak? Anuradha, if there is a God and if you have met Him and if He is willing to listen, then, Anuradha, my soul, tell Him, tell this God, to have mercy upon me. Tell Him I am weary. Of so many fears; so much doubting. Of this dark earth and these empty heavens. (222-23)

Most of Som's questions, though natural to a non-believer like him, would have no meaning to a devout believer. Som's weariness is understandable, but he realizes his mistake rather too late. Leela Sabnis tells him that what he wants is "a mystical identification . . . with a godhead." "You haven't got the faith. You have always been a sceptic. You always will be." (113) He is badly in need of a healing touch of an unqualified faith. We only hope that his deep-seated scepticism and overwhelming rationalism will be cured by the genial effect of his wife, who "trusts like birds fly, like fish swim," and whom trust envelopes "like the amniotic fluid envelopes the embryo, protecting her." (63)

Som's wife is presented as a "sensible, brave" person "aware of certain fundamentals" of life which have remained hidden from her husband. (147) She is, in fact, a "child of another world, traversing, like a plane at a higher altitude, a corridor separate from the dark vestibule." (69) This trust, however, is not the property of religious people alone. Anuradha's mother, for example, who never married the man whom she lived with, had it in abundance, and Anuradha herself, who is described as "nobody's wife," (43) feels it inside her "like one may feel a baby, growing stronger and bigger every day." (134)

In *The Last Labyrinth* the world of dreams, illusions and doubts has been juxtaposed with that of reality and understanding. Words like "dream," "mystery," "doubt," "reality" and "understanding" seem to serve as recurrent motifs—"the minimal dissection of the thematic material."[37] We are reminded of "the miasma of Lal Haveli," (113) where most incidents take place, and of the "morass" of this "tawdry, sensual den, a dead house in a dead city." (108) Benaras, Aftab, Anuradha and their haveli—all appear to Som as "bores, frogs stuck in their ancient marshy wells." (113) Som suffers from the delusions and is condemned to an existence in which "at some point on the horizon all is mixed up." (75) Anuradha, too, looks "mysterious" and there is a "mystery" within Som. (89)

In this "mysterious world" everything is "a haze," (108) and there is "a mystery into which everything fitted." (161) Som's efforts are directed towards perceiving and explaining this very mystery of the world. His struggle, however, is rendered "futile" by his "nagging, enervating doubts." (53) "Of late," says he, "I doubted everything and everybody"; and "my fears, real or imagined, had exponentially increased." (152) He is "torn apart" by his doubts, "the wolves that are going to eat you up." (164) Such a one can hardly perceive the reality of life in true colours. Everything pertaining to life appears to him "such stuff as dreams are made of." Som refers to his dream-like state more than once. He says: "And I dreamt I was in a labyrinth." (82) His past life "had been like a dream" and he is "glad the dream was over." (83) He further remarks: "I dreamt I was in a narrow alley at the end of which a shroud lay. . . . The alley and the houses were deserted." (105) Aftab also "lives in a dream world." (128)

As against this benighted world of dreams and doubts, we have the world of reality and understanding. The river Ganga is seen by Som as "leading to a reality" that he has not yet known. (49) But is it easy to see this reality clearly? Even Geeta admits that "everything is so complicated." (170) "Reality," as Som realizes later, "was so like an iceberg. You never saw the whole of it." (161) An unswerving appreciation of reality is possible if one possesses an understanding born of tolerance and acceptance of all the facts of life with nonchalance.

It is significant to note that the word "understanding" has been used several times in the second half of the novel. K. tell Som: "You don't understand." (209) Aftab describes him as "a secretive devil," (146) and complains that he does not "understand" them because he always works by logic. (217) Leela Sabnis is of the opinion that "if man can go to moon, surely he can make a dent in understanding himself." (79) She herself is said to have "studied and understood and memorized," (79) but it is surprising how little she has "understood the roots of the world's confusion." (80)

Anuradha, Geeta and Gargi are the only ones endowed with proper understanding. Anuradha is "gifted with a special vision" (58) and her eyes are "filled with understanding." (100) Som's wife Geeta is credited with "some subtle understanding" of him, (147) though at times she finds it difficult to "understand what was going on" in his heart. (162) The novel ends with Som's hope that "she understands." (224) Finally, we are repeatedly told that Gargi is "the only one who understood." (203) Som is "keen that Gargi should understand" him. (100) He thinks that she "understood not only what had happened just then but also all that had taken place" between him and Anuradha. (100) Gargi's "intelligent understanding eyes" have a profound impression on Som, but he can "never understand why she had that effect" on him. (202) We are also told that "there is an understanding that only suffering and humiliation bring" and that "Anuradha has that," even Aftab claims to "have a bit of it," but Som is "empty of that understanding." (217)

It is this understanding born of suffering and humiliation that seems to have been presented as a solution to life's meaninglessness in this novel. The novelist suggests that a mere rational approach to life's problems will not do. Einstein once affirmed: "We have to jump out of our mind." The explanation given by thinkers like Darwin and Freud are only partially true. Freud, it is maintained, seems to be "groping in the night of man's mind." (77) And Darwin's theory of evolution fails to give a plausible answer to certain queries regarding life and its riddles. Anuradha says: "Maybe Krishna begins where Darwin left off." (132)

The unwavering faith has been given as a sensible substitute for rationalism. Som's mother had it and she preferred to die rather than relinquish her trust. Fortified by their all-encompassing belief, saints remain "uninvolved, unmoved." (17) Even Som, while climbing the temple, finds the sky turn "lighter, brighter, more hopeful." (180) When he reaches the temple, he comes to know that it is a day for vows. Asked by him if people's wishes get fulfilled there, the *panda* replies: "It depends on their faith. Faith can move mountains." (198)

To get the unwavering faith, however, is not an easy job. One has to make an unqualified surrender of everything belonging to him, including reason and questionings. Aftab tells Som: "You have to sacrifice before you are given. You can't have your cake and eat it too, . . . You want to have faith. But you also want to reserve the right to challenge your own faith when it suits you." (166) Such a matter is not like a marriage of convenience. When Som insists on evidence, Gargi tells him that "God does not work in this simple manner" and that while struggling to know life's dilemma, "we are all children trying to reach up to a crack in the door to peep into a room." (213, 214) Life's problems being what they are, we have no option but to trust and pray if we want to lead a really peaceful life. As Kierkegaard says: "Prayer does not change God, but it changes him who prays." This is what *The Last Labyrinth* also seems to suggest.

Arun Joshi's novels are thus increasingly bold attempts to discover the meaning of life. They try to devise ways and means for eliminating the discrepancy between the individual's pursuits and his fulfilment. Joshi's heroes are lonely and misfits in the world in which they have to live and face the meaninglessness of life. Though they are not religious or saintly, they are humble enough to learn lessons taught to them by life's problems. While experiencing the normal claims of love and hatred, doubts and dilemmas, they try to face challenges of their meaningless life by outstripping the narrow confines of their distraught selves.

Joshi suggests a different solution in each of his novels. He does not care to work out fully the philosophical possibilities of his themes. Nor does he try to probe deeply into his characters's psychology. There is nothing very original about the means suggested by him to counteract life's meaninglessness; they have been described in Indian philosophy and scriptures elaborately, but the way he integrates them in his novels is really remarkable.

One may establish a tenuous relation among different solutions put forth by Joshi, but there is no real progression of thought from novel to novel. He seems to be groping for *the* solution to face the meaninglessness of life, and his search for it, in its present state, remains indeterminate. His novels nevertheless go a long way in affirming the value of meaningfulness in life. They seem to indicate that one can realize the essence of life by liberating the self from the clutches of mercenary civilization and by paying due heed to authentic calls of the inner being. This seems to Joshi to be the only way out of saving man from terrifying degradation and purposelessness of the contemporary sordid, meaningless world.

Joshi's latest novel, *The City and the River*, is far more optimistic than his earlier novels. He does not deny the existence of evil but hastens to reassure that it cannot last for ever and that a new world would emerge in which a new beginning would be made. (167) Since God resides in each soul, "Is not, therefore, always, room for hope? We never know when the soul of a Grand Master is touched and in that hour his life is transformed." (263) We are repeatedly reassured that "all should be well," (29) that "There is season for everything," (114) and that "Time will settle things." (218) But we are equally pertinently reminded that the cure for all problems is to be found "within oneself." (69) Like the earlier novel, Joshi's latest novel emphasizes the significance of prayer, faith, understanding and Truth. Prayers and vows, he holds, perfect a person. (100) Understanding brings tranquillity (9) and enables him to know things by himself. (142) A clear understanding and self-knowledge unfolds Truth, which "destroys falsehood at its very roots." (112) The novelist makes mention of the wheel of *karma* (42, 65, 164) and loosely translates (98) the famous line from the *Bhagavadgita: yada yada hi dharmasya glanir bhavati Bharata/abhyutthanam adharmasya tadatmanam srjamyaham*. (IV/7) In order to "prevent this endless repetition," says the novelist, "this periodic disintegration," human hearts must become pure. The purification of egoism, selfishness and stupidity, however, demands sacrifice. (262-63) The *yajna* of life "burns only on sacrifice" and when the fire is low, "men must feed it with their own life." (166) Doing so, according to the novel, would be fulfilling a great purpose in life.

Joshi claims to have made a steady progress from novel to novel in delineating characters. He wrote to V. Gopal Reddy on 8 January 1981: "Alienation of my characters in the novels which I have written so far ultimately leads them back to community. I realized that in . . . *The Last Labyrinth* for the first time this does not happen."[38] In *The City and the River*, however, a more serious commitment is discernible. The novel explores the relevance of God to man and affirms that "the world indeed belongs to God and to no one else." God is presented as "the highest Truth"; He is "the noblest thing each of us can imagine." (70) The belief in God restores peace to human soul. (76) Even if we do not at times succeed, "In the great hand of God we stand, and can only do our best. For the rest, it is His Law and His Will." (157) Notwithstanding the Grand Master's sceptical ejaculations ("And God – what is God? Where is He? Does he even exist? He must surely have other things to worry about than intervene in the affairs of this city," (219) the final message of the novel is summed up in Yogeshwara's words: "His is the Will, His is the force." (264) An unqualified surrender to His will, according to the novel, is the only solution to life's problems.

VIII

Soon after receiving the Sahitya Akademi award, Joshi told an interviewer that through his novels he tried to explore "that mysterious underworld which is the human soul."[39] His novels delineate the spiritual agony of his lonely questers. Life's meaning, according to Joshi, lies not in the glossy surfaces of pretensions but in the dark mossy labyrinths of the soul. Joshi looks upon human lives as "labyrinths – hopeless mazes where you may get irretrievably lost or discover the shining secrets at the core of life."[40] It is these dark, dismal experiences of the soul that are the subject matter of his novels. The novelist is pre-occupied with what he himself describes in *The Last Labyrinth* as "that core of loneliness around which all of us are built." (54) "We belonged," he adds, "to the same benighted underside of the world." (55) Situated as we are, in this incomprehensible world, we are "like an ant threading through a maze, knocking about, against one wall, then another." (53) The novelist has made sincere efforts to throw significant light on the human mind's journey into a labyrinth, "this going forward and backward and sideways of the mind." (53) His explorations are of considerable value in the modern context.

NOTES

1. *The Liberal Imagination* (New York: Doubleday, 1953), pp. 205, 215.
2. K.R. Srinivasa Iyengar, "The Literature of India," in A.L. McLeod, ed., *The Commonwealth Pen* (New York: Cornell University Press, 1961), p. 140.
3. Meenakshi Mukherjee, *The Twice Born Fiction: Themes and Techniques of the Indian Novel in English* (New Delhi: Heinemann Educational Books, 1971), p. 22.
4. "Fiction in India," *The Reporter*, 28/4 (14 February 1963), p. 59.
5. C. Paul Verghese, *Problems of the Indian Creative Writer in English* (Bombay: Somaiya, 1971), pp. 124, 125.
6. *Man in Modern Fiction* (New York: Random House, 1958), p. 3.
7. *The Spiritual Crisis of Man* (London: Rider, 1952), p. 7.
8. *Adonis and the Alphabet* (London: Chatto and Windus, 1956), p. 124.
9. Sisir Kumar Ghosh, *Modern and Otherwise* (Delhi: D.K., 1975), p. 5.
10. See B. Murchland, *The Age of Alienation* (New York: Random House, 1971).
11. Erich Fromm, et al., *Zen Buddhism and Psychoanalysis* (New York: Harper and Row, 1970), p. 86.
12. C. Wright Mills, *White Collar* (New York: Oxford University Press, 1951), p. 157.
13. Karl Jaspers, *Man in the Modern Age* (New York: Doubleday, 1956), pp. 202, 210.
14. *The Courage to Be* (New Haven: Yale University Press, 1952), p. 142.
15. *The Sane Society* (New York: Holt, Rinehart, 1955), pp. 122, 360.
16. *Alienation: Concept, Term and Meanings* (New York and London: Seminar Press, 1973), p. 46.
17. Melvin Seeman, "On the Meaning of Alienation," *American Sociological Review*, 24/6 (December 1959), p. 786.
18. Karl Mannheim, *Man and Society in an Age of Reconstruction* (New York: Harcourt, Brace, 1940), p. 59.

19. Simon O. Lasser, *Fiction and the Unconscious* (London: Peter Owen, 1960), p. 61.
20. "The Hypnotized People," *Partisan Review*, 27/2 (1960), pp. 311-12.
21. Jasbir Jain, "Foreigners and Strangers: Arun Joshi's Heroes," *The Journal of Indian Writing in English*, 5/1 (January 1977), p. 52.
22. O.P. Bhatnagar, "Arun Joshi's *The Foreigner*: A Critique of East and West," *The Journal of Indian Writing in English*, 1/2 (July 1973), pp. 13-14.
23. *Quest*, 60 (January-March 1969), p. 101.
24. All textual references to Arun Joshi's novels have been given parenthetically. The following editions have been used: *The Foreigner* (Delhi: Hind, 1968); *The Strange Case of Billy Biswas* (Delhi: Orient Paperbacks, 1971); *The Apprentice* (Delhi: Orient Paperbacks, 1974); *The Last Labyrinth* (Delhi: Vision, 1981); and *The City and the River* (New Delhi: Vision, 1990).
25. Jasbir Jain, p. 54.
26. O.P. Mathur and G. Rai, "The Existential Note in Arun Joshi's *The Strange Case of Billy Biswas* and *The Apprentice*," *Commonwealth Quarterly*, 5/17 (December 1980), p. 35. In an interview, Joshi admitted to Purabi Bannerji that he was considerably influenced by existentialist writers. "I did read Camus and Sartre," he said. "I liked *The Plague* and read *The Outsider*. I might have been influenced by them. Sartre I did not understand clearly or like. As for existential philosophers like Kierkegaard, I have never understood anything except odd statements." "A Winner's Secrets," *The Sunday Statesman*, 27 February 1983.
27. *New Ways in Psychoanalysis* (New York: W.W. Norton, 1939), pp. 189, 252, 278.
28. E. Becker, *The Birth and Death of Meaning* (Glencoe, III: Free Press, 1962), chs. 3 and 8.
29. W.S. Maugham, *Razor's Edge* (Philadelphia: Blackiston, 1944), p. 251.
30. W.S. Maugham, *The Summing Up* (New York: The New American Library, 1938), p. 171.
31. *Ibid.*, p. 187.

32. The characteristics of a detached person have been given in the *Geeta*, ch. 4.
33. Existentialistic trends have been noted in the writings of Arun Joshi by Mathur and Rai, and Elena J. Kalinnikova, *Indian English Literature: A Perspective* (Ghaziabad: Vimal, 1982), ch. 5.
34. On the nature of this type of detachment, see Walter Kaufmann, "Introductory Essay" to Richard Schacht, *Alienation* (London: George Allen and Unwin, 1970), pp. xliv-xlvi.
35. C.N. Srinath, "Crisis of identity: Assertion and Withdrawal in Naipaul and Arun Joshi," *The Literary Criterion*, 14/1 (1979), p. 39.
36. Quoted in *Encyclopaedia of Religion and Ethics*, ed. James Hastings (Edinburgh: T. and T. Clark), Vol. XI, p. 192.
37. L. Dolezel, "Towards a Structural Theory of Content in Prose Fiction," in S. Chatman, ed., *Literary Style: A Symposium* (OUP, 1971), p. 76.
38. Quoted in V. Gopal Reddy, "From Alienation to Community: A Note on the Novels of Arun Joshi," *Kakatiya Journal of English Studies*, 7 (1985-86), p. 90.
39. Sujata Mathai, "I'm a Stranger to my Books," *The Times of India*, 7 July 1983, p. 8.
40. *Loc. cit.*

Arun Joshi and the Labyrinth of Life

O.P. MATHUR and G. RAI

Arun Joshi is one of the most significant Indian English novelists of today. For, almost alone among them, he is concerned with the predicament of modern man and his attempt to understand the labyrinth of life. Joshi's angst-ridden protagonists are relentlessly in search of a way to face with dignity a life which is ugly, inescapably painful and always unsatisfying. Ultimately, however, they are able to arrive at some form of personal affirmation.

In his first novel *The Foreigner*, Arun Joshi explores the individual's anguished consciousness of being isolated from the whole apparatus of social convention and ritual. Sindi Oberoi finds himself in the predicament of an outsider. An Indian by origin, brought up in Kenya, educated in London and America, he clearly does not belong and drifts restlessly on the surface of life. He says to Mr Khemka:

> You had a clear-cut system of morality, a caste system that laid down all you had to do. You had a God; you had roots in the soil you lived upon. Look at me. I have no roots. I have no system of morality.... I have no reason to be one thing rather than another.[1]

Like Meursault of Camus's *The Outsider*, Sindi is devoid of emotion, having no respect for society or religion. He believes that "there is no end to suffering, no end to the struggle between good and evil." (43) He feels that his life is purposeless: "Somebody had begotten me without a purpose and so far I had lived without a purpose, unless you could call the search for peace a purpose." (65) His total involvement with self, as he realizes later, results in the death of his friend Babu Rao Khemka and his sweetheart June Blyth. His dissatisfaction with the mechanical apparatus of life leads him onto a quest for identity and integration.

The theme of anxiety arising out of the chaos prevalent in modern life, which makes its first appearance in *The Foreigner*, is more effectively treated in Arun Joshi's later novels. *The Strange Case of Billy Biswas*, like the first novel, develops the theme of man's feeling of anxiety and alienation. The protagonist Bimal or Billy Biswas comes of "the upper-upper crust of Indian society."[2] Though born and brought up in comfort and affluence, his awareness of the deeper layers of his personality makes him something like an existential being, alienated from the superficial reality of life. The ordered, systematized, civilized life which the contemporary man is proud of, intensifies Billy's problem of identity. He develops a bitter aversion for the civilized world and a strong streak of primitivism, "a great force, *urkraft*, a . . . a primitive force," (23) is evident in him even when he is in America. On his return to India he feels like a visitor from the wilderness to the marts of Big city. The *Kitch* culture of the affluent India, which his wife Meena represents, makes him an exile.

In *The Apprentice*, Arun Joshi's third novel, the individual endowed with heightened sensibility feels powerless and isolated from his authentic self as well as from the world outside which has become chaotic, brutal and insensitive. The protagonist is Ratan Rathor, who flouts his values for the sake of a career and is sucked into the vortex of bureaucratic and political corruption only to be shocked out of it after the death of his innocent friend. But in the beginning he is an over-enthusiastic idealist who is gradually forced to come to terms with the hard realities of life. He feels shocked at the atrocities committed by the British people:

> Every now and then someone I knew was imprisoned, maimed, or killed and for days afterwards I felt burdened as though in some way I had been responsible for the killing.[3]

Though his docility and hard work enable him to climb the ladder of bureaucracy, he always feels restless in this unjust and incongruous world. He feels sad after refusing an enormous bribe of ten thousand rupees:

> If earlier, during the days of the inn, my back had nearly been broken by the world's unjust thrashing, I was now struck dumb by its other face, the absurd servility, with which it was willing to turn about and worship the very men whom it had earlier thought nothing of annihilating. (44)

The hopeless mess of life inspires a nausea in Ratan Rathor who thinks of bringing about a change in the existing set-up. He writes a pompous article entitled "Crisis of Character" and distributes its cyclostyled copies. Such a man is fated to be a saint or a sufferer, more probably the latter. He is almost at the threshold of life and is doomed to be caught in its mazes.

The theme of spiritual agony reappears in Arun Joshi's recent novel *The Last Labyrinth*, which explores the turbulent inner world of a wealthy young Indian. Som Bhaskar is an industrialist, married to Geeta, a woman of his choice who has borne him two children. Born of rich parents, educated at the world's finest universities, spending a quarter of a million on his education, he has resources enough for the joy of physical living. But quite strangely he is constantly driven by undefined hungers:

> Through the light of my days and the blackness of my nights and the disquiet of those sleepless hours beside my wife, within reach of the tranquillizers, I had sung the same strident song: I want. I want. I want. I want.[4]

Even at thirty-five, he is "a worn-out weary man incapable of spontaneous feeling." (14) The voids within and without keep him restless all the while:

> It is the voids of the world, more than its objects, that bother me. The voids and the empty spaces, within and without. Voids of caves and voids of the sky; the terrible vacancies of *lokalok*. (47)

His unbearable sorrows never let him be: "I had sorrows that did not let me breathe." (109) He sadly feels that he has no God nor religion to relieve him of the void: "If I believed in God I could pray, maybe run a rosary through my fingers. But that's out." (10) He is envious of those who believe, particularly his mother, who died of cancer, his wife and mistress. As he says, if his wife Geeta's "trademark" is "trust," his is "discontent." (63)

To escape this feeling of restlessness, Arun Joshi's protagonists make relentless efforts. They are anxiously wandering through the mazes of their existence, looking for a purpose of life. Sindi Oberoi is puzzled to see apparent pleasure ending in pain. However, he continues his search and one morning, while sitting on a weathered stone, he suddenly feels greatly lightened:

> All love – whether of things, or persons, or oneself – was illusion and all pain sprang from this illusion. Love begot greed and attachment, and it led to possession. (180)

And therefore, a wise man must love without attachment or desire, and without thinking that the objects of his love are indispensable. Sindi seeks to achieve total detachment in life and withdraws from all action that might cause pain. But he finds it hard to practise it. He is aware that one does not choose one's involvement. The deaths of his friend and his sweetheart resulting from Sindi's own blundering approach to life shake his confidence. A strong urge to roam about the streets of the world overtakes him and he longs to be in a place where he can experiment with himself and start life anew. He thus reminds us of Conrad's Jim who moves ahead in search of a new world entirely free from his past, like a "straggler yearning inconsolably for his humble place in the ranks."[5]

In a mood of despair that envelopes his being like water surrounding a fish, Sindi gets his second insight into the nature of life: "Detachment at that time had meant inaction. Now I had begun to see the fallacy in it. Detachment consisted of right action and not escape from it." (204) In the unjust, corrupt world of Mr Khemka, Sindi gets the opportunity to practise what he has learnt out of his long quest – action without detachment. He offers to do "something meaningful," (14) i.e., something that could make him forget himself. This in itself is a step in the right direction. His preoccupation with self seems to be crumbling and gradually he begins to feel sympathy for the labourers working for Mr Khemka:

> It was a sad sight. The workers' clothes were falling off in rags and sweat poured off their backs as if they had just had a shower. What was the point in all those big men like Mr Khemka talking about God and pain so long as half-naked men had to wrestle with a beastly mass of concrete under a scorching sun? And all for three rupees a day. (209)

He is further involved in sympathetic attachment when he visits Muthu's family. The "accumulated despair of their weary lives" (240) makes him take over the management of the imprisoned Mr Khemka's business: "I felt as if I had been dropped on a sinking ship and charged with the impossible task of taking it ashore." (239-40) His earlier detachment with the world has now been replaced by a fervent but unselfish attachment. He surrenders himself to the cause of others. Deeply aware of this new orientation in his way of life and thought, he gives a new orientation to his name too, and instead of 'Surendra' or 'Surinder' he calls himself "Surrender Oberoi." (242)

Billy Biswas too is interested in his own identity. "Who was I? Where had I come from? Where was I going?" (122) The terrible shock he feels at his degradation intensifies his quest and provokes his flight from a sordid meaningless existence in the so-called civilized world. The urge to live like a primitive man in a primitive world, though experienced since childhood and pushed into the background so far, becomes too strong. In a "devastating apathy" (70) to his own world and his own family, he escapes into the vast hilly tracts of central India where the hill tribes dwell in primitive simplicity. In a minor way this is akin to Siddhartha's renunciation of his wife and child in search of enlightenment. To Billy it is a movement from darkness to light.

Ratan Rathor of *The Apprentice* also, before he attains his own individual "enlightenment," has to "negotiate" (116) with life, always "dancing in the shadows of truth, beating about the bush." (100) He has a Kafkaesque inability to understand the world, the "THEY" who govern his life and take him for granted, before whom he becomes a "NOBODY." (74) Ratan Rathor always plans to do the right thing, but never does it. He accepts a bribe to pass substandard military equipment, resulting ultimately in the suicide of his dearest friend, the Brigadier, and also fails to confess his guilt even to save his friend.

Clearly, he has travelled a great distance from the raw youth who had written so bombastically and confidently on the crisis of character. He is caught in the dark labyrinth of life and is unable to follow the light that is within him. Sometimes he fails to distinguish between right and wrong:

> What was right, what was wrong? What was the measure for doing things or not doing them? . . . The confusion reduced me to the status of those leaves of autumn that are blown here and there, at the mercy of the wind. (72-73)

He is haunted by a sense of futility, "the sorrow of a wasted life." (140) He realizes that, in contrast to his father, he was not a good man:

> I felt deep down, very deep down that *not* being a good man was *not* all right by me. I knew that something was going to have to be done about the matter even though for the moment I did not know what that something exactly might be. (141)

The responsibility for the betrayal of his spirit, he knows, lay only on himself. The words of the Sheikh, uttered out of total darkness, provide him a light. He decides to retrieve his pawned soul by putting himself to use. Through sorrow, humility and a deep sense of guilt, Ratan Rathor finds his way out of the labyrinth.

The search for a meaning is more clearly marked in the protagonist of *The Last Labyrinth*. Som Bhaskar needs to be assured that all is well:

> But I needed the trust – who doesn't? I needed it all the more because I did not trust myself, or my men, or my fate, or the ceaseless travel on the social wheel. (63)

He is very anxious to know what he wants. The desire to know is a labyrinth:

> If only one knew what one wanted. Or, maybe, *to know* was what I wanted. To know. Just that. No more. No less. This, then, was a labyrinth, too, this going forward and backward and sideways of the mind. (53)

He seeks to overcome his hunger by possessing an object, a business enterprise, a woman: "I was a womanizer all right, and a boozer, but my womanizing and boozing had not settled anything." (156) The psychologists whom he consults fail to give a solution to his problem, for, as one of them says to him, "psychiatry doesn't allow certain approaches to problems like yours." (74) Bhaskar's problem is essentially spiritual and remains outside the scope of psycho-analysis. He can meet his wants and desires through another soul: "When you meet the right soul then, of course, things might be peaceful, may even move on towards a higher goal." (74) He believes, for some time, in the powers of the cure of Dr Leela Sabnis, a professor trained in philosophy and an emancipator of women. But his belief soon fizzles out as Leela is unable to provide any cure. He is in need of someone who inhabits both the worlds: "What I needed, perhaps, was something, somebody, somewhere in which the two worlds combined." (82) Benaras, Aftab, Anuradha and their Haveli, all prove to be "bores, frogs stuck in their ancient marshy wells," and Bhaskar decides to go abroad and "get the hell away from this land of obsessions." (113) His visits to Europe and America are of no avail.

In his search of a cure for restlessness, he meets Gargi, the deaf-mute daughter of a sufi *pir* who tells him that "God will send someone to help you. . . . Someone who has known suffering." (118) After Anuradha has left him, he feels dizzy and off his balance. He takes medicines for his fears but nothing happens. (183) The knowledge of his miraculous escape from his heart attack as described by K. (206) drives him into a mysterious world where he learns of an old man travelling nine miles to die near a lake. (192) He also hears of Gargi's father giving eyesight to Aftab and of the Doctor's inability to save his life and of people who, staring into flames which he sees in the temple, can enjoy the Eternal Bliss. (210) He feels shaken and the sense of *deja vu* leaves him numb. (193) Deep inside his heart, Bhaskar feels he is a leper needing a cure but he refuses to yield ground. (126) Though he has sufficient ground for a leap of faith, like Sarah of Graham Greene's *The End of the Affair*, his scientific mind obstructs any such leap. He discards orthodox religion as "half-assed rigmarole" and "gimmick." (208) A man proud of his education, working by logic, a man without suffering and humiliation which bring an understanding, Bhaskar needs evidence till the end. After the disappearance of Anuradha when he has a sense of nothing left, he prays for forgiveness:

> Anuradha, listen. Listen to me wherever you are. Is there a God where you are? Have you met Him? Does He have a face? Does He speak? Does He hear? Does He understand the language that we speak? Anuradha, if there is a God and if you have met Him and if He is willing to listen, then Anuradha, my soul, tell Him, tell this God, to have mercy upon me.... Plead for me, Anuradha. He will listen to you. (222-23)

The long and tedious journey of Arun Joshi's protagonists helps them to arrive at some meaning. The sense of guilt that has oppressed Sindi ever since Babu committed suicide is erased with the traumatic realization that Babu's father is a cheat of great magnitude. The satisfaction he has at the end from the uniqueness of having just one book enables him to settle his account with the past. His eyes are opened to the miseries of the world and he arrives at a re-adjustment of his values. Having become a sort of "Karmayogi," he finds his equanimity and salvation in the land of his birth. Though Billy is shot dead and his search, like that of Querry of Graham Greene's *A Burnt Out Case* and Murphy of Beckett's *Murphy*, is interrupted and ultimately terminated by death, he attains self-fulfilment in the midst of the tribals. He experiences their joys and sorrows, living their beliefs and superstitions while the tribal people soon start adoring him as their king and God. He becomes, as he himself thinks, "some sort of a priest." (191) He finds his fulfilment in the love of Bilasia "the essence of that primitive force that had called me night after night, year after year." (142) He arrives at a parting of the ways in his life and takes the path that leads him to his salvation first in love and then in death. Ratan Rathor too finds meaning in his apprenticeship, viz. wiping the shoes of the congregation outside the temple. He is learning to be of use and he knows that the smell of his hands would prevent him from going astray. No more an island, he realizes the truth of what his father used to tell him, "whatever you do touches someone somewhere." (149) As an apprentice in more ways than one, he has now realized his identity as a small, humble drop in the ocean of the world. However "petrified" (150) our civilization may be, there is hope as long as man is willing to learn, as Ratan Rathor himself has learnt, as he wants his listeners to learn. The novel rightly ends with a dawn which is both outward and inward, though it is a cold one. "But no matter. A dawn, after all, is a dawn." (150)

As different from Ratan Rathor, Som Bhaskar of *The Last Labyrinth* after a long and tiring search seems to have arrived at a state of uncertainty:

> Was this it, then? The terminus? The last of the labyrinth? . . . Was it this that I had wanted all my life? . . . Why was it so unsatisfying? Or, may be, the labyrinth hadn't ended. Something else lay ahead, something more fundamental than a miracle. (211)

However, despite all his disillusionments and uncertainties, Som Bhaskar's only grip on life consists in his selfless, disinterested love for Anuradha. He pays no heed either to his crumbling business or to his lovely wife and his growing children. The departed Anuradha becomes the core of his existence, the crystallization of the meaning of his life. His plea to her to plead to God, if there is one, on his behalf is intensely lyrical. It seems to come from the very depths of his soul:

> Anuradha, if there is a God and if you have met Him and if he is willing to listen, then Anuradha, my soul, tell Him, tell this God, to have mercy upon me. Tell Him I am weary. Of so many fears; so much doubting. Of this dark earth and these empty heavens. Plead for me, Anuradha. He will listen to you. (223)

The remarkable similarity of this cry to the numerous devotional songs, as also Som Bhaskar's reference to Sant Tukaram and to the body as the chariot of God seems to point to a psychological context which might be a harbinger, a "pilot-escort" (223) of a higher faith. He has outlived his hungers of the body and of the mind, the state of "I want. I want. I want. I want." (11) Like a true devotee, he is now unconcerned with the world as such. He seems to have reached the end of his negotiations with the labyrinth of life and only the last labyrinth, that of death, remains to be gone through and he looks forward to it courageously. Even his agnosticism seems to be lined with affirmations and with the possibility of the dawn of faith.

Thus the novels of Arun Joshi explore the "dark mossy labyrinths of the soul that languish forever, hidden from the dazzling light of the sun." (*The Strange Case*, 8) They constitute varied attempts on the part of the protagonists to arrive at self-realization. The outward journeys performed by most of them are symbolic of their relentless quest for a personal salvation and a meaningful goal. Their spiritual hunger brings out with a poignant clarity the utter meaninglessness of worldly prosperity which all of them already have or achieve in the course of their lives. They yearn to transcend the wasteland of wealth into a region of higher values. In the novels of Arun Joshi, man is able to relieve himself from the pressures of anxiety stemming from his terrifying degradation and to regain his capacity for love, affirmation and fulfilment, but only after he has undergone some very painful experiences in the process of his spiritual awakening. Colin Wilson says, "so long as a man is not horrified at himself he knows nothing about himself."[6] In Arun Joshi's novels too, the awareness of self is inspired by a confrontation with some crisis or catastrophe – the death of June Blyth for Sindi, the seduction of Rima Kaul for Billy, the death of the Brigadier for Ratan Rathor and the death of Anuradha for Som Bhaskar.

There are different kinds of labyrinths that a man comes across in this life. There is the incomprehensibility of this world itself in which man is "like an ant threading through a maze, knocking about, against one wall, then another." (*The Last Labyrinth*, 53) Then there is the labyrinth of the mind:

> To know. Just that. No more. No less. This, then, was a labyrinth, too, this going forward and backward and sideways of the mind. (53)

The protagonists encounter all these labyrinths, but their gropings in the dark reach an illumination of some sort or the other. Their dilemmas are modern, and their affirmations too are personal. But all the same the novels seem to restate in modern contexts the eternal quest for self-realization and fulfilment and for a spiritual and cultural identity which has distinctly Indian overtones.

NOTES

1. Arun Joshi, *The Foreigner* (Delhi: Orient Paperbacks, 1968), pp. 143-44.
2. Arun Joshi, *The Strange Case of Billy Biswas* (Delhi: Hind, 1971), p. 9.
3. Arun Joshi, *The Apprentice* (Delhi: Orient Paperbacks, 1974), p. 21.
4. Arun Joshi, *The Last Labyrinth* (New Delhi: Vision, 1981), p. 11.
5. Joseph Conrad, *Lord Jim* (Penguin, 1976), p. 165.
6. Colin Wilson, *The Outsider* (London: Pan, 1956), p. 316.

The Lost Lonely Questers of Arun Joshi's Fiction

THAKUR GURUPRASAD

Arun Joshi's novels are built around dark, dismal experiences of the soul. He gave the impression to an interviewer soon after he received the 1983 Sahitya Academi award for his last novel until then, that he is stimulated into writing to explore "that mysterious underworld which is the human soul."[1] There, he has frankly acknowledged the influence of Camus and other existential writers on his writing,[2] and has put his own philosophical vision of life into the mouth of Som Bhaskar, the narrative-protagonist of his Sahitya Akademi award-winning novel, *The Last Labyrinth* (1981), as he reminisces Azizun's song:

> it reminded you of that core of *loneliness around which all of us are built*. It might have emerged from the slums of Benaras but centuries had gone into its perfection. It rode the night like a searchlight lighting up *the ruins of an ancient abandoned city* with which I, too, was familiar. All my life, at intervals, I, too, had flown across its blacked out skies, flapping my weary wings, not able, for all the striving, to chart a course. . . . *We belonged to the same benighted underside of the world*. (54-55, italics mine)[3]

The above passage pinpoints in Joshi's sensibility the terrible existentialist vision only too often to be found in the modernist and post-modern literature of his time. If anything, it is even more grim than Eliot's vision in *The Waste Land*, where the demented barren woman wandering the heaped up ruins of falling towers,

Jerusalem Athens Alexandria
Vienna London
Unreal,

representing the ravages of all the ancient and modern civilizations of the world – Judáic and Christian, Greek and Egyptian, the Europe of Enlightenment and the British Empire over which the sun never set – envisions "bats with baby faces" to whom she sings a lullaby, fiddling on her long black hair.[4] The bat-face babies in Eliot's image of the wasted world are at any rate perched on the crumbling walls at the violet hour of dusk. The men and women in Joshi's world are fluttering in dark night in the ruined city of the soul, and failing to find their way despite all their efforts: "At once intent and lost." (55)

In one of his fictional observations, Arun Joshi writes that "life's meaning lies not in the glossy surfaces of our pretensions, but in those dark mossy labyrinths of the soul that languish forever."[5] One can say with conviction that the central subject of Arun Joshi the novelist is the dark night of the soul, and his most memorable fictional creations are hopelessly lost, lonely questers after the absurd in the benighted underworld of the inner, dark recesses of existence. As this interviewer has stated, "he sees lives as labyrinths – hopeless mazes where you may get irretrievably lost or discover the shining secrets at the core of life."[6]

Arun Joshi is a connoisseur of souls divided against themselves. Educated mostly in the United States with a degree in Engineering from the University of Kansas with further specialization in industrial management at the M.I.T., he worked in a mental hospital in the States where his uncle was a psychiatrist, and dealt with chronic schizophrenics there. This experience was bound to create a strong impression on his young and sensitive mind. It is quite natural, therefore, that the chief protagonists in all his notable works describe an inner life within the underworld of the soul divided against itself, its aspirations and conflicting urges turned on the will and action – the novelist's search-light carefully scrutinizing it all in full focus. There is good reason to suppose that there is something deeper than empathy for such characters in the novelist's heart. It is not for nothing that *The Foreigner* (1968), *The Apprentice* (1974) and *The Last Labyrinth* are all written in the confessional mode, apart from all of them having a schism in the soul as the *raison d'etre* for the confessional account. The purpose of this paper is to study his literary oeuvre from this angle in some detail.

II

The basis for the kind of approach proposed here is found in *The Foreigner*, his very first novel. The protagonist in this novel, Surrender Oberoi, who narrates the story, is an existential character, rootless, restless, and luckless in a mad, bad, absurd world. He was born in Kenya with an Indian parent but lost both his parents at the age of five and was brought up by an uncle, with whose death some time later, he lost his anchor forever. His life led him to London, Boston and New Delhi. But he was a foreigner wherever he went. In a telling phrase, Sindi describes his whole life as being "alone in the darkness." (189)

The two lasting impressions of his life in London, his escapades with Anna, a minor artist separated from her husband, who was not yearning for him or anybody, "but for her lost youth" (167) and Kathy, who left him after carrying on with him for a few weeks and went back to her husband because "she thought marriage was sacred and had to be maintained at all costs," (168) taught him to practise detachment and non-involvement in human emotions; which cost him dearly, however, when the final crisis of his life approached as he came to Boston, where he got "involved" in a short-lived but passionate love for June, an attractive American girl, in spite of his determination not to get involved.

In his bid to remain uninvolved, Sindi refrained from responding to June's insistent pleas to marry her, and drove her into the arms of Babu Rao Khemka, a doomed Indian student whom Sindi had to receive on his arrival to join college, as a part of his duties as an employee of the foreign student centre. Babu turned out to be totally incapable of coping with the American system of education, and Sindi got involved with him also as he intervened with the Dean to save him from being thrown out of the college for flunking all his courses. Sindi's detachment led to June, in her peculiar proclivity to help those in distress, falling into the pledge of marrying Babu when she found him more and more at sea.

Before the marriage could take place, June got impregnated by Babu, who lost his balance when he failed all his courses again and was thrown out of college, and got killed in a car accident in a fit of reckless driving. As Sindi says: "When I had come close to gaining true detachment and had acted out of goodness, I had driven a man to his death." (174) But worse was to follow. In trying to maintain his detachment, Sindi had left Boston and taken up a job in New York. As a typical existential development, when June broke the news to Sindi that she was with Babu's child and sought his help and advice, he could reach Boston only to be greeted with the news of her death in the course of an abortion. That was his 'absurd' fate.

Witnessing the terrible consequences of practising detachment in America, Sindi decided to leave the country and go to India. "Like many of my breed, I believed erroneously that I could escape from a part of myself by hopping from one land mass to another," (176) for, in another absurd development, on reaching New Delhi, while making a casual courtesy call, he accepts a job in the firm of Babu Khemka's father where he gets "involved" again in spite of his commitment to "detachment" in shoring up the pieces in the interest of employees as Mr Khemka's "empire," founded on consistent tax evasion, goes to pieces! That is where the novel ends.

The above account shows that Sindi is an existential Everyman of our time. As he puts it himself at one place in the course of his narrative, "I saw myself as I had always been. An uprooted young man living in the latter half of the twentieth century who had become detached from everything except himself." (195) He conforms to the copybook concept of Kierkegaardian existentialism that the purpose and direction of life are unknowable. In yet another retrospection, Sindi thus approximates to the Kierkegaardian vision:

> Lying there in the bed I wondered in what way, if any, did I belong to the world that roared beneath my apartment window. *Somebody had begotten me without a purpose and so far I had lived without a purpose*. . . . Perhaps I felt like that because I was a foreigner in America. But then, what difference would it have made if I had lived in Kenya or India or any other place for that matter! It seemed to me that I would still be a foreigner. My

> foreignness lay within me and I couldn't leave myself behind wherever I went. . . . *So far as I knew everybody else did the same thing.* (61-62, italics mine)

It is significant that the lines of the juke-box song in the restaurant that touched his heart most after he visited it on getting his papers cleared for migrating to India have a peculiarly existentialist appeal, and most apply to his own life experience:

> Who knows where
> The road will lead?
> Only a fool can say. (182)

Thus we find in Sindi a quester after absurd wants, with a schism in his soul. The more his experiences prompt him against involvement, the more he gets involved through love and goodness. The schism is externalized when his Western-educated, rational goodness clashes with the dishonest business ethic of Mr Khemka and his likes. A type of them is represented to his sensibility in the bitterest mood by the old men of New Delhi he encountered on the morning after Khemka was arrested and his daughter came pleading that Sindi own up her father's crimes as his own: "I suspected they kept two books like Mr Khemka – one for their neighbours, the other for God." (209) Another type is the consul-general for India who interviewed him for granting him visa, less bitterly than humorously described:

> He was a young person who talked like Sir Anthony Eden. He seemed sad and bored like the rest of his staff, and when he talked, rather than look at me he kept his gaze fixed on a portrait of Mahatma Gandhi on his desk. (177)

It shouldn't be mere coincidence that the novelist has put a great deal of himself into Sindi, who is, like him, an America-trained engineer and has finally come to work in a business and industrial concern in Delhi. It is also remarkable that the novel has been written in the form of reminiscences of things past, and has confessional tone and style throughout. The extracts from three letters of Babu to his sister, Sheila, are thrown in to deepen the inner battle raging within the soul of Sindi in respect of Babu by serving the purpose of confirming his hunches regarding the nature of goings-on between Babu and June as well as what was going on in Babu's soul when he smashed himself to death in the car accident.

III

In the Billy Biswas of his second novel, Arun Joshi portrays how a man of extraordinary obsessions is destroyed by his absurd meandering away from civilization. His story parallels the equally absurd one of the young king who staked his life in the hopeless attempt to sculp the face of God, the episode echoing the one in *The Foreigner* where Sindi, in the agony of the battle raging in his soul between the good impulse of sympathy for Sheila and the rational anger at her father's dishonesty, walking the streets of Delhi too early in the morning, when confronted by a patrolling policeman's question, "Are you looking for something, Sir?," ruefully replies: "Yes, . . . have you seen God?" (208)

The Strange Case of Billy Biswas is yet another variation on the paradigmatic pattern of the doomed existential quest for values in a mad, bad, absurd world. It holds forth the added attraction of the dark, mysterious forces of the universe like Bilasia the tribal girl and the moon rising out of the dark night that magnetize the protagonist and drive him to the doors of death – the last labyrinth that life holds for man in the existential vision.

The Apprentice, the third novel of Arun Joshi, offers yet another variety in evidence of the novelist's skill in the manipulation of his peculiar forte. Ratan Rathor, the protagonist of this novel, conforms to the dot to the dictionary definition of "existential": the doctrine that man forms his essence in the course of the life he chooses to lead. He is born a good man, the son of a martyr in the national movement. But when he goes out of his village to graduate in the life of the crooked world, honesty does not get him even the lowest job, and he makes his essence as he goes along, choosing the life he leads.

There comes a stage when Ratan takes a bribe, he didn't know why, certainly not because he needed the money, which, quite absurdly led to the death of the only person he loved in this wide world – his childhood friend, the Brigadier. He was a good man when he was first offered bribe – and then he needed money – but he refused. But twenty years later it came to be told to him that he was not a good man, because of the consequences of his taking the bribe when he did not need the money. It illustrates exquisitely the course of an existential career. And his next choice, in order to redeem himself, – the grotesque business of shoeshining on the stairway of a temple all unknown to his wife, with his expensive limousine waiting to take him to his office in the Government of India offices, – is also his own, and as Sartre would put it, in his choice lies his freedom, and as Joshi wants us to see, there lies his redemption as perhaps Sindi's lies in working in Khemka's office after the "empire" vanished.

It is worthy of critical attention that this novel is also in the confessional mode. As a matter of fact, the narrator in this novel is an insistent confessionalist; confession is a factor in his redemption, for Ratan has got hold of a young man, an apprentice in the urban life of Delhi, (the same as Ratan himself was over twenty years ago, though now he is an apprentice [148][8] of another sort – apprentice of purified life, as it were) as his confessor, and he probably means to teach him the crookedness of his world that the youngster is going to enter, or has just entered.[9] This is a trump-card in the matter of technique that the novelist has persistently used. It is an indicator of the schism in the soul that is his central theme, his "point of view" as it were.

Ratan's confessional monologue, that is this novel's narrative body, does adequately lay out the horrors harbouring his soul. The most horrendous perhaps in the battleground between human good and evil, masquerading as pursuit of career that is his inner life, is the battle that rages inside himself after he discovered that he was the cause of his friend the Brigadier's suicide, and worse still, that he could have saved the Brigadier by confessing his crime. It left him cracking up. Fear of failure is his tragic flaw, and he knows that "there is no fear like the fear of madness. All other fears are common to men and can, if you have the luck, be shared. Those who descend into madness descend alone." (129) This is the apex of existential wisdom he comes by, and the defence mechanism he discovers against it is the confessional. The shoeshine business is his confessional unto himself.

Yet another existential aspect of Ratan's labyrinthine life is the dilemma he shares with Sindi on the one hand and with Som and his father on the other. It is the dilemma about God. As a matter of fact Himmat Singh the Sheikh is his mentor. He diagnoses for Ratan the malady – the crookedness of the world; and he discusses the cure:

> But if it was God's darkness, he asked, what was the cure? What was the cure of a crooked world. None, perhaps. Revolution, perhaps. Or, perhaps . . . perhaps . . . he seemed to hesitate a long time . . . perhaps God Himself. God alone perhaps could remove His darkness.
>
> But where was God, he cried out again, suddenly excited, his voice ringing with despair. *What* was God? And *where*?" (145-46)

This uncertainty, this ultimate existential "unknowable" is the lifelong problem facing Ratan. When his boss in the Temporary War Office where he got his first job cryptically answered his question whether he should have accepted the first bribe he was offered, by saying, nothing but God exists, (45) it left him puzzled. And puzzled he remained throughout, for he found a pimp in the *pujari* of the temple when he wanted to pray for atonement. (124) He never entered a temple again. He sought his redemption through shoeshining at the stairway of the temple. Thus far he could go, but no further into a shrine.

The extraordinary novelty of this novel is that in it Arun Joshi, apart from making the exquisite study of the underworld of the soul in people like Ratan Rathor, Himmat Singh the Sheikh and the Secretary, not to say the Minister, as individuals has actually covered social psychiatry. The broader topic of this novel is the rotten soul of a whole generation in a nation, the generation of post-independence India emerging between 1947 and the Chinese war of 1962, in the words of the narrator, "frustrated men sailing about in a confused society, a society without norms, without direction, without even, perhaps, a purpose." (74) It is a nation of hundred million men gone existential.

IV

The Last Labyrinth may not be Arun Joshi's most powerful novel the Sahitya Akademi award notwithstanding. But one thing is certain. The warp and woof are closer between this one and his first one. He has put as much of himself in Som Bhaskar in a way as he had put into Sindi Oberoi in another. Som Bhaskar, too, is a Western-educated industrialist. He, too, though an Indian by birth and domicile, and a Brahmin at that, is unable to make head or tail of the mumbo-jumbo of Hindu religion, depending on which his mother sacrificed her life as a victim of cancer, nor of the *tantra* practised in the ancient city of Benaras. He, too, is unable to believe in God, and contemptuously treats the idol of Krishna just as a "wooden creature," (69) and the mysterious disappearance of Anuradha on Janmashtami night due to her impregnable superstition he squarely blames on this wooden creature, as much perhaps as he blames on it his mother's death. Though he has learnt the business acumen of cornering companies, it is by no means by mastering the business ethic of Khemka, but by relentless application of business administration learnt in the U.S. that even Sindi might have learnt, and which was certainly based on Cartesian logic.

And yet there are conspicuous variations and notable novelty. *The Last Labyrinth* can be seen as a tale of two cities, Benaras and Bombay—one symbolizing Western, rational, industrial and technological, the other Oriental, occult, feudal and treacherous. At one level, it is a story of shrewd Bombay businessman trying to grab an inefficient plastics company owned by a feudal Benaras *jagirdar*, getting involved in "a game of chess," also into winning the owner's concubine, and capturing the worthless business while almost losing his life to the tantric manoeuvres of the tricky Aftab Rai operating from the mysterious Lal Haveli full of myriad labyrinths, and certainly losing the mistress he desired more than everything else in the world. Detectives are used to trace the missing shares of the company, and the novel has enough of the element of fantasy to pass muster as a mystery novel. It is close in spirit, from this angle, to *The Strange Case of Billy Biswas.*

Another remarkable innovation is the symbolism latent in this novel. The Lal Haveli is a symbol of life itself, its last labyrinth of death. Anuradha symbolizes the "elusive, unattainable" in life, Som's "dark and terrible love." (157) Gargi is yet another symbolic, mysterious character who turns the purposelessness of existential philosophy into the mystery of life. In one of her memorable statements in reply to Som's "I want. I want," not knowing what he wants, the deaf-mute wrote: "We are children trying to reach up to a crack in the door to peep into a room." (214) One can go on and on giving a symbolic explication of this dark tale.

And yet, it is essentially, like any other, a typical novel of Arun Joshi the connoisseur of the underworld of the soul. Som Bhaskar is a troubled soul. He is an insomniac who writes out the novel to relieve the tension in his soul for a somewhat therapeutic purpose as he uses his womanizing and his boozing. He has a morbid urge for knowing, in which he is a greater incarnation of Sindi or Billy Biswas. This is a sure sign of the schism in the soul. He suffered from voids within, as he puts it in his narrative. (48) Even though he is married to a beautiful wife, Geeta, whom he loved, and who gave him two children, he is existentially alone, and all his business wizardry is existentially purposeless. Even K., his physician and companion, is of no avail. Not only does he fall hopelessly in love with the mysterious dark beauty, Anuradha, and loses her after possessing her most intensely for a while; there were many more women in his life, and he boozed and boozed to shut up the voices in his incurable voids. As he writes in his confessional, "I was a womanizer all right, and a boozer, but my womanizing and boozing had not settled anything." (156) As his philosopher girl-friend Leela Sabnis put it, he was "a compulsive fornicator." (80) He stumbles over wine and women again and again to survive each new existential crisis, as he explains his womanizing in his confessional, talking of his necking with his future wife in his seaside villa:

> Watching her I was moved and I took her in my arms. Just like that. Without notice. I had done that to other women, taken them by surprise, not the surprise of a Casanova because, as one of them had explained it for me, something about the deployment and pressure of my limbs communicated that it was not that, but the pleasant, asexual surprise hug of a fellow survivor after a crash-landing. (69-70)

One of the sources of the schism in Som's soul, perhaps, is two generations of Western education. His father had a bruised soul, for deep-drenched as he was in Cartesian science, he tried to trace everything to the First Cause and, having never got over his wife's death due to cancer after all treatment, had died one day, suffering from melancholia. Som had gone much further, in Western education, his father having spent millions on it. It is a curious fact that Godlessness is a common feature of most of Arun Joshi's protagonists – Sindi, Ratan Rathor and Himmat Singh the Sheikh, Som Bhaskar and his father.

And then, there is the clash of cultures. Som could never understand the superstitious faith of his mother in Krishna (she thought he would cure her cancer), nor of Anuradha in the astrology of Benaras *sadhus,* and the *tantra-mantra* goings-on in Aftab Rai's Lal Haveli. To Anuradha, after she is lost, he can only make the pathetic prayer of a defeated existentialist:

> Anuradha, listen. Listen to me wherever you are. Is there a God where you are? Have you met Him? Does He have a face? Does he speak? Does He hear? Does He understand the language that we speak? Anuradha, if there is a God and if you have met Him and if He is willing to listen, then, Anuradha, my soul, tell Him, tell this God, to have mercy upon me. Tell Him I am weary. Of so many fears; so much doubting. Of this dark earth and these empty heavens. Plead for me, Anuradha. He will listen to you. (222-23)

Som Bhaskar is as lonely an existential man as any. Like Ratan Rathor, he, too, generalizes on the loneliness of all men, in his earlier-quoted narrative comment on Azizun's song, which is used as the theme song for this paper, and may well be the theme song of the fiction of Arun Joshi, the industrialist who writes to know and, in an existentialist tone, claims to be a stranger to his own writing.

NOTES

1. Sujata Mathai, "I'm a Stranger to my Books," *The Times of India*, July 7, 1983, p. 8.
2. *Loc. cit.*
3. Arun Joshi, *The Last Labyrinth* (New Delhi: Vision, 1981).
4. See T.S. Eliot, *The Waste Land*, ll. 374-82.
5. Arun Joshi, *The Strange Case of Billy Biswas*, quoted in Sujata Mathai.

6. Sujata Mathai.
7. Arun Joshi, *The Foreigner* (New Delhi: Orient Paperbacks, 1968).
8. Arun Joshi, *The Apprentice* (New Delhi: Orient Paperbacks, 1974).
9. The novel begins with the narrator's dramatic monologue which looks like the reply to a newcomer's enquiry about a place in the metropolitan Delhi.

From Detachment to Involvement: The Case of Sindi Oberoi

K. RADHA

From detachment to involvement – these words sum up the career of Sindi Oberoi, the chief protagonist of Arun Joshi's first novel, *The Foreigner*.[1] Sindi's parentage and early life made him the ideal "foreigner," the man who did not belong anywhere. He was born in Kenya, of an Indian father and an English mother. Both of them died in an air crash near Cairo long ago so that he had no recollection of them and it was as if they never existed for him. He was brought up by his uncle in Kenya who too was dead. He had his early education in Kenya and later in England and finally in America. Thus he was not an African because neither of his parents belonged to Africa. He was not an Englishman because his father was an Indian. To America he was not in any way attached: "It is much too sterilized for me. Much too clean and optimistic and empty." (89) And he had not seen India till he was twenty-six. Even then his coming to India was not by deliberate choice. It was decided by the flip of a coin. (175-76) Thus he was one who did not have roots anywhere in the world.

> I wondered in what way, if any, did I belong to the world that roared beneath my apartment window. Somebody had begotten me without a purpose and so far I had lived without a purpose, . . . Perhaps I felt like that because I was a foreigner in America. But then, what difference would it have made if I had lived in Kenya or India or any other place for that matter! It seemed to me that I would still be a foreigner. My foreignness lay within me and I couldn't leave myself behind wherever I went. (61)

He felt an alien who did not belong to any place and his words and behaviour created the same impression in all those with whom he came into contact. Very early in her acquaintance with Sindi, June remarked: "I have a feeling you'd be foreigner anywhere." (33) And Sheila told him sometime after he came to India: "You are still a foreigner, you don't belong here." (141)

A person so alienated and rootless as Sindi was bound to become cynical, misogynístic and detached. Babu Khemka, a student at Boston, wrote to his sister Sheila that Sindi was "terribly cynical" (52) and June's mother told Sindi: "You are just a cynic, my boy." (102) Even as a boy he was tired of living and had contemplated suicide. (166) His flatmate Karl once said to him, "I didn't know you could laugh." (72) Sindi's reply was as significant as the remark that provoked it, "I can if I'm drunk enough." (72) "You are the saddest man I have ever known," Sheila once said to Sindi. (140) Sindi himself confessed: "I was cynical and exhausted, grown old before my time, weary with my own loneliness." (152) Babu's father Khemka was not far wrong when he said to Sindi that he was "living, but as bad as dead." (137) To Sindi nothing ever seemed real or very important. (107) His disgust with his own life is expressed by him in very strong terms:

> Twenty-five years largely wasted in search of wrong things in wrong places. (92)

And all that he had to show was "a ten-stone body that had to be fed four times a day, twenty-eight times a week. This was the sum of a lifetime striving." (92) He thought that people existed only for dying. (62) Sindi sums up for Khemka the uprooted and alienated man of the world – a man with no ambitions, no aim in life, no attachments:

> Look at me, I have no roots. I have no system of morality. What does it mean to me if you call me an immoral man. I have no reason to be one thing rather than another. You ask me why I am not ambitious; well, I have no reason to be. Come to think of it I don't even have a reason to live. (136)

It was part of his cynicism and sense of alienation that he was utterly indifferent as to what he studied and what profession he followed. He had a very successful academic career at the London University and at Boston where he took a doctorate in mechanical engineering – not that he cared for mechanical engineering a bit more than any other subject: "I cared two pins for all the mechanical engineers in the world." (14) His professor rated his abilities so high that he offered him a place in the college faculty. But Sindi opted for a job in New York from where he came to New Delhi. He accepted a job in Khemka's factory only because it would keep him away from himself. (14)

Sindi had, as he said, no system of morality. Morality and immorality did not have any distinction for him. One day he asked Sheila while they were discussing June's virginity: "so you think one of these Marwari girls is really superior merely because of a silly membrane between her legs ?" (57)

Nowhere is his cynicism more in evidence than in his attitude towards love and marriage. He said to June that he "didn't believe in marriage" because "marriage was more often a lust for possession than anything else. People got married just as they bought new cars. And then they gobbled each other up." (66) He believed that love that wanted to possess (in marriage) was worse than no love at all:

> One should be able to love without wanting to possess. . . .Otherwise you end up by doing a lot more harm than good. (66)

In most marriages, he believed, love soon ended and hatred took its place: "The hand that so lovingly held mine would perhaps some day ache to hit me." (69) He was really, he said, one not "cut out for marriage" and he did not "believe in marriage" (105): "I was afraid of possessing anybody and I was afraid of being possessed, and marriage meant both." (106)

Sindi made friends with a Catholic priest in Scotland and he had long talks with him. One morning it came to him in a flash: "All love – whether of things, or persons, or oneself – was illusion and all pain sprang from this illusion. Love begot greed and attachment, and it led to possession." (170) Sindi was of the view that "one should be able to detach oneself from the object of one's love." (66) He did not want to get involved: "Everywhere I turned I saw involvement." (70) He wanted to remain free, detached. In his cynical way he tells June: "You can love without attachment, without desire. . . . Love is real only when you know that what you love must one day die." (170)

To have views is one thing, but to act up to them is another. While in England he had a number of affairs – with Anna, Kathy and others. But he remained "fancy free." They were not affairs of the heart and he came out unscathed. He cherished the false notion that he could ever continue to remain free and uninvolved. But he soon realized that his relationship with June was quite a different affair and he became nervous:

> How long could I stay free! . . .The commitment had already been made the moment I had seen June at the dance. Now it was only a matter of time. Our hands would soon give place to our bodies and then the worst will come; our souls will get involved. It was only a matter of time. (70)

Things developed as he had anticipated. After their first sexual union, he says: "I stayed awake, counting the broken pieces of my detachment. I counted the gains and the losses and the losses mocked me like an abominable joker." (81) They spent several evenings: "We lived like animals when we went out on those holidays." (84) But gradually "a strange tenderness" grew within him and he set apart for her a drawer in his flat. Here he kept her blouses well-folded. He felt as if he was taking care of a child. He would buy small presents for her, and the food that she liked, and when she was away he missed her. (84-85)

The story of Sindi's relationship with her is a story of the gradual breaking down of the barriers of detachment and non-involvement that he had built up all his life. He was quite conscious of what was happening and tried valiantly to resist it, but in vain.

When Babu appeared on the scene there grew up a friendship between him and June. But June was still very much in love with Sindi and she suddenly asked him one night after they had made love: "Why don't we get married?" (105) Sindi put forward his usual view on love and marriage and excused himself. As she put on her dress and combed her hair their eyes met in the mirror:

> She smiled softly at me and a strange sadness grew in the pit of my belly. My eyes grew misty. I got up and grasped her shoulders. I

> clung to her with an unusual fierceness and pressed my lips against her neck.
>
> "Oh my darling," I whispered, "you don't know how much I love you." (108)

Sindi realized that he had "exchanged the steady tranquillity of [his] being for the excruciating moments of ecstasy in a woman's body" (118) and his decision "to remain detached under all circumstances" was slowly giving way. He was yet to realize that "objectivity was just another form of vanity." (119)

After Sindi's refusal to marry June it was perhaps natural that June and Babu should meet more often and avoid Sindi. One day Sindi telephoned June and requested her to dine with him. But she declined the invitation: "I'm sorry, Sindi. I will not be able to see you anywhere, I mean not as I used to. Babu and I are getting married soon." (131)

Sindi begged her to see her once, but she said she was sorry. When he put down the receiver, he pressed his face hard against the metal of the telephone and cried. (131) By this time all his carefully-cultivated detachment had vanished and he was utterly miserable. He said: "The edge of pain was so intense that it left me completely numb." (141) He lay in a state of coma for a time. Gradually the coma wore out, as he was aided by his work at the college. Still he behaved like the typical lover, not the man immune to all emotions as he thought he was. Every now and then he found himself in places where he had been with her:

> Here is where we met, here I bought her a book, there she wanted me to kiss her, and my heart would sink with the burden of my memories and I couldn't help whispering to myself, "My darling! Oh, my darling!" (142)

These are not the words of "one who should be able to detach oneself from the object of one's love." (67)

But worse was to follow. The rest of this episode may be briefly narrated. Sindi did not know that "Babu *had* been sleeping with her" (183) for June had lied to Sindi about this. (158) She told Sindi that she did not really love Babu. (159) So when June made advances to Sindi one night in his apartment Sindi yielded to her. Later she drove to Babu's flat where they had a quarrel and she admitted that she had been sleeping with Sindi. He suddenly left the flat and drove off blindly in his car and was killed in a crash. Sindi and June knew that Babu had really committed suicide. He had been sent out of his college as he had failed in all his examinations. He had been disowned by his father for intending to marry June. And on the top of it all came June's confession.

Sindi felt that he had driven a man to death. Well might June accuse him and say: "Look, what your detachment has done." (174) He could not stay longer in America. He decided to leave the country. While he was waiting for the necessary papers, a worse blow struck him.

To avoid being in Boston Sindi had accepted a job in New York. He received a letter from June informing him that she was carrying Babu's child in her womb. She was in the fourth month. She requested him to come to Boston for she wanted to see him. He could not leave New York for a few days. When he called at her house he found it locked. He was told by a neighbour that June had died after an abortion. Her mother had gone away from the house. The death of June left Sindi desperate. All his objectivity broke down.

Thus we find that the armour of indifference and non-involvement which he was wearing was made of wax and the slightest warmth of love had melted it away leaving him naked and helpless. He thus learnt by bitter experience that true detachment "consisted of right action and not escape from it" (192) which is also the lesson that the *Gita* teaches us. While Sindi's detachment is non-involvement and a close ally of callousness, the detachment preached in the *Gita* is indifference to the result of one's actions. As Eliot puts it in "The Dry Salvages": "And do not think of the fruit of action/Fare forward." (ll.161-62)

So much about his much-valued detachment. We have now to examine whether his oft-proclaimed cynicism and aimlessness in life were really more than skin-deep. He had chosen to take a degree in mechanical engineering though he had no special aptitude for it. He did not mind whether he was going to Nigeria or India. However, when Sindi got his papers ready to fly to India, he felt unusually exhilarated. "I loved the world. . . . I had a new lease of life. In a way, I was born again." (179) In New Delhi he was not keen on accepting a job in Khemka's factory. When the Income Tax people raided Khemka's office and his house and took away incriminating documents, Sindi told

Khemka to his face that he was a crook who deserved the punishment which he was sure to get. He then walked out, determined never more to have anything to do with him or his business which was sure to be ruined.

Sindi searched for a new job and secured one in Bombay. But before his departure, he went to the house of Muthu who was a low-paid employee in Khemka's office. He lived in a one-room tenement with a dozen other people. Sindi was deeply touched by the squalor of the place and the wretchedness of Muthu's lot. Muthu made an impassioned plea to Sindi to take charge of Khemka's business and save him and others like him from starvation. Sindi did not want to get involved. But Muthu convinced him that "sometimes detachment lies in actually getting involved." (225) Sindi thereupon took over the office and with the willing co-operation of the staff effected several economies and set all kinds of wheels in action (227) with the result that the business soon showed visible signs of looking up. The cynical exponent of non-involvement became overnight, as it were, a warm-hearted and purposeful man of action.

Joshi also gives us ground to hope that it will not be long before Sindi will find a loving and loved wife in Babu's sister, Sheila. Clear indications are given of a growing mutual tenderness and attraction that promises a closer relationship. (57, 143, 144, 205, 211, 218)

Sindi, the cynical, alienated young man, belongs to a prolific genre, both in life and literature. "What way I fly is Hell; myself am Hell" – this seems to be the cry of the uprooted angry young men of the modern age. Among the tragic legacies of the British Raj in India is the class of Indian intellectuals – anglicized greatly in their outlook and way of life and, at the same time, without their roots fully cut off from the soil of their motherland. They are a completely alienated lot. Sasthi Brata is one such "herd abandoned deer." In his "bold and irreverent" autobiography, *My God Died Young*, he has uninhibitedly laid bare the tradition-bound society in India. He is equally critical in his accounts of the West, especially England and America. He complains that British rule in India produced men like himself who can neither feel and identify with his own people nor accept "the glare, the steel-muscle concept of human life" in the western countries.

Another of the vain seekers of a home, a refuge, for their tortured souls is V.S. Naipaul. After a brilliant school and college career in his adopted country, West Indies, he went to England where he spent eight years and married an English girl. Still he felt like an alien in England – he described himself as having achieved the "Buddhist ideal of non-attachment." He came to India, the home of his ancestors, to discover his identity. But this voyage of discovery proved a thorough failure as we see from his travelogue *An Area of Darkness*. He was a Brahmin-cum-Englishman in Trinidad, an Indian in London, a European in India.

Like Sasthi Brata and Naipaul Sindi felt like an alien, a foreigner in whatever country he was – Africa, England, America or India. But he differs from them in that he seems at last to have discovered his home in India where he took up challenging work and probably found the woman after his own heart.

The very name of the novel *The Foreigner* compels comparison with other novels with very similar names, Kamala Markandaya's *Nowhere Man* and Camus's *Outsider*. But the contrast with the heroes of the other two novels Srinivas and Monsieur Meursault is obvious. Sindi, as we have seen, progresses from isolation and alienation to involvement. But Srinivas progresses (or retrogresses) in the opposite direction. He starts as a member of an affluent South Indian family, fully absorbed by the relationships in his own family and even in the neighbouring family to which his close friend Vasu and his future wife Vasantha belong. He is interested in his studies and later gets involved in the national movement. This involvement leads to his departure to England where he settles down with his wife. Later a series of mishaps conspire to make him the "nowhere man." The death of his wife and his second son, the marriage of his anglicized first son, Laxman, to an English Lady and his complete separation from him, the collapse of his business and finally his contracting leprosy – the accumulation of all these misfortunes makes him a lonely and pathetic figure. But even at the height of his desolation, he has a companion in an equally solitary woman Mrs. Pickering who brings some light into his life in his last years. Srinivas is altogether unlike Sindi in mental attitude. He does not go about proclaiming his nowhereness to others. Srinivas bears all his misfortunes, and they are real unlike Sindi's, with uncomplaining stoicism.

Sindi is also different from Camus's hero, Monsieur Meursault in *The Outsider*. Meursault remains the outsider, detached and indifferent to whatever happens to him, the illness and death of his mother, his imprisonment and even the sentence of death passed on him. At the trial he makes no attempt to save himself, and the sentence of death leaves him quite unmoved. His only wish is that "on the day of [his] execution there should be a huge crowd of spectators and that they should greet him with howls of execration."[2]

While Sindi's cynicism and detachment are only a thin veneer at the surface interlinked with the inclemencies of life's weather, detachment is woven inextricably into the very texture of Meursault's being.

NOTES

1. Arun Joshi, *The Foreigner* (Delhi: Hind, 1968)
2. *The Collected Fiction of Albert Camus* (London: Hamish Hamilton, 1962), p. 68.

Filial Relationships in *The Foreigner*

MAHENDRA KUMAR MOHANTY

Arun Joshi's first novel, *The Foreigner*, was published in 1968. It centres round a youngman, Sindi Oberoi, who, as Meenakshi Mukherjee aptly observes, "is an alien everywhere physically as well as metaphorically."[1] Sindi Oberoi is an Indian Kenyan who returns to India after years in the West and finds himself incapable of achieving any emotional involvement with the milieu of his racial origin.

Sindi Oberoi is a born "foreigner," a man alienated from all humanity. "The only son of an Indian father and English mother, and born in Kenya he is orphaned at an early age. He grows up without family ties and without a country."[2] "My foreignness lay within me," (61) he confesses. He has very vague memories of his parents. When his American beloved June Blyth asks him how long he has been affected by asthma, he answers, "As long as I can remember. They say my mother had it."[3]

At Delhi, when Babu's father Mr. Khemka questions Sindi about his parents, he brusquely replies: "I lost them when I was four." Sindi hates to talk about his parents for "I hated pity I got from people."(11) This assertion of course appears dubious in the context of the situation at Boston when June and her mother Mrs. Blyth come to know of Sindi's parentless life. They become visibly moved. At this Sindi gets a feeling of genuine sympathy that people have for orphans: "This really hit the cockles of Mrs. Blyth's kind heart. I almost expected her to fly at me and weep on my shoulder. Even June appeared visibly moved but she said nothing." (64)

He is obviously glad on being addressed "Child" by June's mother and feels as if parents are for soothing words and a soothing life. He experiences a balming effect while discussing with June about Babu's authoritative parents, Sindi expresses a peculiar sense of parental void: "I only know what it is not to have a father; I don't know how it would have been if I had one." (123) In Sindi's life, except for a very short time that he spends with his uncle, there is hardly any parental influence. Yet the filial love of his uncle adds definite meaning and purpose to his life. As his uncle's death snaps the last thread of parental love, life becomes a purposeless existence for him. He says:

> Somebody had begotten me without a purpose and so far I had lived without a purpose. . . . I hadn't felt like that when my uncle was living. . . . The thought that he moved about in that small house on the outskirts of Nairobi gave me a feeling of having an anchor. After his death the security was destroyed. Now I suppose I existed only for dying. (61-62)

Parentlessness has its manifold implications in the different facets of his life, like his religion and his love for June Blyth. He tells June: "Anyway, I can't really be called a Hindu. My mother was English and my father, I am told, a sceptic. That doesn't seem like a good beginning for a Hindu, does it?" (33) His love for June ends tragically both for the girl and his friend Babu Rao Khemka, primarily because "Sindi is afraid of marriage and its demands of possessing anybody and of being possessed."[4] He is masculine but frustrates June by his peculiar sense of rootlessness. When Sindi proposes love to June for the second time, she is afraid of being the beloved of Babu. When Babu dies of an accident, Sindi, in a state of despair, feels guilty like an erring child and dreams of his father: "My parents, my uncle, my lovers, Babu and June, their parents, and finally myself, one by one all were called by the invisible judges and asked to give their evidence." (195)

Sindi is a child to none. A stranger to the world of filial relationships, he learns about four families, directly or indirectly. Sindi's first exposure to the filial situation is with Mrs. Blyth's family at Boston. Mrs. Blyth is a divorcee who lives with her only daughter June. June loves Sindi, a student at Boston. Her father's memory is alive and she yearns for a father: "I asked her if she missed him. 'Yes' she said 'I would have liked to have had a father but it does not matter much now. You get used to things.' She apparently didn't want to talk about her father." (45-46)

June first loves Sindi, then Babu and then Sindi. But what she wants is not only love but motherhood. When there is the threat of her illegitimate pregnancy caused by Babu, she becomes panicky and decides to abort it. She dies of abortion. The absence of a father in Mrs. Blyth's family leads it to total destruction.

Karl comes of another American family. He is a friend of Sindi and has a stepmother, who brings her lover after the death of Karl's father. The worst happens when the nymphomaniac stepmother makes an attempt to seduce Karl. So Karl runs away from home. He tells Sindi: "I hated the way my stepmother brought lovers home after my father died. And one day when she got drunk and tried to seduce me, I left." (27)

Sindi, while working for his doctoral degree at Boston, meets Babu Rao Khemka. He is an oversheltered son of a Delhi tycoon. His association with Babu gives him a clear picture of an educated and rich Indian family. He comes in contact with the father and children of Babu's family.

Babu's father Mr. Khemka brings up his son with all the love and care as is expected. He tells Sindi: "I had brought him up with all the care that a father can give to a child. . . . Even as a child, I had myself taught him what was right and what was wrong." (136) Mohan Jha aptly observes that Babu has innocence and simplicity but not the seriousness and toughness of experience as one thinks of his childhood's moralistic training. "Ever since his childhood, he has been fed on the hygienic diet of morals, even so he does not apply himself to his pursuit with the seriousness that is expected of him."[5]

Sindi finds Babu as only "a kid," as an innocent little rich father's boy and tells Babu: "that father of yours who has made this bloody mess of you." Sindi also tells Sheila in this context: "Innocence concoted by you and your father." (56)

Babu was sent to America for his higher studies. Sindi feels it was not so much for Babu as for his father's needs and social prestige. It is perhaps because a son is a proud possession of an Indian family. Sindi tells Sheila: "he sent Babu to America so he would come back and add that much more weight to your family's social status. He could talk to friends at the club about his foreign-returned son." (56)

With the nature of Babu's upbringing he becomes unfit to face America in the absence of his father and sister: "Babu with his dependence on his father, his craving for his friends, his ignorance of American patterns is a square peg in a round hole."[6] Even as Babu continues his studies at Boston, his fear for his father continues. June observes: "This father of his seems to be an awful bully. I am sure things would be much simpler if he were not always there in the background, sending those long sermons and telling him what's wrong with him and how he should carry himself." (123)

Babu's world is confined to his sister and his father. He loves his elder sister Sheila but is terribly afraid of his father. As a result, there is lack of communication between Mr. Khemka and his children. In the absence of the mother, the family is low-keyed and unemotional. The filial awe of Babu is remarkable when he fails in the examination and frustrates the expectations of his father. He writes in a letter to his sister: "Don't show this letter to father. He would get angry, I'm afraid." (52) Babu is less concerned with his career than the fact that his failure would disgrace his father. He tells Sindi: "'What would father say when he comes to know about all this?' And he started crying again. . . . He kept on worrying about what his father would say, 'They would all be ashamed of me.'" (111)

Babu comes in contact with Sindi's beloved June and finds an emotional anchor in her love. But he is conscious of the attitude of his father towards love and marriage. He tells Sindi: "He would be very angry if he found out that his son was running around with strange women." (21) When June asks Babu to marry her, he expresses his helplessness: "'I'm an only son you see,' he added with a touch of pride and regret. . . . 'He'll be very angry if I married here.' 'You must have a terrible sort of a father,' June said mockingly. . . . 'He is not terrible,' he said sullenly. 'He is quite orthodox.'" (90) When June asks Babu as to why he was so afraid of his father, "For a moment Babu nearly clammed up. Finally he said he was not at all afraid of his father; it was just that he had a deep respect for him." (113)

When Babu's engagement to June is relayed to Mr. Khemka by Sheila, "He was furious. For two days he neither slept nor ate. Then he sent off a cable threatening to cut Babu off from his property if he married June." (54) Mr. Khemka also tells elsewhere: "It is ridiculous. I had wanted him to gain some polish. But how would I have known he would abandon all his morality in the process?" (136) Sindi's observation about Babu's father sums up his character. He tells Sheila:

> Your father loved him like a factory. Babu was a pawn in your father's hand with no will or life of his own. That's why he couldn't bear the thought of Babu marrying June. It didn't fit his plans. He wanted to marry Babu to a fat Marwari girl whose dowry might bring him half a dozen new factories. (56)

As Babu in a state of frustration drives into an accident and dies, Sheila says: "He knew how much we all loved him and he had all these factories to come back to." (136) The grief-stricken Khemka says, "We never wanted him to do anything of the sort. It was bad influence on him that led him astray." (136) In the next moment, we find Mr. Khemka perfectly composed as he feels that the entire generation of Babu is unfit for life: "Living, but as bad as dead." (137)

Babu's elder sister Sheila is an M.A. in History and a record holder at the all India level. Babu tells June that Sheila is modern: "She has very progressive views." But she is an obedient daughter. She is next to her father in running the business concern. She loves her father and her father's business. When the income tax people seal the office and Sindi informs her, she begins to sob. Like Babu, Sheila has also never ventured to explore the world. In that way, she is traditional: "Sheila, his daughter, living on the brink of life but never entering it." [7]

Mr. Khemka is an anxious father. He thinks of the well being and welfare of his children. When Sindi accuses him of the lies and fabrications on which his business is based, he says: "I have worked hard just so that my children can live in comfort." (215) But Sindi is not satisfied with this explanation. He tells Sheila: "Your father is a selfish old man." (217)

In the economically weaker section, parental affection is better displayed than what one finds in the upper crust of the society. Mr. Khemka as a father is inferior to Muthu who is a low-paid employee of his business establishment. He leaves an indelible imprint on Sindi's mind: "Muthu . . . a rather poor assistant makes him (Sindi) reverse his direction."[8]

Muthu struggles not only for his own livelihood but also for all his children and for his brother's children. His fatherhood is more intense and wider. He narrates all this when Sindi visits Muthu's "dingy shade." He thinks of the future marriage of his daughter when she is hardly a girl of about eight: "I have to start thinking of getting my daughters married." (220) Muthu is not only good as a father but also as a son. He performs his duty to his father both during his lifetime and after his death. He risks his role as a father to be a good son: "I sold my land to pay my father's debts." (225) When Sindi questions Muthu if he is frightened, he replies: "'Yes . . . it becomes difficult to remain calm when you find so many children going hungry most of the time.' Muthu had been trying to sound objective and cold, but his voice became thicker as he continued." (225) Problems with his peculiar philosophy of detachment: "Sometimes detachment lies in actually getting involved." (225)

The two American families stand in direct contrast to their two Indian counterparts. Both the foreign families are economically well to do and matriarchal in nature. In Mrs. Blyth's family, the husband has divorced and left. Karl's father is dead. Mr. Khemka's family is rich and educated. Muthu is poor and lowly. In both these Indian families, mothers do not figure at all. Mr. Khemka sounds traditional only in his authoritative exercises, but Muthu presents a high tradition of parental sacrifice where filial relationship is warm and intense. In June's family, her mother is loving and affectionate, so also is June. In Karl's family, on the other hand, there is nothing mother-like. In Mr. Khemka's family, love for the children is visibly absent. Muthu's family, on the other hand, is full of parental emotion and sacrifice in the midst of poverty. Sindi comes across all these families but accepts the ethics of Muthu's family as his life's guideline. Of all the novels of Arun Joshi, it is only in *The Foreigner* that one finds the portrayal of the life of non-Indian families.

Joshi's heroes never come of ordinary families. They are sons of parents with social recognition, either material or cultural, with noble and lofty ideals. Babu's father is an industrial magnate. Bimal of *The Strange Case of Billy Biswas* is the son of a Supreme Court Judge. Ratan of *The Apprentice* is the son of a freedom fighter who died in the country's struggle for Independence. Som of *The Last Labyrinth* comes of an engineer-father's family. All have their childhood days in a world of make-believe, their growth becomes, as it were, a 'Pilgrim's Progress,' a process of realization that the world outside is the hard reality whose full perception is inhibited within the confines of their families.

Babu with the high voltage of parental authority in his upbringing fails to adapt himself to the society, and ends his life as an oversheltered seedling. Billy from the family of a Supreme Court Judge enjoys traditional love of parents, absorbs them all from the older generation but does not reciprocate it to the old parents, nor transmits it to his children. He dies as an unruly son and as an irresponsible father. Ratan's father dies for mother India but Ratan has no time even to look after his own widowed mother. As a son, he is shameless and as a father, brazen-faced. Som Bhaskar is the son of a scientist and industrialist father but as a father, he is insignificant. The older generation is warm both as son and as father, but the younger generation is rather cold and self-centred in both the roles of the filial relationship.

NOTES

1. Meenakshi Mukherjee, "The Prospect," *The Twice Born Fiction* (New Delhi: Heinemann, 1971), pp. 202-3.
2. M.K. Naik, *The Ashok Pillar, Independence and After: Arun Joshi*, pp. 220-30.
3. Arun Joshi, *The Foreigner* (Delhi: Hind Pocket Books, 1968), p. 36.
4. M.K. Naik, pp. 230-31.
5. Mohan Jha, "*The Foreigner*, A study in Innocence and Experience," *The Fictional World of Arun Joshi*, ed. R.K.Dhawan (New Delhi: Classical, 1986), pp. 173-74.
6. C. Malathi Rao, "*The Foreigner*, Arun Joshi," *Literary Criterion*, 8(4), 1969, pp. 76-77.
7. Jasbir Jain, "Foreigners and Strangers: Arun Joshi's Heroes," *The Journal of Inidan Writing in English*, Vol. 5, Jan. 1977, No. 1, pp. 52-53.
8. R.P. Rama, "Arun Joshi's *The Foreigner*--A Review," *Indian Writing Today*, July-Sept. 1970, pp. 164-65.

Philosophical Reverberations in *The Foreigner*

SUSHEEL KUMAR SHARMA

In an interview with Sujata Mathai,[1] Arun Joshi reveals that he was influenced both by Camus and existential writers on the one hand and by Gandhi and the *Bhagavadgita* on the other. Besides these influences, the influence of evolutionary philosophers can also be traced in his writings. It is not only the attributes of different philosophies that are present as an undercurrent in Joshi's fiction but the characters too sometimes discuss various philosophies and philosophers. For example, the protagonist of *The Foreigner* quotes certain verses from the *Bhagavadgita* and tries to practise the principle of detachment preached therein. Similarly, the characters in *The Last Labyrinth* discuss evolutionists like Darwin and Lord Krishna: "May be Krishna begins where Darwin left off."[2]

Despite the fact that Arun Joshi admits in one of his interviews: "Sartre I did not understand clearly . . . as for existential philosophers like Kierkegaard, I have never understood anything except odd statements,"[3] there are instances and descriptions in the novel which make the novel read as an existential quest to find a meaning in the absurdity of life.

The protagonist of the novel Sindi Oberoi goes on hopping from one land to another because he finds his life meaningless and rootless, therefore valueless and purposeless. Born of an English mother and Indian father in Kenya, he finds his life a burden after the death of his parents. So he contemplates "suicide." To relieve himself of this burden, he reached London but was "very soon tired of the class-room lectures"[4] and continued his search for "meaning of his life." (167) It is in this effort that he goes to Soho and washes even dishes; this does not lead him anywhere. In a Scotland village he discusses his problems with a catholic priest, who does not give him any solution. Though the books on philosophy, which he reads during his three-month sojourn there, give him some light as he comes across some reality (170-71) yet that is not ultimate and permanent. There is no substantial change in his attitude to life that he is living at the superficial level because he does not belong anywhere. He realizes the vanity of human achievements and purposelessness of his life at the bare age of twenty-five when normally a youngman is full of enthusiasm and gusto for life. He gives expression to his feelings thus:

> And yet all shores are alien when you don't belong anywhere. Twenty-fifth Christmas on this planet, twenty-five years largely wasted in search of wrong things in wrong places. Twenty-five years gone in the search of peace, and what did I have to show for achievement: a ten-stone body that had to be fed four times a day, twenty-eight times a week. This was the sum of a lifetime of striving. (98)

Thus, the problem that Sindi is facing is that of finding a meaning in the absurdity around him. Since he considers this life to be full of illusions, he is unable to find his roots anywhere in the world. His problems multiply particularly when he feels insecure after his uncle's death. (61) Thus, Sindi's is a psychic case. For an insecure man, everybody around him is an enemy and everything is purposeless. He ruminates on the purposelessness of his life:

> I wondered in what way, if any, did I belong to the world that roared beneath my apartment window. Somebody had begotten me without a purpose and so far I had lived without a purpose, unless you could call the search for peace a purpose. Perhaps I felt like that because I was a foreigner in America. But then, what difference would it have made if I had lived in Kenya or India or any other place for that matter? It seemed to me that I would still be a foreigner. My foreignness lay within me and I couldn't leave myself behind wherever I went. (65)

Sindi's case in *The Foreigner* is not a study of an individual but "the whole lot of mankind" suffering from the modern malaise of rootlessness, powerlessness, normlessness, cultural estrangement, social isolation and self-estrangement. In a bid to find solace within and without, Sindi moves from person to person, place to place and country to country because he feels that individuals and places have their own limitations in a given set of circumstances and he hopes to meet individuals and places which will give his suffering soul solace. Because of his hopping nature, he is not able to cultivate a culture[5] or even become a part of it. He confesses to Mr. Khemka that he has no sense of morality and he does not belong to any culture. Though he realizes the vanity of his thinking when he says: "Like many of my breed, I believed erroneously that I could escape from a part of myself by hopping from one land mass to another,"(187) yet this realization is too late, for his efforts to belong somewhere did not bear any fruit. He himself is conscious of the fact: "In truth it had only been a change of theatre from America: the show had remained unchanged. I had met new people with new vanities. They merely had different ways of squeezing happiness out of the mad world. *And they suffered differently.*" (220, emphasis added) Thus, Sindi like an absurdist finds this world full of suffering and, therefore, unbearable at one point of time.

In order to get relief from pain and get the answer of some perennial questions, Sindi takes refuge in Occidental and Oriental philosophies. After the death of his parents, he goes to Scotland and works in a library in a small village for three months. There he not only discusses things with a catholic priest who initially is interested only in converting him but discusses religion, God and mysticism later on. (179) Besides the discussions, Sindi did a lot of reading there but the reader is not told what that is about. However, the conclusion Sindi reaches is that of a Vedantin: "All love--whether of things, or persons, or oneself—was illusion and all pain sprang from this illusion. Love begot greed and attachment, and it led to possession." (180) Thus, it is apparent that Sindi did a lot of reading of Oriental philosophy and he found some solace therein.

The first part of the *jnana* attained by Sindi is a part dealt with in *The Bhagvadgita*. While Arjuna saw his relatives standing in the battlefield ready to fight, he suffered from *moha* and as a result attachment and pain:

> My limbs quail, my mouth goes dry, my body shakes and my hair stands on end. Gandiva slips from my hand and my skin too is burning all over. I am not able to stand steady. My mind is reeling.[6]

It was due to this *moha* that Arjuna fell a victim to "greed and attachment":

> I do not long for victory, O Krsna, nor kingdom nor pleasures. Of what use is kingdom to us, O Krsna, or enjoyment or even life? Those for whose sake we desire kingdom, enjoyments and pleasures, they stand here in battle, renouncing their lives and riches. Teachers, fathers, sons and also grandfathers; uncles and fathers-in-law, grandsons and brothers-in-law and (other) kinsmen. These I would not consent to kill, though they kill me, O Madhusudana (Krsna), even for the kingdom of the three worlds; how much less for the sake of the earth?
>
> *The Bhagavadgita*, 1: 32-35

> Even if these, whose minds are overpowered by greed, see no wrong in the destruction of the family and no crime in teachery to friends. *The Bhagavadgita*, I: 38

It is to dispel Arjuna's *moha* that Lord Krishna talks of *Jnana Yoga* and *Karma Yoga* which are "distinguished on account of the distribution of emphasis on the theoretical . . . and practical aspects."[7] Lord Krishna talked about *Jnana Yoga* in the context of body and soul and impressed upon Arjuna that ultimate reality is soul because it never dies. But Sindi does not see the ultimate reality. He bothers himself about dead parents, dead uncle, dead Babu and dead June. *The Gita* preaches that "wise men do not grieve for the dead or for the living." (*The Bhagavadgita*, II: 11) A man who practises *Jnana Yoga* treats "pleasure and pain, gain and loss, victory and defeat" alike. (*The Bhagavadgita*, II: 38) But, Sindi makes a difference in pleasure and pain, gain and loss and victory and defeat. Nay, he wants to enjoy pleasure, gain and victory but wants to run away from pain, loss and defeat. In order to justify his actions he takes the help of the concept of *Karma Yoga*. *The Bhagavadgita* preaches, "To action alone hast thou a right and never at all to its fruits; let not the fruits of action be thy motive; neither let there be in thee any attachment to inaction." (*The Bhagavadgita*, II: 47) Sindi forgets the last tenet altogether. He misinterprets the first dictum also for he acts (e.g. he courts June Blyth) but he believes that accepting its fruit is not right; rather he tries to disown its fruit. He does it on the pretext of not wanting any involvement and wanting detachment. Therefore, he refuses to accept the result of his courtship and flatly refuses to marry her. Actually, Sindi wants to become a *Yogi* without acquiring the pre-requisites for becoming one. Describing some of the characteristics to become a *Yogi*, Lord Krishna says:

> He who draws away the sense from the objects of sense on every side as a tortoise draws in his limbs (into the shell), his intelligence is firmly set (in wisdom).
>
> Even though a man may ever strive (for perfection) and be ever so discerning, O Son of Kunti (Arjuna), his impetuous sense will carry off his mind by force. *The Bhagavadgita*, II: 58, 60

Sindi does not even think of applying a check on his senses but talks of acting as if in detachment. Sindi does not come under the purview of persons described by Lord Krishna as "he who controls the senses by mind without attachment engages the organs of inaction in the path of work . . . is superior." (*The Bhagavadgita*, III: 7) But Sindi is a man of false conduct for "he who restrains his organs of action but continues in his mind to brood over the objects of sense, whose nature is deluded is said to be a hypocrite." (*The Bhagavadgita*, III: 6)

Lord Krishna preaches the philosophy of detachment in the following verse: "Fixed in Yoga, do thy work O winner of wealth (Arjuna), *abandoning attachment* with an even mind in success and failure for evenness of mind is called yoga." (*The Bhagavadgita*, II: 48) The Lord says that one has to work in detachment but Sindi misconstrues the whole philosophy of the *Gita* and says time and again that since he wants to remain detached he will not get involved. "I don't want to get involved," he says repeatedly (74) meaning thereby that he will not act.

To justify his stand, he ruminates like a philosopher: "Nothing ever seems real to me, leave alone permanent. Nothing seems to be very important." (113) But the root cause of such rumination is *avidya* (ignorance): "The world is not an illusion, though by regarding it as a mere mechanical determination of nature unrelated to God, we fail to perecive its Divine essence. It then becomes a source of delusion . . . it breeds ignorance."[8]

In actual practice of life Sindi is a pleasure-seeker like the epicureans as is evident from his revelling and developing illicit relations with Anna, Kathy, Judy, Christine and June on both shores of the Atlantic. But whenever there is a question of marriage, he tries to be excused on the pretext of remaining detached. In the daily routine also, he wants to be freed from commitment and involvement. For example, he does not want to fall in love because "To love . . . is to invite others to break your heart." (82) Yet he falls in love with at least five girls and is in the process of falling in love with the sixth when the novel closes. His escapist tendency is also evident from his trying to find out jobs in Calcutta and Bombay after he finds a mess in Mr. Khemka's business. He pretends to be a misogamist for "marriage was more often a lust for possession than anything else. People got married just as they bought new cars. And then gobbled each other up." (71) But, it is merely a pretext for not owning responsibility and not sharing concern in marriage. Sindi does not know that a person who escapes from his duties has nothing in store but pain. Since Sindi does not want to discharge his duties he feels the pangs of pain time and again:

> That was the first time I came face to face with pain. Until then I had heard and read about it, but now it was real, and it seemed to permeate everything, like the smell of death in an epidemic. All that I had thought was pleasurable had ended in pain, and after all this I was as far from finding the purpose of my life as I had been to start with. . . . I spent a whole year wandering through the maze of my existence looking for an answer. (179)

Sindi's fatal flaw is that he forgets his duty but remembers detachment[9] which for Lord Krishna is a vital necessity to do one's duty.

For a person who is above love and hatred, terms like pleasure and pain have no meaning as he becomes a *sthita prajana*. (*The*

Bhagavadgita, II: 38, 55-68) But, this is not the case with Sindi nor is he immune to anger and hatred as he himself confesses:

> My love for June was streaked with hatred and anger. And with every passing day my love fed upon my anger and both grew stronger. It was as if two high voltage electrodes had taken root in my head and each of them kept spitting venom into my brain. The strain grew so great that I almost lost all ability to think logically for any length of time. Often I suspected I was going mad.[10] (137)

Of course this is not the behaviour of a detached person but one who is "possessive, selfish and greedy." (127) Sindi, though he wants to be and considers himself to be a detached person, yet he loves June to the extent of possessing her. He as a matter of fact remained unresponsible towards June because he was convinced that "June would not leave me, not for Babu anyway. What would she find in Babu that I didn't have?" (126) The extreme case of infatuation with the self and June becomes even more apparent when Sindi muses: "what if June has left me? . . . Was I not supposed to remain detached under the circumstances? But I also knew that the more detached I became, the farther June would move away from me." (126) Detachment in Sindi's case is another name for inaction. It is only when June dies that the realization dawns upon him. He confesses: "Detachment at that time had meant inaction. Now I had begun to see the fallacy in it. Detachment consisted of right action and not escape from it." (204) It is not because of a foreign land that Sindi felt alienated there and considered himself a foreigner but because he did not understand the real meaning of detachment.

Sindi has reached his meaning of detachment because he considers this world to be only illusion (Maya) since it is not permanent. He tells June explicitly: "Nothing ever seems real to me, leave alone permanent. Nothing seems to be very important." (113) Therefore, he wants to know "the real" and his relationship with it in the manner of an Indian sage:

> I climbed a hill and sat down on a weathered stone. The sun had just risen and the valley seemed strangely ethereal in the clear light. Suddenly, I felt a great lightening, as if someone had lifted a burden from my chest and it all came through in a flash. . . . Birth

> and death are real. They are the constants. All else is variable. . . . According to the Hindu mystics there is a reality beyond all this. But I don't know. I would like to know some day. (179-80)

Unlike Arjuna he confesses his ignorance yet he sticks to his concept of "detachment" and "non-involvement" until he meets Muthu who is really a *karmayogi*. It is from him that Sindi learns his lesson of *karmayoga*. It is Muthu who teaches him that some persons "mistake the action of their senses for their own actions." Muthu also suggests that Maya (illusion) keeps the reality hidden: "It is all Maya." (46) Sindi realizes that detachment in the real sense of the term should not only be from the world but also from one's own self. It is only when one is detached from one's self that one can do some good to others. Sindi therefore comes to realize that he was the cause of Babu's and June's death: "I had learnt to be detached from the world, but not from myself. That is when the fatal error was made that ultimately led to Babu's and then to June's death." (207) The realization of self-delusion continues even further. Sindi realizes: "In many ways the past had been a waste, but it had not been without its lessons. . . . We could have acted more responsibly, with greater detachment. . . . Circumstances and events had led to my detachment from all of them. . . . But . . . I couldn't be detached from the world and remain attached to myself." (234) Sindi has to struggle too hard to get freedom from the psychic fear of involvement: "Still, the old, nagging fear of getting involved with anything, anyone, was pushing through the mists of reason--a line of reasoning that led to the inevitable conclusion that, for me, detachment consisted in getting involved with the world." (239) Muthu's meaning of detachment though not codified in philosopher's language ("Sometimes detachment lies in actually getting involved" [239]) prevails on Sindi and he accedes to Muthu's request of taking over Mr. Khemka's business. Sindi works in a truly disinterested manner: "The fruit of it was really not my concern." (242) Sindi's action in the right earnest brings him and his companies peace and happiness.

The concept of *Karma*, enunciated in *The Kathopnishada*, also finds a mention in this novel. We are taught in the theory that no action of ours goes unrewarded or unpunished. Sindi uses the concept both in right and wrong senses. He uses it in the wrong sense when he blames

Mr. Khemka, Sheila and the civilization for Babu's death: "Behind Babu lay the stupidity of his father and his sister and his entire civilization." (193) If Babu died, it was for his own faults and not for anybody else's faults. According to *Karma* theory it is according to one's own deeds that one is rewarded or punished. Thus, Sindi's interpretation of the causes of Babu's death and laying the blame at someone else's door-step is untenable.

But Sindi analyzes his behaviour in terms of *Karma* rightly when he utters: "In the past I had let life lead me by the nose and I knew the damage I had caused in the name of goodness. I did not have any desire to be good anymore, I merely wanted to do my duty. And it did not quite seem that my duty lay in paying for the sins of Mr. Khemka," (207) and further: "Mr. Khemka had to suffer for his own actions. *In the past I had tried to put the consequences of my actions on others, or presumed to take over their actions as my own*. Both had boomeranged. In the end, both had done more harm than good." (221, emphasis added) Sindi also uses the theory rightly while explaining to Mr. Khemka: "I have sinned, and God knows, I have paid heavily for them. This time it is your name that is being called. It is you who must answer. That is the only hope of salvation you have left" (228); and also in the passage: "But you can't get rid of your sins by just turning me out. They will stalk you from every street corner just as they have stalked me. We think we leave our actions behind, but the past is never dead." (229)

There are some traces of Marxism too in the novel. This philosophy is made use of by the novelist to highlight the class-consciousness and class-conflict. Mr. Khemka advises Sindi not to care for the talk of the workers in his concern. In the manner of a shrewd capitalist, he (Mr. Khemka) says: "Never trust these lower classes. They have to be made use of, but kept in their place." (140) Arun Joshi hints at the class-conflict by highlighting the contrast in the living standards of Mr. Khemka, the employer, and Muthu, the employee. On the one hand is Mr. Khemka's air-conditioned house in the posh locality of the city; on the other is Muthu's one room in the lowliest area. While Khemka's house has been furnished lavishly, "luxuriously and tastefully," (14) Muthu lives with eleven other members of his family in one single room. While Mr. Khemka hosts parties every now and then, Muthu can barely make his both ends meet. The irony of the matter is that Mr. Khemka keeps himself busy in maintaining fictitious account books while Muthu works hard honestly. The class struggle becomes even more apparent when Sheila Khemka suggests to Sindi that he must own up the responsibility of keeping two accounts and should go to jail instead of Mr. Khemka.

The fact that Muthu despite being an honest worker faces the crisis of losing his job for no fault of his own clearly hints that in the class struggle it is only the lowliest who suffer: "Now some big banker was going to turn [Muthu] out of that also, *not because he did not want to work but because another big shot had made stupid mistakes and hadn't the guts to face up to them*." (238, emphasis added) The struggle between the haves and have-nots becomes even more apparent when the haves are blamed for the miseries of the have-nots by Sindi:

> It is not I who should be ashamed of, Mr. Khemka, but you yourself. I have only been one of your victims. It is you who have swindled those miserable wretches in rags who push carts on your streets and die at twenty-five. It is you who have been telling lies and fabricating documents just so that you could air-condition this ostentatious house and throw gigantic parties for the horde of jackals who masquerade as your friends. (227)

Thus we find that Arun Joshi makes a use of existentialism, Vedanta, the philosophy of *Karma*, and Lord Krishna's concepts of "detachment" and "involvement" to bring out the inner recesses of the protagonist Sindi Oberoi. Since in the novel June and Babu die, it can very safely be concluded that Arun Joshi rejects the American way of life (June was an American) and also the ignorant-Indian approach symbolized by Babu. But Sindi being a round character learns and modifies himself and saves himself from the doom. Despite the fact, that these philosophies are mentioned and practised by different characters in *The Foreigner*, the novel does not have an overdose of philosophy and does not tend to become a philosophical novel like those of Raja Rao or any communist-propagandist's fiction. Joshi suggests like Gautama Buddha does that there is misery in this world and it is generally caused by misconceptions of certain ideas. Joshi suggests that there is always a way out of misery for a wise man who is ready to learn and know. It is in this respect that his vision is different from existentialists and absurdists.

NOTES

1. Sujata Mathai, "I'm a Stranger to My Books," *The Times of India*, July 7, 1983, p. 8.
2. Arun Joshi, *The Last Labyrinth* (New Delhi: Vision, 1981), p. 132.
3. "A Winner's Secrets: An Interview with Purabi Bannerji," *The Sunday Statesman*, February 27, 1983.
4. Arun Joshi, *The Foreigner* (Bombay: Hind Pocket Books, 1968), p. 167.
5. A man acquires culture only when he has roots. Both T.S. Eliot and W.B. Yeats subscribe to this view.
6. *The Bhagavadgita*, I:29-30, trans. S. Radhakrishnan (1948, rpt. Bombay: George Allen and Unwin, 1971).
7. S. Radhakrishnan, "Introductory Essay," *The Bhagavadgita*, p. 53.
8. *Ibid*, p. 42.
9. Dr. S. Radhakrishnan explains the meaning of the term thus: "We have to act in the world as it is while doing our best to improve it. We should not be defiled by disgust even when we look at the worst that life can do to us, even when we are plunged in every wind of loss, bereavement and humiliation." *Ibid*, p. 69.
10. Almost a similar idea of the process of the loss of intelligence has been described in *The Bhagavadgita* (II:63).

Having and Being: A Study of *The Foreigner*

USHA PATHANIA

> There is Heaven when one goes out to one's neighbour, and Hell when one turns back to oneself. Hell is the state of being without affectionate relationship. One may go through circle after circle of Dante's Inferno, down and down, and although there are always crowds there is never relationship.
>
> Grace Stuart: *Narcissism*, p. 160.

For Arun Joshi fiction is neither a source of entertainment nor an instrument of publicizing some sets of ideas. Unlike Mulk Raj Anand, he does not use his genius for propagating any political or social creed, nor does he escape from the world of human struggle and seek aesthetic relief in an imaginary place as R.K. Narayan does. He shares with us the doubt and despair arising out of the awareness that, notwithstanding unprecedented scientific and technological advancements, which have added immensely to his physical pleasure and comforts, the contemporary man finds himself in a tragic mess. No wonder, Joshi is intrigued by acute trying situations in human life. He has been, for more than two decades, experimenting with the medium of literature to delineate man's predicament particularly with reference to the negative feelings of loneliness and meaninglessness that have come as an emotional fall out of worldly success, material prosperity and disintegration of all bonds of love and solidarity. The loneliness of the contemporary man he articulates in the following lines in his first novel *The Foreigner*: "We'll see you then, she called. They waved and drove off. So they would see me, would they? That is the loneliness of our times, I thought as I rode up in the elevator. Strangers promise to see you without even knowing your name. You are a King in a deck of Kings, shuffled and reshuffled, meeting fifty one similar Kings but never saying anything sensible, never exchanging names."[1] "My novels," says Joshi "are essentially attempts towards a better understanding of the world and myself. If I did not write, I imagine, I would use some other medium to carry on my exploration."[2]

In his novels *The Foreigner, The Strange Case of Billy Biswas, The Apprentice* and *The Last Labyrinth* Arun Joshi portrays a world where man is confronted by the self, feeling fractured and fragmented under the burden of many unanswered questions and unresolved dilemmas related to human existence. Living in an era of rampant materialism and individualism, his protagonists are unhappy people. Their material prosperity, academic achievements and hedonistic life-style fail to lead them to a state of peace within and calm around. Sindi Oberoi, Billy Biswas, Ratan Rathor and Som Bhaskar are lonely, anxious, depressed and dependent people who are painfully aware of the "mess they are in," and are oppressed with the "sadness of living." In their struggle for survival, they find themselves in a wilderness where, as Yeats would describe it,

> The things fall apart
> The centre cannot hold.[3]

All order is gone out of their life. There is no plan, no peace; nothing to keep them within the pattern of everyday living.

These works read like the spiritual odyssey of the twentieth-century man who has lost his spiritual moorings and is roaming bewildered and confused; searching an answer to the question whether pleasure and possessions could be a satisfactory answer to the universal desire for meaningful human existence. By delineating the turbulent inner world of his protagonists, he highlights the fact that the need for a profound change in our modes of living emerges not only as a psychological demand arising from the pathogenic nature of our present social character, but also as a condition for the sheer survival of the human race. Through his fiction, he brings out the relative merits of the two basic modes of human living – the having and the being.

The alternative of having versus being does not appeal to common sense. To have is a normal need of our life. In order to live we must have things. Moreover, we must have things in order to enjoy them. In an age, in which the supreme goal is to have and to have more and more and in which one can speak of someone as "being worth a million," how can there be an alternative between having and being? On the contrary, it would seem that the very essence of being is having, that if one has nothing, one is nothing.

Yet, the great masters of living have made the alternative between having and being a central issue of their respective systems. The Buddha teaches that in order to arrive at the highest stage of human development, we must not crave possessions and selfish individualism. Buddhism sets up a world in which actual life attains an ideal harmony. According to this principle "no one being will exist by itself and for itself, but the world will move and act in unison as if the whole were under general organizations."[4] Jesus teaches: "For whosoever will save his life shall lose it; but whosoever will lose his life for my sake, the same shall save it. For what is a man advantaged, if he gains the whole world, and lose himself or be castaway." (Luke 9 : 24-25) Master Eckhart taught that to have nothing and make oneself open and "empty," not to let one's ego stand in one's way, is the condition for achieving spiritual wealth and strength.[5] Marx taught that luxury is as much a vice as poverty and that our goal should be to be much and not to have much.

By having and being, Erich Fromm refers to two fundamental modes of existence, two different kinds of orientation toward self and the world: to two different kinds of character structure the respective predominance of which determines the totality of a person's thinking, feeling and acting. In the having mode of existence my relationship with the world is one of possessing and owning, one in which I want to make everybody and everything my property. In the being mode of existence, one identifies two forms of being. One means aliveness and authentic relatedness to the world. The other form of being is in contrast to appearing and refers to the true nature, the true reality of a person or a thing in contrast to deceptive appearances.[6] The fundamental concern of my paper is to establish that Arun Joshi's first novel *The Foreigner* is primarily an attempt to explore the hazards of the having structure of existence. True happiness and real salvation are found, it is argued here, in one's relation with others. Person in communion with person can transcend his narrow, isolated selfhood and realize himself fully in a living dynamic reality.

The Foreigner is a poignant portrayal of Sindi Oberoi's unhappy, lonely and meaningless existence. His bright career prospects and enviable academic achievements are of no avail because, from all around, he is overwhelmed by a nagging sense of loneliness and "the chaos of his being." (43) He is painfully aware of "twenty-five years largely wasted in search of wrong things in wrong places. Twenty-five years gone in the search of peace, and what did I have to show for achievement: a ten-stone body that had to be fed four times a day, twenty-eight times a week. This was the sum of a lifetime of striving." (92) What oppresses him most is the realization that he is a "lonely man who has failed to see in what way, if any, did he belong to the outside world?" (61) His girl friend June Blyth finds him to be a "queer person" because he lacks the spontaneity and warmth of a person who enjoys being with others. She tells him: "There is something strange about you, you know, something distant. I'd guess that when people are with you they don't feel like they're with a human being. . . . I have a feeling you'd be a foreigner anywhere." (33) He himself knows: "My foreignness lay within me and I couldn't leave myself behind wherever I went." (61)

A person in the being mode enjoys interacting with people because he can transcend his own egocentricity and is capable of responding spontaneously and productively. He forgets about himself, about his knowledge, the position, the thoughts and ideas he cherishes. His ego does not stand in his way and he can fully respond to the other person and that person's ideas. Unfortunately, this is not the case with Sindi Oberoi. He has a purely detached, business-like attitude towards life and people. Sitting expressionless, he watches the world go by. June tries to involve him in a conversation with a view to knowing more about him. But it makes him uneasy. He feels "embarrassed by her personal talk" (34) and changes the subject to save himself from the discomfort of talking about himself. He, all along, desires to "physically possess her" (62) but "wildly struggled to remain uninvolved." (63)

Emotionally fulfilling primary bonds provided by an affectionate mother and a protective father inculcate in a child the feelings of fellowship and communion with the people. Unfortunately, the death of Sindi's parents in an accident deprives him of the opportunity to learn to establish meaningful interpersonal relationships with people. Later on, the death of his uncle destroys all sense of security provided by family bonds:

> I hadn't felt like that when my uncle was living. It wasn't that I loved him very much or anything – as a matter of fact we rarely exchanged letters – but the thought he moved about in that small house on the outskirts of Nairobi gave me a feeling of having an anchor. After his death the security was destroyed. (61)

Sindi, now, wanders from place to place and person to person in search of peace and meaning of life. Not having enjoyed the sense of well-being and happiness provided by emotional bonds, he remains suspicious of all involvements and makes detachment the creed of his life. His belief in detachment, however, is a mask to cover his inability to reach out to people, to love them, to belong to them and to understand them. June's sincere efforts to involve him in a loving union fail because he stubbornly refuses to loosen his grip on his creed of detachment and non-involvement. He enjoys making love to her as it feeds his vanity to know that there is someone who finds him worthy of love. He gloats over the fact that "he held the key to June's happiness." (196)

Being engrossed with his own self he fails to "return her love." (167) Nothing productive comes out of his encounter with June. He remains stifled within himself because of an anxious concern for retaining his detachment and non-involvement. In a mood of confession he admits: "Instead of Babu's child she could have been carrying mine. I didn't want to get involved. One didn't choose one's involvement, however. Wasn't Babu's child my own, in a way? Hadn't I driven her into his arms?" (187) Their conversations hardly ever reach the plane where it is no more an exchange of commodities in the form of information and knowledge and become a dialogue in which it does not matter any more who is right. The duelists begin to dance together and they part not with triumph or sorrow – which are equally sterile – but with joy.

Sindi's desperate attempts to remain locked within the having mode and persistent refusal to become active and fully alive in human company interferes with his own freedom and impedes the way of his self-realization. Freedom in the sense of being unfettered, freedom from the craving for holding on to things and one's ego, is the condition for love and for productive being. But Sindi is incapable of this freedom in his interaction with anybody as June observes, "I thought you never loved anybody except perhaps yourself." (157) This, in fact, has been his undoing and in a subtle manner paves the way for the ultimate tragic end of both Babu Khemka and June.

Babu Khemka's sudden death followed by June's tragic demise comes as a rude shock to him. He realizes the full meaning of the words June spoke to him after Babu's death: "Look, what your detachment has done." (174) The whole episode leaves Sindi baffled. Babu's death drains something out of him. At one blow most of what he had cherished in life is taken away. He admits: "Babu has kicked out all my beliefs and disproved all my theories. I felt like a desert or like a vast field of naked oaks in winter time. I felt more alone and naked in the world than I had ever felt before." (175) The feeling of his nakedness in the hands of existence urges him to once again roam the streets of the world. He wants to go to a place where he could experiment with himself. Arbitrarily he decides to go to Delhi.

The mystery of human existence terrifies and unnerves Sindi totally when he learns about June's death due to abortion. In this shattering moment he sees the fallacy of detachment. He sadly remembers how June was deprived of her vivaciousness because he took all precautions to thwart her affiliation wants by showing no interest in her psychic needs. He dismissed them by saying "It is none of my business." June dies when he fails even to respond to her call for help. Babu's death taught him only half the lesson; the remaining half comes to him now, revealing the full meaning of the word detachment that has been his most reliable prop in all situations where he was expected to transcend his immediate self-interest. He confesses: "Detachment at that time meant inaction. Now I had begun to see the fallacy in it. Detachment consisted of right action and not escape from it. The gods had set a heavy price to teach me just that." (193)

Sindi's decision to go to Delhi, and more specifically the way it is made by a flip of the coin, reveals that now careful choice and thoughtful planning, the hallmarks of the having mode of existence, have lost their charm for him. This is an unmistakable sign of his progression from the having to the being mode of existence in which an individual approaches a situation by preparing nothing in advance. He admits: "It meant an escape from a bit of myself that appeared the most decayed." (176) He feels like a river "that hopes to leave its dead wood behind by taking an unexpected plunge over a steep precipice." (176) The futility of being clever and taking precautions dawns on him. For the first time, he confronts his own reality: "I saw myself as an uprooted youngman, living in the latter half of the twentieth century, who had become detached from everything except myself. Where Kathy and Anna had taught me to be detached from others, June's death finally broke my attachment to myself. "It was here that my hope lay." (195) In this moment of crisis he wishes to talk to some one about her. His agonizing sense of loneliness is deepened when he realizes that he had no friends. Vyvyan Richards in his *Person Fulfilled* rightly remarks: "Isolation and neglect are men's hell: fellowship his heaven."[7]

On his arrival in India Sindi does not find peace and belongingness waiting for him in Delhi. What he finds is another trap in Mr Khemka's invitation to work as his personal assistant to help him in all his activities. The mode of life and the set of values which Khemka and his friends follow offer a more sickening version of the having mode of life which Sindi had already experienced in America. Their shameless and immoral attempts to own objects and people confuse and confound him. He confesses: "I took a long time figuring out how I was expected to behave. I had no desire to cause a disturbance. Ultimately I decided to forget about the figuring. It would have been impossible for me to behave as the others." (15) The irony of his predicament is, that though labelled as an Indian, he is an outsider, a stranger, a foreigner in India too. The social parties arranged frequently at Mr Khemka's house are all a bit of a hoax. Everybody knew it, but, there was no point in talking about it. These were the occasions when "old men fat with success came with their plump wives. They drank and then they had gorgeous dinner. They talked of money and how to make more of it. They left the impression that they could buy up anybody they wanted. These fat men left me with a distinct feeling of being out of place." (16)

In fact, he only finds it to be a change of theatre: the show remains the same. Here he finds different people with different vanities and different ways of squeezing short-term happiness out of this mad world. He is filled with disgust to know how Mr Khemka and his tribe exploited needy people like Jain and Muthu so that their empire could grow. When, after an income tax raid, Mr Khemka is under trial and there are rumours of his firm being bought over by some other greedy shark, Muthu requests him to take over the office so that the poor workers of the factory are not retrenched. The heroic struggle of Muthu to provide food to his own family and the family of his brother, who is unemployed, reveals to Sindi the real meaning of life which one finds in developing sympathetic understanding of the needs of the other person and responding to them warmly. Muthu, an almost uneducated person in comparison to Sindi Oberoi, a Ph.D. in mechanical engineering from the prestigious university of America, teaches him the distinction between detachment and involvement: "Sometimes detachment lies in actually getting involved. He spoke quietly, but his voice was firm with conviction." (225)

Muthu defines for Sindi the ideal of non-attachment or non-involvement as it is preached in the *Gita*: "Duty should be done with indifference, renouncing all results. He who gives up the fruit of action is the true renouncer. And, finally, the supreme state (of non-involvement) which transcends all work is attained by him whose understanding is attached, who has subdued his self, and from whom all desire has fled."[8] Muthu becomes for him the most appropriate example of the ideal man – the man of steady wisdom. In the *Bhagavad Gita*, the Blessed Lord said: "Whose mind is undismayed (though beset) by many a sorrow, who for pleasure has no further longing, from whom all passion, fear, and wrath have fled, such a man is called a man of steadied thought, a silent sage."[9]

After his meeting with Muthu a major change is discernible in Sindi's attitude towards the real pursuit of human life. He cancels his visit to Bombay where he has been offered a job. He refuses to be a wanderer any more. After dinner, much to the surprise of his servant, he unpacks his things and puts them "back as neatly as possible in their old places." (226) It is a symbolic act affirming his new-found sense of belongingness. His search for the meaning of life comes to an end when he decides to hurl himself headlong into the battle of survival which the workers of the factory could not have won without his help, cooperation and guidance. When he decides to infuse new life into the ruined business of Mr Khemka he takes the most heroic decision to transcend self-interest and help out all those employees who earn their family's daily bread by working in that factory.

Sindi's orientation in the being mode is complete when he is filled with the desire to serve others with joy and gladness of heart. Such an attitude not only minimizes psychic conflicts arising out of the feelings of loneliness and worthlessness, it creates one of the deepest forms of human happiness, shared enjoyment. Vyvyan Richards rightly argues: "Every touch of kindness that opens one's isolated self to others and theirs to us, begins to enrich and perfect our being."[10] To Sheila's question how long he plans to stay with the company, he replies, "I don't know. As long as I am needed, I suppose." (230) In his interpersonal relations, he ultimately succeeds in imbibing the rare and enviable quality of forgetting his separateness and individual identity. The journey from America to India has been a long journey indeed. He has reached his destination. The most coveted goal of peace within and around, emanating from a meaningful existence and a sense of belongingness has been attained. He is no more afraid of love, of freedom, of growth, of change, of the unknown; he becomes himself. Sindi has ultimately discovered what Erich Fromm calls man's "own nature, and with this self-knowledge he has . . . entered manhood. For he is the only creature who is able to say not only 'no' to life but 'yes' and to make for himself a life that is human. In this decision lie his burden and his greatness."[11]

Thus the mutually contradictory tendencies for having and being are everpresent in human beings. The desire to have, to possess, owes its strength to the biological factor of the desire for survival: the desire to be, to share, to give, to sacrifice, owes its strength to the specific conditions of human existence and to the psychic need to overcome one's isolation. In order not to feel utterly isolated which would condemn us to insanity, we need to find a new unity: with our fellow beings and with nature.

The discussion is concluded with the observation that *The Foreigner* reveals to us Arun Joshi's keen awareness of a deeper social reality of our times. He helps us peep into the anguished psyche of that affluent section of society that tries to buy its way to happiness. A reading of the novel suggests that this mode of living is littered with emotional landmines that derail even the most successful fast tracker. It can safely be argued that the pursuit of material possessions, individual identity and the creed of noninvolvement results in dissonance and despair for people with refined sensibilities. The self-complacent attitude of those who are wedded to the having mode of living does not continue for very long. For the soul, which is thus isolated from others, grows penitent of its pride and unsocial behaviour and, at last, step downs from its lofty positions to join the common life and share its sorrows and its joys. A search for authentic existence ends when one achieves the state of a happy co-existence and harmony with his fellow mortals. The very last verse of the *rigveda* is a beautiful expression of this supremely blessed state of human existence:

> Let your aims be one and the same;
> Let your hearts be joined together
> May your minds be in accord, and
> At peace with all, so may you be.[12]

NOTES

1. Arun Joshi, *The Foreigner* (Delhi: Hind, 1968), p. 186.
2. Reply to M.R. Dua, dated September 3, 1971.
3. W.B. Yeats, "The Second Coming," *W.B. Yeats: Selected Poems*, ed. A Norman Jeffares (London: Pan, 1962), p. 199.
4. Wing-Tsit Chan and Charles A. Moore, *The Essentials of Buddhist Philosophy* (Honolulu: T.H., 1956), pp. 43-44.
5. The source of Eckhart quotation is Erich Fromm, *To Have or To Be*? (New York: Bantam, 1988), p. 59.
6. Erich Fromm, p. 134.
7. Vyvyan Richards, *Person Fulfilled* (Cambridge: W. Heffer), p. 37.
8. R.C. Zachner, *The Bhagavad Gita* (Great Britain: Oxford University Press, 1968), p. 219.
9. *Ibid.*, p. 52.
10. Vyvyan Richards, p. 11.
11. Erich Fromm, p. xvi.
12. The source for this quotation is John M. Koller, *The Indian Way* (U.S.A.: Macmillan, 1982), p. 56.

The Foreigner: A Study in Techniques

JOY ABRAHAM

Arun Joshi's *The Foreigner* examines the problem of isolation and involvement and man's despair at being unable to find a meaning in existence and attempts to explore its genesis, course and cure. The novel is "a well-plotted briskly written piece."[1] It has a remarkable degree of maturity and technical competence that calls for a critical discussion.

The Foreigner has a story interest. It opens with a morgue where Sindi Oberoi has to identify his dead friend Babu Rao Khemka. Sindi Oberoi, a Kenya-born Indian reaches Boston after his studies in England. While he is working for his doctoral degree in mechanical engineering, he meets June Blyth at a foreign students's party. She begins to like him but he fights hard himself to escape "another affair." His involvement with a married woman Kathy, and her subsequent separation have made him realize that "all love--whether of things or persons, or oneself--was illusion and all pain sprang from this illusion."[2] In spite of his attempts to keep away from another affair, he gets involved all the time regretting that he has exchanged the steady tranquillity of his being for the "excruciating moments of ecstasy in a woman's body." But, when June proposes that they get married, Sindi makes a clean refusal saying that "some people are not really cut out for marriage" and that he is afraid of possessing and being possessed and marriage means both. But for June to love somebody, make somebody happy, bring up children who contribute to society, seems to be the most attractive prospect of life.

June, a devoted passionate lover, finds Sindi too cold and cynical, develops an affair with another Indian boy Babu Rao Khemka, the son of a rich industrialist. A love triangle gets formed with Sindi, June and Babu. Sindi allows June to slip out of his hands although he is conscious of being "jealous." Babu, a freshman at the University--as in life--and coming as he does from a conservative background is subjected to severe tensions in having to reconcile his weakness for the glamorous life with the strong pulls of a conservative conscience. The boyish impetuousness and the frank, heady passion of Babu has a strong pull for June especially after her disappointment with Sindi. There is a peculiar, almost a non-human detachment in Sindi which makes June accept her defeat and find comfort in Babu's callow, but open, arms. But, for Babu his first affair itself proves to be disastrous for he dies even when he is half-way through his love affair. Babu has all along been too naive to guess that Sindi has something to do with June all along that she has shared bed with him. When he comes to know about it, the knowledge proves fatal, for he drives himself to a suicidal accident, followed not long afterwards by June's death at the time of abortion. Thus, Babu, June and their child all perish. It is too late for Sindi to realize his own guilt in the circumstances which have caused the death of Babu Khemka and June and he is full of remorse and repentance:

> Wouldn't Babu still be living if I had not surrendered my body to June that night we went out for a ride? I thought I was acting out of detachment but was it not merely a desire to prove that I still held the key to June's happiness? . . . And if Babu had not killed himself June would still be living. (196)

In order to forget his conflicts, at least at the conscious level, he wants to leave America. He wants to decide by tossing a coin and the toss turns out to be in favour of India. But, strangely enough, in India he straightaway lands into Khemka's at Delhi and becomes private secretary to him. When Khemka's tactics of tax-evasion threaten to ruin his business, Sindi decides to take up the management after having been solicited by the employees threatened with unemployment. Mr. Khemka has no chance of success against the Government when the novel ends, but Sindi and Sheila, the daughter of Khemka, "begin to understand each other" ensuring a sub-plot to the novel.

The story is told in a series of flashbacks, with a clever ordering of past events, throwing together the past and the present, the real and the remembered, the world of imagination and reality to maximize the suspense. *The Foreigner* is apparently theatrical both at the beginning and at the end. The novel begins with the death of Babu in a tragic accident the cause of which is not known until the reader has finished two-thirds of it. It is true that the car accident which kills Babu Rao Khemka, the finding of the photograph of June from his wallet, the identification of the dead body by Sindi Oberoi, and Sheila's instant handing over a "frayed envelope" which contains Babu's letters, all that evoke the atmosphere of a "detective story"[3] and the suspense of a thriller. But the deft handling of the narrative makes it all the more inevitable in order to create "curiosity" and sustain "inquisitiveness."[4] Further, Joshi's subjects are such that even a thriller-writer would not dream of handling them. At the very outset of the novel, having gripped our attention, Joshi goes on to create Sindi Oberoi's background and his relationships throwing together the past and the present. The chronology is maintained though the past is triggered by questions asked by Sheila who is anxious about the death of her brother Babu.

One of the major challenges of the novelist is to control the weight of the details by his narrative art. It must be said to the credit of Arun Joshi that he manages his material with admirable dexterity.

The point of view in the novel is that of autobiography, for the narrator-protagonist enters the novel as an "I" character. The purpose and effect of narration demand this technique; for the novelist tells the reader about the protagonist's psychical contact with society and his psychological developments which enable him to solve his problems, at least temporarily. Karl Kroeber says:

> Point of view functions as an indicator of the novelist's relation, more exactly his conception of his relation, to his readers.[5]

Secondly, Sindi keeps always "detached" and not interested in the events of his life as events, but in terms of the meaning hidden in them as he finds himself "involved" towards the last. The first person narrative enables the writer to keep his character neutral, who can have his own identity as much separately as from other men and women in the book as from the author himself and render only what he can hear, think, or feel.[6]

His very conception of the novel and of the narrative techniques help Arun Joshi to take up the happy position of surveying both the East and the West in an objective manner. He has chosen Sindi Oberoi, a Kenya-born Indian as the hero of the novel. Devoid of love, familial nourishment and cultural moorings, he grows rootless with a built-in fissure in his personality. He is a "foreigner" both for the East and for the West. In a way he is as near to these cultures as he is far from them, for his mother was a British and his father a Kenyan-Indian. It is this mixed parentage that helps him to look at the situation from the human rather than from the cultural perspective. Here, Sindi, the narrator-protagonist, strikes us as the most suitable for the role of a hero, more suitable certainly than the heroes of many other novels on the East-West theme. It is not the confrontation between two sets of values or a value judgement on any one of them as we may see in Raja Rao and Kamala Markandaya. The foreigners in his novels are not very important characters and their contribution lies in their individual reactions and responses and not in any kind of representation of a set of values.

Sindi is a "foreigner" everywhere. His rootlessness "is not merely one of geography or nationality, it is rooted within his soul like an ancient curse and drives him from crisis to crisis."[7] His psychic aberrations which emanated from his orphaned and neglected childhood keep him always a foreigner. His emotional involvement with several girls in England leaves a streak of pain in him. Although they share the most intimate and intense moments of their passion with him, he cannot get entangled with any one of them in marriage as he comes to the conclusion that,

> Marriage was more often a lust for possession than anything else. People got married just as they bought new cars. (66)

His dilemma stems out from the fruitless attempts to establish his identity through his contact with others. But when one comes closer, he is threatened with the fear of the loss of his identity. D.H. Lawrence's Paul Morel is a case in point. In his *Sons and Lovers*, Paul seeks to confirm his identity through his relationship with Miriam. Happily he loves her keeping a distance in between them. When Miriam turns out to be possessive Paul feels his self is threatened.

> I can only give you friendship--it's all I am capable of--it's a flaw in my make-up.[8]

Therefore

> One should be able to detach oneself from the object of one's love. (66)

In America Sindi is involved with June, a gay and sincere American girl, who likes to mix with foreign students. Sindi's cold detachment has paved the way for her to fall back on Babu Khemka, who in all his craze for America is projecting an image of indefatigable Indian Casanova abroad. To him America turns out to be a dreamland of free sex and there is no use of coming to America if one is not to play around with girls. He is a typical Indian snob who declares: "I would never go back to India if I had the choice." (89) But Sindi and even June know better that Americans are not "very congenial towards foreigners." It is here that Arun Joshi explores the cleavage, the prejudices and illusions of the East and the West. The author reveals through Mrs. Blyth how Indian poverty becomes the subject of laughter and derision in America. He also brings forth the snobbish and the patronizing attitude of the Americans in their charities they give India. In the cultural stampede he also finds the Hindu nonsense about idols and its "mealy-mouthed philosophers!" and the Gandhian non-co-operation being mocked at in America. Sindi rightly questions Mrs. Blyth:

> And what use have you made of your extra height and extra years? You carry heavier guns and have a longer time to make each other unhappy, that's all. Can you call that an achievement? (101)

He also finds America "a place for well-fed automatons rushing about in automatic cars," and much "too clean and optimistic and empty."

Against this social and cultural milieu lies the personal problem of Sindi, June and Babu. If Babu's hair-thin morality is indiscreet, Sindi's detachment is unwise. While Babu is incapable of making resolutions

Sindi doesn't make them because the pain of breaking them is too unbearable.

> They were two aspects of the same psychology--one foolish, the other unwise. One was under-controlled, the other over controlled. Both were basically cowards.[9]

Sindi, therefore, ponders over his detachment and objectivity, not realizing that objectivity is just another form of vanity. Detachment either in the West or in the East is mistaken to mean inaction, but now he has begun to see the fallacy in it. Detachment consists of right action and not an escape from it. Even in India he sees a kind of fakeness about life, its vanities and its money-grabbing morality saps away all that is human. To Mr. Khemka and his daughter Sheila, June is a foreigner who cannot be happily married to Babu as she does not know the language, the customs, the traditions, and the religion of India. Sindi laughs in his sleeves on the Indian brag of tolerance and says, "Foreigners don't fit in our homes because we don't want them to fit in." (56) Sindi scoffs at the sex-centred morality of India when Sheila accuses June of not being virtuous on the grounds that she is not a virgin:

> So you think one of these Marwari girls is really superior merely because of a silly membrane between her legs? (57)

whereas the fact remains that she finds no fault with the tax-evasion morality of Mr. Khemka. Sindi, thus, finds himself as much a foreigner in India as he has been in America. "The spatial development of the novel now reaches the depths of human problems of exploring the peculiar predicaments in which they are placed beyond their geographico-historico-socio-cultural existence."[10]

As a study in cross cultures, the novel is indeed a success. Human beings with their vanities are the same everywhere:

> In truth it had only been a change of theatre from America: the show had remained unchanged. I had met new people with new vanities. They merely had different ways of squeezing happiness out of the mad world. (207)

Strangely enough, Sindi who sheds off his detachment begins to like Sheila towards the end of the novel. As a critic has observed,

> *The Foreigner* is not only a novel with a fine aesthetic vision rendering the subtle complexities of attitudes and emotions, in a language which has verve, ease, and suppleness, but it also marks a definite improvement over all other novels in English on East-West muddle.[11]

It has been pointed out that there is a colourless cosmopolitan quality about the novel.[12] The writer of this essay likes to say that almost all the present-day novels are in a sort of experimental form that breaks away with the pre-occupied themes of socio-political trauma and turns to the inner man.[13] Even though the novel lacks the philosophical profundity of Raja Rao in his *Serpent and the Rope*, it is a powerful statement on the theme of the meeting of the East and the West at the level of human emotions. Sindi Oberoi, the hero of the novel, is himself an embodiment of cosmopolitanism, his only identity being that of a human being. He is an uprooted young man living in the latter half of the twentieth century who has become detached from everything except himself. June's remark about Sindi in the beginning of their relationship is highly significant, as it indicates the very characteristic core of his personality:

> There is something strange about you, you know. Something distant. I'd guess that when people are with you they don't feel like they're with a human being. Maybe it's an Indian characteristic, but I have a feeling you'd be a foreigner anywhere. (35)

Back in India, this is what Sheila, too, stresses, "You are still a foreigner, you don't belong here." (144) Further, the atmosphere of Boston is skilfully etched. The creation of setting or locale is undoubtedly a part of the English novelistic tradition in the line of arguing for cosmopolitan outlook. Boston is not only a city but a state of mind. Joshi's use of motifs to strengthen the central design shows a great deal of craftsmanship. Twice in the novel he recapitulates the jukebox song to deepen the existentialistic appeal in the life experience of the protagonist who saunters in the hopes to migrate to India.

> Who knows where
> The road will lead?
> Only a fool can say. (193)

Whereas the loneliness felt by the other Indian students in America is caused by the rather unfriendly, hostile environment, in the case of Sindi it is self-imposed. His alienation is self-generated. This alienation is set off even by the way in which nature is portrayed in this novel. The bleak chilly evenings create a background appropriate to the prevailing mood of the character. Sindi with all his strangeness finds beauty in those stone buildings even in glorious weather. The whole work is overflowing with the American atmosphere of hectic, mechanized life. In a narrative that is swift, firm, sensitive and penetrating, a variety of human relations are touched off.

The sub-plot of Khemka, his daughter Sheila and Sindi is inextricably woven into the texture of the main plot of Sindi, June and Babu. Mr. Khemka is a pompous businessman who has sent his son to America, so that he can talk to his friends at the club about his widely-travelled son. Mr. Khemka, we are told, has been cheating those miserable wretches in rags who push carts on the streets and die at twenty-five; telling lies and fabricating documents for business gain so that he can air-condition that ostentatious house and throw "gigantic parties" for the hordes of jackals who masquerade as his friends. His moral,

> I did it because everybody does it. You can't run a business these days without doing these things. (212)

reminds the justifications put forth by Joe Keller in Arthur Miller's *All My Sons*:

> It's dollars and cents, nickels and dimes; war and peace, it's nickels and dimes, what's clean? Half the Goddam country is gotta go if I go![14]

Khemka is a contrast to Sindi in many ways. While Sindi is never sure of himself, Khemka is always so sure of himself. He is of the strong conviction that people who don't have money are envious of those who have. There is nothing wrong in making money and only clever people can make money. To him money is the only reality. Sindi decides to leave Khemka's "tumbling universe" when he is sacked by the income-tax people only because he is reluctant to pay "for the sins of Mr. Khemka." He decides to hold the reins of business out of sheer sympathy for the employees who face removal from service. The cynical exponent of detachment becomes a purposeful man of action overnight--being of use to another human being, the golden rule of June Blyth. And it is here that he "belongs."

Now, as a study in rootlessness and detachment, *The Foreigner* does not make much of an impact.[15] This can be mainly due to two reasons. First, happenings are drawn up with clean moral conclusions. It is a little bit difficult for a twentieth-century reader to believe that there are such easy solutions as "detachment." Second, we fail to see in him any zeal to fight society for its cramped and convention-bound values and we do not find him being tested against real crisis or dangers. His is a problem of existence, seeking fulfilment in terms of human relationships. His sufferings and loneliness are self-inflicted ones and even his rootlessness is somewhat unreal. Further, his moral conclusions are stronger than the values held by Babu, June and Mr. Khemka. His search appears to be a "marginal occupation"[16] as the society to which he does not belong is rather friendly to him. Not only that his uncle and aunt want Sindi to have a sense of belonging, Sindi himself says:

> They had fervently hoped they could give me a place to anchor on this lonely planet. (186)

When Sindi talks of suicide his uncle understands his mental anguish and sends him to London to study Engineering. A number of events happen in the course of the novel, each contributing to the hero's own search for wisdom. Even the death of June is a revelation to him:

> Where Kathy and Anna had taught me to be detached from others, June's death finally broke my attachment to myself. It was here that my hope lay. (195)

Sindi is seriously concerned for June when he trembles to think of what June would do if she suddenly discovered one day that she had married a kid. He senses that Babu's innocence will invariably lead to destruction of both of them. A situation might come when Babu would not get from June what he wanted and he would be helpless to do anything about it. It could be seen that Sindi has a clear vision of Babu's situation.

His sadness is philosophical and partly the result of the futility of his own efforts to love. The writer is not much interested in psychological probing. Sindi accepts the situation as inevitable and his detachment arises out of his philosophical acceptance of it. Detachment, which he clings to with perverse obstinacy, misconstruing the lofty concept in a manner suiting his awareness, is an euphemism for self-isolation, callous indifference, gross selfishness and inhuman passivity.[17] He is disillusioned at the prospect of achieving a better understanding of the human relations:

> Sindi's view of love and life, based as it is on experience enjoyed in complete disregard of the value of human relations, naturally leads to his obsession with detachment and non-involvement. Mere myopic sentimentality, thus, masquerades as intellectual profundity.[18]

Yet, what he obviously wants is to be loved. He is unnecessarily making things difficult for himself by too much brooding and introspection. In the last few paragraphs of the fifteenth chapter, we once again meet him seized with the problems of detachment. His dependence on June becomes a constant need for her and he feels lost without her. "The real Sindi is not of the cynical image he wishes to project – the real Sindi is a lonely individual wanting to love and be loved but afraid of committing himself."[19] Detachment as revealed to him is the opposite of worldly entanglement, a desire to possess. It is a sort of love in a detached manner and "sometimes detachment may even lie in involvement" and all love is "illusion" and all pain springs from this illusion.

Most of these thoughts are used to give colour to the existential terms of alienation and involvement obtaining in the novel. It is not by chance that a critic writes:

> There are moments when Arun Joshi's handling of ideas appear phoney: Indian philosophy grafted on experience which is the usual stuff of existential literature.[20]

Hence, it is the flow of the narrative in *The Foreigner* rather than the theme of alienation that keeps up our interest. It is nothing but the craft of Arun Joshi, his narrative art which sustains the reader's interest in the novel in spite of the theme of alienation that runs through it and hampers the story. The flow of the narrative is too swift and vigorous for us to feel the tedium of introspection and inner life. "It is the deft handling which transmutes a philosophical concept into fictional enactment."[21]

Even in the case of Sindi Oberoi, the alienation is not as real as it seems to be. It is the particular narrative technique used in the novel with Sindi himself as the narrator which helps to create such an impression. In other words, the "alienation" of Sindi as well as his "existential predicament" do not evolve in a convincing manner. The use of the outsider point of view for satire is well combined with a view of life as in Camus imparting to it a strong punch. The satire becomes all the more direct especially when he focuses on Indian economic disparity and the moral code. Evidently, he argues for the half-naked struggling labourers against the rich who swindle both the Government and the people. In his short story, "A Trip for Mr. Lele,"[22] the author throws light on the unscrupulous way of modern manufacturers who have no qualms of conscience in employing any deceptive method for the sale promotion of their goods. Mr. Lele is one of the highest-paid vendors of toothpastes in the country. He is second only to his boss. He is so much attached to his daughter that he cannot miss a birthday of hers. She reminds him of "all the beautiful and perishable things with which so much of life's mansion is furnished." He was confused and muddled up when he was detained on a sales promotion tour and could not present himself on the birthday of his daughter. He is thrown out of his office as he doesn't keep to the advertisement campaign of the company. In the eyes of the manufacturer, his goods are more precious than the inmost feelings of a father for his club-footed daughter. In his protest against the dehumanizing influence of our civilized life and emphasis on the worth of dignity of the individual, Arun Joshi has close affinity with the existential writers of the West.[23]

Arun Joshi's detached observation is not without faults. It stands in the way of delineation of character. Except June and perhaps Sheila, all the other characters are mere satirical sketches. June grows into

Bilasia of *The Strange Case of Billy Biswas* and Anuradha of *The Last Labyrinth*. Babu's portrait is badly exposed to ridicule. His inexperience, recklessness and naivete are made clear. Babu is a typical Indian student abroad; Mr.Khemka, an Indian businessman; Mrs. Blyth an American snob. Babu's innocence leads him to his death. Babu is real but we see him only from outside. Lacking the fighting spirit and unable to face the stark realities of life, he commits suicide. Mr. Khemka is corrupt; so he is detained behind the bars. Babu's innocence and naivete are brought out against his father's stupidity, wretchedness and "childish pomposity." (213) The more he speaks to June Blyth about his fortune at home, the more does she consider him to be "a sweet little boy." (96) While Babu represents the fragility, Sindi stands for the toughness and durability of experience.[24] As against this, June is one of those rare persons who have a capacity to forget themselves in somebody's trouble. And this is exactly what she does to both the Indian students in America. She wants to be of use to others. She likes meeting people from different countries, especially people from Asia. Despite these pitfalls it is essentially the story of Sindi Oberoi touched into shape.

The force of the point of view carries the narrative which mainly consists of retrospective summary and scenes. The structural layout of splitting chronology in simultaneous threads running along, then merging into one, is surely a technical ingenuity of the storyteller's craft. The division of the novel into three parts is in accordance with the progression of events. In the first are the beginnings of relationships; in the second, growth and decay; and in the last, death and destruction. It is difficult to conjecture the purpose of placing the scene of Babu's death in the beginning of the novel. It may have been done with a view to kindle the curiosity of the reader and to reduce tragic intensity from the last part.

A definite achievement, of course, is the narrative design of the novel. It is the restraint in the narration which makes the death of June tragic. The restraint is also there in the emotional restrictions of Sindi to June's death. The techniques of suggestiveness are not contrived ones and are made use of effectively along with parallelisms, juxtaposition and overlapping of dialogue sequences. The writer conducts the characters through the interplay of move and countermove, and always within the framework of the chosen consciousness. Hence, the question of organic wholeness[25] does not arise.

Indian English novelists have used myths both as digressional methods and as structural parallels in the use of which Raja Rao is the most outstanding.[26] It is difficult to find out any mythical pattern in *The Foreigner*. Yet, we can perceive a sustained mythical parallel only incidentally illuminating certain aspects of situation and character. As B. Rajan in his novel *The Dark Dancer* identifies his hero with Karna, the great character in *The Mahabharata*, Joshi's character Sindi can also be equated with Karna, for to Karna too the problem was one of "belonging." Even Karna could not "belong" anywhere. Sindi in this novel finds himself placeless and rootless:

> An uprooted young man living in the latter half of the twentieth century who had become detached from everything except myself. (195)

Karna at first seems to be a convenient figure to represent the predicament of the modern man who suffers from a loss of identity; but a close study will prove that Sindi's situation in *The Foreigner* is by no means parallel to that of Karna. In *The Mahabharata* the problem of belonging is crucial and brought out by fate and destiny controlling the fortunes of many great men, nations and empires. But in Sindi, it is a self-inflicted one. There is no doubt that Karna always knew his Kshatriya origin. Further, what Karna lacked was not exactly a sense of belonging, but social recognition. Sindi's craving for social recognition is a marginal quest as the societies to which he belongs are relatively friendly to him. Further, Karna the man of action is in no way comparable to Sindi who is worried about his identity and detachment. There is no earnest attempt on the part of Karna to win Draupadi at the "swayamvara." He was present there but not as a suitor. Sindi, even though he does not want to be involved and possess June he is jealous of her being whisked away from his hands. So, any attempt to find a mythical parallel for this novel in the story of Karna can give only a pseudo-mythic equation.

Sindi Oberoi's quest for identity can be viewed as a *yatra*, a pilgrimage from "Existentialism to Karmayoga."[27] It charts the moral growth of Sindi, who after a prolonged conflict between the "saint" and the lusty beast in him, hits upon a solution of right action.

The formative part of the novel develops in the backdrop of the West and the final stage is set in India. The hero of the novel begins his pursuit to get beyond the advertised version of reality and learn "how to live." This is the only question he wants his Nobel laureate Professor to answer him. He feels sad and unhappy about his education which does not teach him a thing about life. Eventually, in order to gain experience he tries his hands as a dishwasher in the night club in Soho:

> I didn't work to earn money. My mind was full of thoughts and I wanted a different kind of experience to sort my ideas out. (167)

He is found thrown out to the maze of his existence looking for a purpose in life as we find in the *Puranas*. The *yatra* the pilgrim undertakes seems to be a testing ground. Almost all the incidents in the novel like academic success, ruptures in love and friendship, suicide, death, and the downfall of the Khemka empire are the touchstones to test his moral principles and beliefs contributing to his wisdom. It is a sort of voyage to the different islands of consciousness. He appears very much a stranger to Khemka only because of his obsession on the impermanence of things. And like the outsider Meursault of *L'Etranger* (literally meaning the "foreigner"), he is anti-ambitious and detached, yet with a difference. In fact he cultivates detachment as a virtue. Meursault remains the outsider, detached and indifferent to whatever happens to him, the illness and the death of his mother, his imprisonment and even the sentence of death passed on him. While Sindi's cynicism and attachment are only a thin veneer at the surface, these are woven inextricably into the texture of Meursault's being.[28] Joshi's protagonist though not religious or saintly is humble enough to learn lessons from the problems of life.[29] His conception of all love as illusion that leads to possession and greed sounds like the message of *The Bhagavadgita* which emphasizes the importance of non-attached action:

> Karmany evāh dhikāras te mā phalesu kadāchana
> mā karma phala hetur bhūr mā te ṣangoh stv akarmani
> Seek to perform your duty; but lay not claim to its fruits.

> Be you not the producer of the fruits of karma; neither shall you lean towards inaction.[30]

The events of life are uncontrollable and one gets involved. Sindi finds, "one does not choose one's involvement." The death of his friend Babu and his sweetheart June is a rub in the sore wound which drains out his confidence. Under normal conditions, this would have been painful but after the shock of June's death it comes as a great "therapeutic process" as if some indefatigable surgeon cleans up his soul with the sharp edge of a scalpel. In a mood of extreme despair, he decides to stop the destruction. He understands that involvement without undue attachment is the key to a balanced life. With this knowledge comes peace and happiness. His earlier detachment with the world has now been replaced by a fervent but unselfish attachment, he surrenders himself to the cause of others and calls himself Surrender Oberoi. (242) Further, Babu's love for his father, sister and June makes Sindi envy him. He says that Babu probably had received more love than he had and consequently had more to give. Thus, Babu makes Sindi analyze the validity of his detachment and the necessity of love and involvement in this world. The sense of his guilt is partly erased with the realization that Babu's father is a great cheat. The satisfaction he derives from "the uniqueness of having just one book" enables him to settle his account with the past. His journey to the West and the East helps him to arrive at a meaning. There is an outer path of the journey as well as an inner path. "Having become a 'Karmayogi' he finds his equanimity and salvation"[31] in the land of his ancestors. It is this steady reflectiveness that enables him to accept Muthu's suggestion to take charge of the factory. Sindi comes to terms with his "foreignness" and feels that even if the future is as meaningless as the past, there would be "useful tasks to be done," perhaps a chance to redeem the past. The dawn breaking the dark water indicates the emergence of light within him. Sindi comes across a bronze figure of dancing Shiva in the luxuriously and tastefully furnished drawing room of Khemka. The god "Shiva" is the confluence of both the destructive and constructive forces. The purpose of the dance is to release man from illusion. Leaving behind his state of inertia, Sindi now begins to move on. Thus the entire novel itself presents a pursuit after awareness--the Advaitic method of searching for one's identity which is typically Indian.

"Fiction is movement,"[32] says Robert Scholes. A story is a story because it tells about a process of change. A man's situation changes, or he himself is changed, or our understanding of him changes. These are the essential movements of fiction.

The action in the novel has a definite movement despite the fact that Arun Joshi has used the techniques of flashback and perceiving the things through the eye of the protagonist. After coming back to India, Sindi looks back at his life and events in Boston and London in juxtaposition. Thus, the present grows out from the past, and the past directs the present. Further, the qualities the novelist attributes to his characters determine the action, and the action in turn progressively changes the characters and thus the story is carried forward to the end. The plot of the novel wants to move us along and the design makes us pause and see the "counteraction of these two forces as one of the things which enables our experience of fiction."[33] Thus, *The Foreigner* has a beginning, a middle, and an end.

The language is well suited to the narrative imparting seriousness to the novel. A critic[34] cites the following passage as an example of the degeneration of style into that of popular love stories published in pulp magazines:

> Hypnotized, I would watch her dark liquid eyes flashing laughter, her small hands creating patterns of beauty with the tinkle of tiny bangles. I would watch the subtle swell of her golden belly showing beneath the gauzy sari and I would become aware of my own loneliness. (16)

As an answer to this comment one can quote B.C. Chakravorthy: "The biological attraction between man and woman beyond the conventional limits . . . has received wide recognition at the hands of the modern novelists."[35] It is therefore misleading, if not wholly incorrect, to say that Joshi exposes things in an unabashed style.

Most of the images in the novel are related to death and are from technology as Joshi himself admits, "The world which I knew well is the industrial world which has not so far been handled in a novel."[36] Sindi describes June Blyth to Sheila just as he describes an automobile, "Tall and slim, with blonde hair and large blue eyes." (57) The image seems to be muddled when he says, "I stood in the graveyard of cars." Phrases from Eliot like "the irredeemable time" and "the eternal joker snickered within me" are used. We can sense something artificial about the setting when June and Sindi incidentally meet in a nearby wood and begin to love each other.

The author uses metaphors and symbols for variations of mood and intensity of emotion. Sindi Oberoi, the main character in the novel, is drawn analogous to a tree without roots. He is an orphan for whom the only reality of his parents is "a couple of wrinkled and cracked photographs" and he doesn't particularly miss them. The sudden fall of the spider from the ceiling which aimlessly walks upside down "exploring his inverted universe" and the playing of cards are the symbols of man's deplorable position in the universe. Thus, the title *The Foreigner* gains a symbolic value in the larger context of human existence. The idea of foreignness is kept before the reader throughout the novel. It again portrays the protagonist's sense of metaphysical anguish at the meaninglessness of human condition. The unreality, insecurity and transitoriness associated with the word "foreigner" form the entire edifice of the novel providing the necessary texture and structure to it. From this point of view, *The Foreigner* has a remarkable degree of maturity and technical competence well-suited to its theme.

NOTES

1. K.R.S. Iyengar, *Indian Writing in English* (Bombay: Asia, 1962, rev. 1973), p. 513.
2. Arun Joshi, *The Foreigner* (London: Asia, 1968), p. 171.
3. Elena J. Kalinnikova, trans., *Indian-English Literature: A Perspective* (Ghaziabad: Vimal, 1982), p. 177.
4. E.M. Forster, *Aspects of the Novel* (London: Edward Arnold, 1927, 1963), p. 83.
5. Karl Kroeber, *Styles in Fictional Structure* (Princeton: Princeton Univ. Press, 1971), p. 43.
6. Anne Sherril and Paula Robertson-Rose, *Four Elements: A Creative Approach to the Short Story* (New York: Holt, Rinehart and Winston, 1975), p. 78.

7. The blurb of *The Foreigner.*
8. D.H. Lawrence, *Sons and Lovers* (Penguin, 1948), p. 271.
9. O.P. Bhatnagar, "The Art and Vision of Arun Joshi," *Arun Joshi: A Study of his Fiction*, ed. N. Radhakrishnan, (Gandhigram: A Scholar Critic Publication, 1984), p. 33.
10. O.P. Bhatnagar, "Arun Joshi's *The Foreigner*," *The Journal of Indian Writing in English*, 1, No. 2 (July 1973), p. 13.
11. *Ibid.*, p. 14.
12. Iyengar, p. 514.
13. Kamal H. Dhalla, "Indo-English Short Story Anthologies (1945-75)," *The Indian P.E.N.*, 44, Nos. 5 & 6 (July-August 1978), p. 1.
14. Arthur Miller, *All My Sons* (New Delhi: Allied, 1973), p. 125.
15. D.R. Sharma, "The Fictional World of Arun Joshi," *The Indian P.E.N.*, 43, Nos. 9-10 (September-October 1977), p. 2.
16. R.P. Rama, "Arun Joshi's *The Foreigner* – A Review," *Indian Writing Today*, 4, No. 3 (July-September 1970), p. 166.
17. S. Rangachari, "T.S. Eliot's Shadow on *The Foreigner*," *Arun Joshi: A Study of His Fiction*, p. 2.
18. Quoted in Shyam M. Asnani, "A Study of Arun Joshi's Fiction," *The Literary Half-Yearly*, 19, No. 2 (July 1978), p. 101.
19. Jasbir Jain "Foreigners and Strangers: Arun Joshi's Heroes," *The Jo urnal of Indian Writing in English*, 5, No. 1 (January 1977), p. 53.
20. Rama, p. 167.
21. C.N. Srinath, "The Fiction of Arun Joshi," *The Literary Criterion*, 12, Nos. 2 & 3 (1976), p. 119.
22. Arun Joshi, "A Trip for Mr. Lele," *The Survivor* (New Delhi: Sterling, 1975), pp. 70-81.
23. O.P. Mathur & G. Rai, "The Existential Note in Arun Joshi's *The Strange Case of Billy Biswas* and *The Apprentice*," *Commonwealth Quarterly*, 5, No. 17 (December 1980), pp. 30-31.
24. Mohan Jha, "The Foreigner: A Study in Innocence and Experience," *The Fictional World of Arun Joshi*, ed. R.K. Dhawan (New Delhi: Classical, 1986), p. 174.
25. Murali Das Melwani, *Themes in Indo-Anglian Literature* (Bareilly: Prakash, 1977), p. 64.
26. Meenakshi Mukherjee, *The Twice Born Fiction* (New Delhi: Arnold Heinemann, 1971), p. 132.

27. O.P. Mathur & G. Rai, "From Existentialism to Karmayoga: A Study of Arun Joshi's *The Foreigner*," *Alien Voice: Perspectives on Commonwealth Literature*, ed. A.K. Srivastava (Lucknow: Print House, 1981), p. 107.
28. K. Radha, "From Detachment to Involvement: The Career of the Chief Protagonist of Arun Joshi's *The Foreigner*," *Contemporary Indian Fiction in English*, ed. K. Ayyappa Paniker, p. 90.
29. R.S. Pathak, "Human Predicament and Meaninglessness in Arun Joshi's Novels," *The Fictional World of Arun Joshi*, p. 139.
30. *The Bhagavad Gita*, trans. Swami Chidbhavananda (Tirupparaitturai: Sri Ramakrishna Tapovanam, 1970), p. 172.
31. Mathur, p. 115.
32. Robert Scholes, *Elements of Fiction* (New York: Oxford Univ. Press, 1968), p. 15.
33. *Ibid*., p. 37.
34. Rama, p. 168.
35. B.C. Chakravorthy, *Rabindranath Tagore: His Mind and Art* (New Delhi: Young India Publications, 1971), p. 206.
36. "A Winner's Secrets: An Interview with Purabi Bannerji," *The Sunday Statesman*, 27 February 1983.

The Strange Case of Billy Biswas: A Psychograph of an Alienated Hero

SUSHEEL KUMAR SHARMA

Elizabeth B. Hurlock in her book *Personality Development* identifies three syndromes of alienation viz. "recessive," "socially disinterested" and "socially ineffective." According to her, these three syndromes "include traits that make a person disliked by others." Further, she mentions the following characteristics of an alienated person: reserved, listless, having withdrawn behaviour, self-bound and concerned with his own interests and welfare. Such a person, according to her, causes trouble to others by being noisy, boisterous and show-off, by resisting authority, ignoring rules, regulations and rejecting the accepted cultural moves regarding behaviour, speech and dress. She goes on to write:

> In general, the alienation is marked by such unsocial behaviour as teasing and bullying, making unpleasant comments, being hypercritical, intentionally annoying people, lying and being sneaky, rising alibis or projecting blame on others, and being sullen, sulky and moody. People characterized by the socially ineffective syndrome are annoying to others, while those characterized by the recessive and socially disinterested are so distasteful that others have no desire to have anything to do with them.[1]

In the *Encyclopaedia Britannica*[2] the following variants of alienation have been mentioned: (i) powerlessness (ii) meaninglessness (iii) normlessness (iv) cultural estrangement (v) social isolation and (vi) self estrangement. In the modern world of growing hostility, mechanization, urbanization, changing values, depersonalization, disorganization, self-misgivings, delusions, rootlessness, discontent, psychological and other maladjustments, alienation has become a part of life. The result is that estrangement from self and from society is almost a common experience.

A novel, being "a perpetual quest for reality" and "the most effective agent of the moral imagination"[3] in the present-day world, deals with the problems faced by modern man, and the writings of Indian novelists are no exception to this. In these writings the thematic aspect takes within its purview problems like maladjustment, crisis of consciousness, cultural and psychological deviancy and human predicament in general. Therefore, a modern novelist has withdrawn himself from "the outer world" to "the inner world" in order to explore the "essence of human living." Arun Joshi is no exception to this trend of the contemporary literary world as he himself has admitted in one of his interviews that he was stimulated into writing to explore "that mysterious underworld which is the human soul."[4]

Arun Joshi writes for expounding his ideas vis-a-vis understanding his own true self; for he "essentially attempts towards a better understanding of the world and of [himself]."[5] His statement echoes the influence of Albert Camus, Sartre and Kierkegaard. Arun Joshi admits this indirectly when he says, "I liked *The Plague* and read The *Outsider*."[6] The trio of the existentialists mentioned above has not only contributed to existentialism but has also given new dimensions even to alienation by dealing with this theme in their creative as well as philosophical writings. Arun Joshi treats the theme of alienation at full length in *The Strange Case of Billy Biswas* which is an attempt to find out viable alternatives for "the most futile cry of man . . . in . . . smart society"--the predicament of an alienated personality of the modern world. Romi (Romesh Sahai) the narrator puts it in the following words at the very opening of the novel:

> As I grow old, I realize that the most futile cry of man is his impossible wish to be understood. The *attempt* to understand is probably even more futile. If in spite of this I propose to relate Billy's story, it is not so much because I claim to have understood him as it is on account of a deep and unrelieved sense of wonder

> that in the middle of the twentieth century, in the heart of Delhi's smart society, there should have lived a man of such extraordinary obsessions.[7]

The idea of being "understood" is directly related to a person being rooted in a place and tradition.[8] Billy's predicament becomes a special case when the reader comes to know that Billy's was a split personality-split between "primitive" and "civilized." Tuula Lindgren who is getting advanced training in psychiatric social work at Columbia gives it an expression when she ruminates: "Billy feels something inside him, but he is not yet sure. Sometimes he is afraid of it and tries to suppress it. . . . A great force, *urkraft*, a . . . a primitive force . . . it is very strong in him, . . . It can explode any time." (19) Such is the struggle of the man who finds his identity lost in the so-called civilized world. Though this conflict is termed a conflict between the primitive and the civilized by Tuula, who is a Swedish, yet, to Arun Joshi, it is a recurring conflict of "an essentially Hindu mind."[9] At a later stage, Billy himself gives an account of his forsaking the existence which was powerless, normless and meaningless because of living in the fast degenerating society:

> What got me was the superficiality, the sense of values. I don't think all city societies are as shallow as ours. I am, of course, talking mainly of the so-called upper classes. I didn't really get to know the others. I don't think I have ever met a more pompous, a more mixed-up lot of people. Artistically, they were dry as dust. Intellectually, they could no better than mechanically mouth ideas that the West abandoned a generation ago. Their idea of romance was to go and see an American movie or go to one of those wretched restaurants and dance with their wives to a thirty-year-old tune. Nobody remembered the old songs, or the meaning of the festivals. All the sensuality was gone. So was the poetry. All that was left was loud-mouthed women and men in three-piece suits dreaming their little adulteries. (176-77)

Naturally, Billy left this world of the so-called civilized men in search of a place where he was not treated as an outcast, not culturally uprooted, socially isolated and self-estranged. Billy's retrospection of his life at this juncture makes it evident that two of the three syndromes of alienation are dominant while the third one is dormant. Billy, therefore, rejects "the post-independence pseudo-Western values,"[11] and reaches a place where "Nobody . . . is interested in the prices of foodgrains or new seeds or roads or elections and *stuff like that*" (111, *emphasis added*); where friends "can die for each other" (110); where lies "not Bilasia . . . but [his] future, indeed the very purpose of [his] life." (111) It is in such a world that Billy is able to discover himself and to find out his life force: "that bit of himself that he has searched for all his life and without which his life is nothing more than the poor reflection of a million others." (140) And whenever the idea of forsaking this life-force comes to Billy's mind, he starts crying: "I sat with my hands pressed against my eyes. I don't think I made much noise but my chest heaved something terrible. In a little while I could feel the tears running down my wrists and forearms and getting soaked into my trousers at the elbows. . . . I was terrified, as a child is terrified in the dark." (117)

It is not only in India that Billy is unable to cling to his roots but also in "white America" during his sojourn there. Billy stays at Harlem in New York though he could very well afford to live in some other area like Manhattan; for, he comes of an "upper-upper crust of Indian society." (5) But his persistent quest for self-realization beckons him constantly to live at "the most human place" (5) where he may nurture a sense of belonging, a spirit of succour and superintendence by wholly preserving his identity. Just for not losing his identity, he studies Anthropology and not Engineering which his parents want him to. Though he makes all his efforts to keep his identity, yet he is not successful. His constant discomfiture to identify himself with his environs is reflected in his aberred behaviour which, in turn, is projected in his way of living, eating and dressing and even thinking. Romesh's host describes him as an "anarchist" and "thoroughly crazy even by Indian standards." (5) These epithets are generally attributed to an alienated person as has been mentioned by Elizabeth B. Hurlock. That Billy felt culturally estranged at New York also becomes clear from Romesh's description of the party where Billy goes on sitting silently without moving, without drinking and suddenly beating the bango drums. Romesh and Tuula are unable to find out an explanation for Billy's aberred behaviour. Romesh goes to the extent of asking Billy himself for an answer. Billy's reply is quite evasive because he says, "I must have been disgustingly drunk . . . what else?" (18) But Romesh's description of Billy's "[eating] little and [talking] even less" (16) drinking almost nothing, sitting silently in a corner even though there was plenty of eating, drinking and merry-making at the party, proves that Billy feels secluded there. He does not drink much to have forgotten himself but makes a contrived effort to attract the attention of the persons at the party. Billy gets success in his attempt and sees that everybody's eyes are rivetted on him. But Billy largely remains an alien in that land. Even on his return to India, he does not feel homely, well-entrenched or the true son of the soil, who is culturally well-rooted and socially well-beleagured. A sense of nothingness pervades him: he suffers from a sense of a loss of socio-cultural ethos, finding himself wrapped in a vacuum, which his entire being is unable to comprehend. It dawns upon him when he listens to the *aarati*. In this realization, the whole life becomes meaningless and futile to Billy:

> Returning home one evening, finding myself in a state of considerable agitation, I stopped at a temple. It was the hour of the evening *aarati*. I stood before the idols my hands folded, my head bowed, incense of *dhoop* tickling my nostrils. I stood there while the pious voices of men, women, and children, rose and fell about me like little waves of a benevolent sea. What I had hoped to achieve by my visit I do not know. . . . As I stood there, my eyeballs restive behind the quivering lids, it *suddenly dawned upon me that it was all a great waste*, that the god who awaited me now was one to which no temples could be built. What awaited me now, I realized, was Fate. (93-94, emphasis added)

It is at such weak moments only that a man takes certain decisions to fill up the void of his life. Billy's visiting the temple proves that he is trying to adjust himself socially and culturally but once again he feels totally disenchanted by the utopia and this results in the realization of wasting his time by living in a civilization where people are simply busy "making and spending . . . money." Billy's antipathy to the people and their civilization is reflected in the following extracts from his letters written to Linda at different times:

> I see a roomful of finely dressed men and women seated on downy sofas and while I am looking at them under my very nose, they turn into a kennel of dogs yawning (their large teeth showing) or snuggling against each other or holding whisky glasses in their furred paws.
>
> ... the so-called thinkers and philosophers and men like that ... are merely hired to find solution, throw light ... on complications caused by this making and spending of money.
>
> ... we are swiftly losing what is known as one's grip on life. Why else this constant blurring of reality? Who am I? Who are my parents? My wife? My child? (92-93)

These letters show his concern for civilization, society, individuals and also himself. His pinpointing several weaknesses, hypocrisy, and the fact of leading his life on a superficial plane, show how much alienated from all that is around him he feels though he, also, wants to stick to it in one way or the other.

The products of this "bloody old phony" and "materialistic" civilization disappoint him even more. His frequent change of "beloveds" is really a search for a true life-partner. His marriage with Meena Chatterjee, a pretty young daughter of a retired civil servant, is an impulsive action, no doubt, but this is prompted by Billy's search for viable alternatives. In that condition of mind, he finds no better girl than Meena. Perhaps Billy thinks Meena's bonds will be strong enough to chain up his split personality. It is just like Shudhodan's getting his son married with Yashodhara to chain up Siddhartha. The result is drastic as Billy does not find in her a good partner for she is too much down-to-earth for Billy. Meena is worldly wise and is a product of money-machine culture. She wants nothing but money and glamour which Billy hates. If he has a soft, tender and delicate heart and the mind of a mystic and a naturalist, Meena is just the opposite of Billy's temperament. She does not even attempt to understand Billy and establish a communication with him. In America, Billy's Swiss girlfriend used to help him come out of the strange hallucinations. Being a psychiatrist, she also advises Billy not to give a free hand to them as they were "very dangerous" for Billy. In India their frequency increases suddenly. Perhaps Billy thought that his marriage with Meena would put a check on the hallucinations and Meena like Linda would help him. But Billy is in the wrong as Meena could never establish a rapport with Billy. This marriage being a case of "uneven minds" results in utter failure. Meena's nature of drawing a line is realized by Situ in her very first meeting. Situ sketches her character beautifully when she says: "Did you see how she looked me up and down? . . . As if she herself was no less than Miss India or something. Did you notice her hair?" (67) Such a snobbish and "self-possessed" character as Meena's could never have helped Billy as a partner. Though Meena realizes that she is incapable of handling the situation with Billy, she complains of Billy's alienated behaviour which is reflected through his losing his temper on minor provocations, quarrelling "all the time," "snapping at everybody," remaining in a "dark mood," not touching his wife "for six months," always making fun of Meena, not keeping his promises to his wife, and the sense of resignation in Billy, which was perhaps the result of losing the battle every time. But, Meena simply complains: "Things are falling apart" (70) and "Billy is getting stranger and stranger with every passing day." (71) She does not make any effort to improve upon the situation. She confesses to Romi: "You see, I just can't handle the situation anymore . . . . It is all probably my fault. Perhaps I just don't understand him as a wife should." (72) On the other hand, instead of making compromise with the situation to save it from worsening, she spies on him: "Tell me, Romi, do you think he is having an . . . an affair?" (74) She suggests three solutions to get rid of the rut: (i) "Go to your cannibals, if you find me so intolerable" (76); (ii) "I wish I were dead" (76) which she repeats twice in her eight sentences; and (iii) "I will go away if that is what you want." (77) These three sentences of Meena estrange Billy even further as he undergoes mental agony but his reply is that of a well-composed man: "That is not what I want, Meena. You know that." And while saying this Billy is "more depressed than annoyed." (77) Thus, Billy's last attempt to find a refuge also goes waste. And the second syndrome of alienation becomes even more conspicuous.

Billy is not only sensitive in the literal sense of the term but also conscious of the identity of his being. He, therefore, himself feels concerned with the eternal questions like "Who was I? Where had I come from?" (120) at a small age of fourteen. At this age he could realize that "something has gone wrong with [his] life." (123) And throughout his life he goes on making efforts to seek his "identity" which he sees missing everytime. He tries to find his identity in individuals like Linda and Meena; in societies like the American and the Indian; and in civilizations--the Western and the Eastern, but everytime he feels frustrated and thoroughly cast down. During all these attempts, he moves away from his own self so much so that there is a danger of his identity being lost. It is at such a sensitive moment of self-estrangement that he listens to the voice of his other self. He has hitherto been denying it either in the form of curbing the hallucinations; or coming back from Bhubaneshwar where, he feels, he belongs; or the call from Bilasia. His other self grows even stronger than and attractive to his temporal existence, which ultimately makes him realize that he has been running after shadowy and illusory appearances. It goes on reckoning him:

> Come, come, come, come. Why do you want to go back? . . . You thought New York was real. You thought New Delhi was your destination. How mistaken you have been! Mistaken and misled. Come now, come. Take us. Take us until you have had your fill. It is we who are the inheritors of the cosmic night. (119)

Billy readily responds to the call and finally decides to abjure this world to join tribals to find not only his roots but also identity. He tells Dhunia, the tribal-chief: "I am fed up of those slimy bastards who are camped across that river, and I am fed up of the millions who surround me in that wretched city where I come from." (144) Dhunia welcomes him calling *mahaprasad* (an intimate friend). The so-called civilized world called him a rebel but the tribals look upon him as their friend; he succeeds in endearing himself to the tribals by curing Dhunia's niece Bilasia. He makes a contrived effort to join the other world of civilization. Moreover, this was not an impulsive action but a well thought-out plan--Billy thought over this question the whole night. His abandoning of the civilization cannot be termed to be a simple case of rebellion of an angry child as Billy has tried to find roots and identify himself with individuals, society, civilization before bidding it farewell but all of them have disillusioned him. It is only when he is on the brink of breaking himself (self-estrangement) that he decides to join the other civilization which welcomes his entry. Billy moves out of the civilization so deftly that he leaves no trace of his slipping away to the "world of primitivism." He gets it rumoured that he has been eaten away by a man-eater. Symbolically, it represents the permanent breaking of bonds between the "civilized world" and Billy.

Billy is all happy so long as he is in the company of tribals because he has adjusted himself there alright. His behaviour is not deviant in the tribal society. Reaching there, Billy feels quite at peace with himself. He gives a vent to his exhilarating experience: "It was that passing moment that rarely comes in a man's life, when he feels that he has suddenly discovered that bit of himself that he has searched for all his life and without which his life is nothing more than the poor reflection of a million others." (140) Though Billy makes this statement in order to describe his experience of "desire--too mild a word" which was aroused at the sight of Bilasia, nevertheless this is the whole experience of Billy at getting his roots. In a mood of celebration, he ponders over reaching the place where he belonged:

> Had he not known that every four weeks there was a moon like this, that there were hills as blue as these, and people in the hills that were all that he had ever wanted to be. Why did it take him thirty years to discover this. For all his so-called courage, he thought, he, even he, had been afraid, afraid and foolish, squandering the priceless treasure of his life on that heap of tinsel that passed for civilization. (139)

Billy reaches a world in Maikala Hills which is just the opposite of the world of rat-race which he has abjured. The life in this materialistic world has become so obnoxious because of several complexes that when a man reaches a place. where people are so simple that you can "look through their hearts," he cannot take human relationships for granted. Even the narrator Romesh wonders at this equation between human beings and says: "I marvelled at the intense beauty of this human relationship that was born out of so much love." (141) Billy tells Romi the formula of his happiness in the tribal civilization: "the earth, the forest, the rainbows, the liquor from the *mahua*, an occasional feast, a lot of dancing and love-making, and, more than any thing else, no ambition, none at all." (146) And he is very right because it is the "ambition" which alone causes anxiety and rivalry, makes one forget one's values and ultimately leads a person to alienation; and only a tragic and catastrophic end lies in store for an alienated man. It is in this friendly, simple, pure, and disinterested (in the sense of the *Bhagavadgita*) atmosphere that new vistas of knowledge are opened before Billy. He is not only recognized as the king of that part of Chhattisgarh but is also treated as endowed with many divine gifts such as chandtola starts glowing because of Billy's presence; he can revive a dead man; tigers run away at his sight and so on. All these "news-items" remain only sensational ideas for Romesh as he never gets a proof for substantiating the veracity of these impressions. But he realizes Billy's power of profound faith and unfathomed knowledge when the latter could do almost the impossible (i) by predicting rains when there was no sign of relief from the scorching sun; and (ii) curing Situ's migraine which had escaped cure in spite of the treatment given by the doctors of the "civilized" world for almost ten years. These are only stray examples of the knowledge possessed by Billy, which is just like the tip of an iceberg of the knowledge acquired in perfect harmony by belonging to microcosm and macrocosm; living and non-living; nature and human beings. Although Billy laughs away the idea of his practising magic and he being considered the king, there is nothing but truth in it. Tribals, hearing the news of Billy's death, turn out in a huge crowd and the officers dare not carry away even dead Billy from the spot.

The tragedy takes place when the so-called civilized world impinges upon the world of simple tribals. In terms of alienation, the tragedy takes place when an established man is forced by the people whom he hates and abandons (and in turn alienates himself) for their petty gains to uproot himself. Situ is tempted to send the news of Billy's re-appearance to Meena and Billy's father. That Billy hated Meena is not only clear from their retrospective relationship but also from Rima Kaul's statement. It may be noted that Billy was emotionally attached to her (Rima) so much so that he started crying at the news of her death. Billy was not attached to his son, wife and father, so Rima's statement that Billy "had nothing to come back to" (87) becomes all the more relevant. Romesh tries his best to pacify Mr. Biswas and also Meena. But for them Billy's is the case of annoyance of an ordinary son. They do not realize Billy's malady and insist on meeting Billy even without his consent. They do not let any opportunity go unused and the matter is reported to the Chief Secretary who threatens to punish Romesh. Consequently, the power reaches the hands of Rele, the Superintendent of Police, who is no better than an instrument to penalize people who revolt against the norms of society. They are unable to understand Billy's problem. They fail because they are rational in their approach while Billy's problem is emotional. Rele and his men enter the village where Billy resides along with his tribal wife and two sons. None of the villagers is ready to give a clue to Billy's existence but the mountebank intellectuals of the so-called civilized world have their means of getting success. An item of news is spread that Billy has killed a constable. The result is that far away a constable shoots a man who appears to be a tribal in dress and habit, but it is Billy. Billy dies uttering "You bastards," (231) which again shows his contempt for the values of the "civilized world" which does not hesitate even to snatch his life. The most tragic part of the story is that none tries to understand Billy's problem even after his death. Mr. Biswas, Meena, the Chief Secretary, Rele along with his men and even Situ are "the representatives of a society which, in its middle-class mediocrity, bracketed men like Billy with irresponsible fools and common criminals and considered it their duty to prevent them from seeking such meagre fulfilment of their destiny as their tortured lives allowed." (229-30) The *havildar* is troubled to know that he has shot the Governor's son dead and Meena simply wants *havildar* to be brought to book. None of these persons realizes that Billy was making a "search for truth" (175) which is hard to come across and even more difficult to understand. Romesh says that Billy's case was disposed of without considering any of the factors which led to the ultimate tragedy--it was "disposed of in the only manner that a humdrum society knows of disposing its rebels, its seers, its true lovers." (238) Romesh suggests that "nothing but blind blundering vengeance, howsoever camouflaged, awaits all those who dare to step out of its stifling confines. It is a confrontation whose outcome is as certain as the end of solitary boats beating against a maelstrom." (238) Billy was perhaps in the know of this fact as is also suggested by Romesh but the fact remains that Billy took refuge in the tribal civilization only when there was no option before him and there was every possibility of his breaking down. He sought his identity with the civilization, society, individuals and in the process felt like losing his own self and remained rootless. It was only to find out his roots that he went to the tribal world which "guarded him as his own" (239) until his reappearance from "the sanctuary of the great god of the primitive world." (239)

In short, Arun Joshi in the first part of the novel narrates the story of a person who finds himself alienated from individuals, society and civilization as such. Though Billy goes on making efforts to remain a part and parcel of the society and civilization by pinning his hopes on individuals (the smallest unit of a society), yet he fails in all his efforts. Billy instead of breaking himself (self-estrangement) prefers to abjure the civilization as such to join the world of tribals. It is in this part of the world that Billy finds his identity. Instead of feeling "rootless" (as he is an outsider there), he feels "established." But when some external forces try to uproot him from there, he prefers dying to succumbing to their wish.

NOTES

1. Elizabeth B. Hurlock, *Personality Development* (New Delhi: Tata McGraw Hill, 1976), p. 41.
2. *Encyclopaedia Britannica* (1977), p. 574.
3. Lionel Trilling, *The Liberal Imagination* (New York: Doubleday, 1953), pp. 205, 215.
4. Sujata Mathai, "I'm a Stranger to My Books," *The Times of India*, July 7, 1983, p. 8.
5. Arun Joshi's reply to M.R. Dua, September 3, 1971.
6. "A Winner's Secrets: An Interview with Purabi Bannerji," *The Sunday Statesman*, February 27, 1983, p. IV.
7. Arun Joshi, *The Strange Case of Billy Biswas* (Bombay: Asia, 1971), p. 3.
8. T.S. Eliot and W.B. Yeats have emphasized this point in their writings. Both of them believe that a culture is the product of deep-rooted traditions in the soil of a particular place.
9. Reply to M.R. Dua.
10. "A Winner's Secrets."

The Strange Case of Billy Biswas: A Serious Response to a Big Challenge

D. PREMPATI

Critical studies of *The Strange Case of Billy Biswas* are yet to settle down in identifiable stereotypes. Not that the novel has not attracted much critical attention. Unlike Desani's *All about H. Hatterr* which is the critics's novel, Arun Joshi's *The Strange Case* was meant to be the readers's novel in every meaning of the term. Perhaps the refusal to anticipate the strange pattern of the critics's idea of the novel has contributed not a little to the somewhat hesitant and tentative explorations the novel has induced since 1971 when it was first published.

Often *The Strange Case* is described as existentialist in certain aspects. One doesn't know whether the problem posed in this formulation is literary or existential. If by existentialism the critic means no more than a literary perception of one's existence, all literary creation being involved in some measure in the problems of existence is indeed existentialist. The literary critic's perception of existentialism has been pretty chaotic, to go by the glib discussions of this school in critical works. And yet there are certain critics who rush to seek in this novel large doses of one of the several, and often contending, schools of existentialism. It gives rise to a suspicion that existentialism being as all-encompassing as the blue sky above is the critics's latest hold-all for every kind of literary creation under the sky. The so-called existential approach to *The Strange Case* goes only to slur the specificity of Arun Joshi's artistic thrust in this novel, besides vulgarizing all schools of existentialism as known universally to the schooled eye.

The other approach as one finds has been to pin it down to only problems of identity. A criticism of this sort is grossly superficial, for it does not take into account the conditions of the making of a work of art, nor does it show up the totality of the conflicting forces which make the novel what it turns out to be.

In *The Strange Case* Arun Joshi seems to be mediating between New Delhi and the Satpura Hills, between the two distinct cultures that these two geographic locations have come to embody not so much to dramatize the yawning gap but to make the situation plain, to reveal what has been lost and to reinforce the utter falsity of the so-called refinement of the Indian upper crust. What comes through is not a primitive celebration of the primitive Satpura life. The novel, so to say, lives through a tension between the two ends of a given civilization, between the two distinct tribalisms spanning the complex divide of a strange society. By no means is it an idyllic encounter between the primitive and the sophisticated in some sort of wilderness setting.

The Strange Case is a study in the total alienation of its protagonist Billy Biswas from the modern bourgeois society of India. The achieved significance of the novel lies in the conscious espousal of an anti-bourgeois outlook. Not that the novel takes a problem of some human interest, weaves around it a narrative of some sequel and conveys a desperately-needed message. An apocalyptic light spreads over the novel. The Promised Land gets lost in the Promised End. A rare spiritual regeneration is what the novel structurally lives through, each device dramatizing the central contradiction between spiritual regeneration and spiritual decay.

On whichever plane one were to confront the novel it is a strident criticism testifying to a loss of confidence in the anglicized Indian tradition of high culture, a tradition more flawed than its western parent. Arun Joshi needed Billy's *urkraft* – a primitive force – to see and show the sterility of this tradition which we ourselves do not see and show. It is, however, extremely doubtful if Arun Joshi sought to project in Billy any counter-culture framework as opposed to the thinness of the social structures of the anglicized ruling class of India.

Though not identical to but in many ways reminiscent of the Satpura Hills is New York's Harlem, a sequel to the western loss of innocence. Harlem is not simply the product of a generation gone awry. It came into being as an enduring indictment of the larger society, the white-dominated distortion which brought into being the sore it grew into. It was also a witness to the myth of the American South floundering on the rock of the ever-deepening bourgeois relations. In American literature the Harlem Renaissance of the 1920s worked as an undercurrent giving the Blacks a distinct culture, opposed as much to technological industrial capitalism as to pre-capitalist, traditional Southern agrarianism. The Great Migration of the American blacks from the South to the North was not merely a physical migration but, in essence, a process of urbanization seeking not only an ethnic but also a class identity.

It should be interesting to contrast the Harlem Renaissance with the New Criticism which was the white man's response to the black cultural resurgence. The formalist emphasis on the New Criticism was an upshot of the proven debility of capitalism to confront its crises on its own, and of its helpless escape to pre-capitalist modes such as Southern agrarianism so that the latter take care of the crippling social contradictions which threatened to wreck the society at large. While the Harlem Renaissance tried to politicize art, the formalists not knowing how to confront the crisis between the decaying and the emerging attempted to turn life to aesthetics. It is given in the nature of man's trials and tribulations that history occasions certain crucial points of conjunction. While the Blacks used this turning point to advance to the center of sharpening contradictions, the white ruling class recoiled from its responsibility and sought to snap the life-sustaining bonds between the people and its culture.

Conversely the Harlem Renaissance proved to be a profound expression of the revival of the culture of black people and of the demand for positive images in art and literature. It sought to make literature an active agent, and not a life-negating aesthetics, historically the breeding ground of fascism.

The Harlem and the white ruling class polarity is not without some specific interest to the student of Indian literature. One finds in *The Strange Case* a similar polarity albeit on a lower key between the Satpura bhils and New Delhi's anglicized ruling class, the two making a taut nexus of conflicting forces. It was, therefore, not surprising that *The Strange Case* opens in New York's Harlem, the black ghetto of America. On the part of the novel's protagonist Billy Biswas it was a conscious choice to take residence in Harlem, not a safe and dignified place by middle-class standards. It appeared as though he took refuge in Harlem from the white dissipation around.

Though a student in a New York university, Billy belonged to the anglicized ruling class of India. His father Mr Biswas was a judge of India's Supreme Court. How come Billy belonging as he did to the smart set of the ruling New Delhi culture and having had his schooling in Europe chose Harlem for his residence! He was a rebel impulsively, and the sham and false anglicized culture of the Indian upper crust repelled him right from childhood. When he came to New York, Harlem, and not Manhattan, was his obvious place of residence.

Was he a freak? Somewhat caddish? A historical anachronism? The narrator quotes him: "Perhaps, as he once said, before the eye of each one of us, sooner or later, at one time of life or another, a phantom appears. Some, awed, pray for it to withdraw. Others, ostrich-like, bury their heads in sand. There are those, however, who can do naught but grapple with such faceless tempters and chase them to the very ends of the earth. These last, he might have added, run the most terrible of perils that man is capable of." (7-8)[1]

An individual of such grim determination defies all known theories of rebellion. What is so fascinating about Billy is that he vehemently denounced the culture out of which he sprang. The rejection was total. He argues:

> I know. What got me was the superficiality, the sense of values. I don't think all city societies are as shallow as ours. I am, of course, talking mainly of the so-called upper classes. I didn't really get to know the others. I don't think I have ever met a more pompous, a more mixed-up lot of people. Artistically, they were dry as dust. Intellectually, they could no better than mechanically mouth ideas the West abandoned a generation ago. Their idea of romance was to go and see an American movie or go to one of those wretched restaurants and dance with their wives to a thiry-year-old tune. Nobody remembered the old songs, or the meaning of the festivals. All the sensuality was gone. So was the poetry. All that was left was loud-mouthed women and men in three-piece suits dreaming their little adulteries. (178-79)

An outright rejection of this sort hardly comes from a negative attitude. He did project how he came by his own sense of values and perceptions. Billy thought he would forever hold himself in contempt for what he did to Rima Kaul. He seduced her. He realized he started to behave in a manner that in other men it would have excited his greatest contempt. What made the situation much worse was that she remained as yet fond of him. It was his degeneration, he began to realize:

> It gradually dawned on me that a tremendous corrupting force was working on me. It was as though my soul were taking revenge on me for having denied it for so long that Other Thing that it had been clamouring for. "Here, you swine, if you haven't the guts to break away from this filth, well, then, I am going to wallow in it until it makes you sick." (189)

It was the Other Thing for which he continued his quest: "That Other Thing was, and is, after all, what my life is all about." (189) The narrator asked whether he meant his desire to become a primitive. Billy hesitated. He said: "I don't want to sound too pompous, old chap. Becoming a primitive was only a first step, a means to an end. Of course, I realized it only *after* I ran away. I realized then that I was seeking something *else*. I am still seeking something else." (189) What was he seeking? Was it God? No, that sounded too pompous. Could it be something like that? Yes, something like that, he agreed, though reluctantly.

For Billy being primitive was only a first step. It was, however, not an absolute dedication to Primitive such as we often find in the American Westerns glorifying the Return of the Redskins. A conscious primitivization is like disrobing oneself of the rotten apparel which corrupted him both from within and without.

What gives *The Strange Case* its basic irony is the device of a point of view carefully focused through the vision of the narrator Romesh Sahai, one of the two characters to have had a measure of sympathetic understanding of the enigmatic Billy. Arun Joshi made a deft use of memory-monologues, and largely through the central vision of the point of view protected the monologues from being one-sided affair an egoistical narration of only one dimension.

The sharp contrast between the sophisticated Meena and the primitive Bilasia reinforces the central vision of *The Strange Case.* Bilasia, when Billy first saw her, appeared to be the essence of that primitive force that had called him night after night, year after year. It was to this call he responded in his childhood off Bhubaneswar. It was, again, to this call he responded when the little Negro girl was moved – sexually – to him, playing a pair of bongo drums. It was only to respond to this call that he did to Rima what he never wanted to do: "It was as though a master mind had arranged the whole thing to give me a preview of what awaited me if I continued to defy its call. Poor Rima had crystallized for me the alternatives, although I did not realize this until I sat outside my tent that fateful night. I had two clear choices: I could either follow this call, this vision, whatever the cost, or be condemned to total decay." (189-190) The collapse of his marriage with Meena was again due to this phantom or hallucination. He destroyed his family – the mighty New Delhi family of the Supreme Court judge Mr Biswas. Perhaps, for the same urge, for the same craving, he destabilized the primitive harmony, too, up the far-away Satpura Hills.

Billy's violent end marked the destruction of the weighty family into which he was born. Not that the novelist was glorifying violence in some sense. In a way the family symbolized the insalvability of the Indian upper crust. Perhaps violence alone was to accelerate its demise.

The epigraph – "It irk'd him to be here, he could not rest" (6) – reveals the making of the spirit soaring higher and higher to the invisible vision or the Chandtola of the primitive concept. Are we condemned simply to get on with the business of living ? Mustn't we have the Dream, the vision ? We cannot really understand that we have lost these things largely through the passivity we have elected to go by. And we cannot understand what we have lost unless we are prepared to look critically at the culture in which we live and which we take so much for granted.

Billy aflame with vision and vitality was not the person to rest and rust. He is all for a difficult choice:

> Sometimes I think the human mind is equipped with a built-in apparatus for compromise. As soon as you are faced with a difficult choice this apparatus is switched on. It runs about here

> and there, brokering between various parts of man, rationalizing this, postponing that, until what is left is the conventional expedients of the age and hardly a choice. Deep down we are afraid that the price of making such choices is terrible, not realizing that the price of not making them is even more terrible. (190)

The Strange Case of Billy Biswas is likely to sound strange only to such pedestrians as are terribly scared of making choices. The rebels, the dreamers and the visionaries who are the main motive force of history are the stuff who realize that the price of not making choices is even more terrible. They are not likely to pigeon-hoie Billy Biswas as a strange case such as the nameless bureaucracy did in order to dispose of the file.

Imagine the faceless bureaucrat studying *The Strange Case*. He will bring a legal and formalist approach to the business of scanning the vision embedded in this novel. The exercise may be identical to the formalist abstraction of the New Critics who in a panicky reaction sought to glorify the American South agrarianism. In either case the attempt clearly seeks to snap the bonds between the novel and the readers. I read *The Strange Case* from the context of Indian culture. I found myself placed in a continuity of which we are a sequel as well as actors. It was this active aspect which led me to explore the regeneration-corruption theme in the novel.

To the extent Arun Joshi has brought about a sharper awareness of the principal contradictions of the modern Indian society the novel *The Strange Case of Billy Biswas* is likely to remain extraordinarily responsive to the successive generations of its active Indian readers.

NOTE

1. Arun Joshi, *The Strange Case of Billy Biswas* (Delhi: Hind, 1971).

The Narrative Strategy in *The Strange Case of Billy Biswas*

JOY ABRAHAM

In *The Strange Case of Billy Biswas*, Arun Joshi explores the contemporary man's inner crisis of being isolated from the whole apparatus of convention and ritual of society upholding our glorious cultural ethos. If in *The Foreigner*, his first novel, the crisis of identity arises out of conflict between three different cultures, in *The Strange Case of Billy Biswas* it is a conflict between more basic and greater forces, namely civilization and primitive life or between nature and art. In the case of Billy his experiences are mainly intellectual and psychic and he is a lonely quester, whereas Sindi in *The Foreigner* is a person who is assisted by others in his search. It is a movement from the almost contemplative world of Sindi Oberoi to the dynamic, vital and active world of Billy.

Billy Bimal Biswas from the "upper-upper crust of Indian society," the only son of a Supreme Court Judge, with a pronounced sophisticated English accent acquired in the schools of England, is sent to America to study engineering. On his arrival in New York he takes up his lodging in the outer skirts in Harlem famous for slums because "white America is much too civilized for him." He abandons his study of engineering in favour of Anthropology and is already half-way through his doctoral work in that subject. That is where he meets Romi, the narrator, with whom he shares his lodging and forms a thick friendship.

The death of the narrator's father compels him to return to India. Back in India he joins the Indian Administrative Service. He is one of those handful young men churned out of a mass of four hundred million whose welfare they are meant to be entrusted with. Billy, after his Ph.D. in Anthropology, lectures at Delhi University and apparently settles down. He is married to a pretty aristocratic, convent-educated girl, named Meena. Billy inwardly suffers from pangs of conscience which keep him in a perpetual state of irritation against the social set up in which he is placed. He becomes highly impatient and intolerant of that society. The ordered systemized civilized life which contemporary man is proud of intensifies Billy's problem of identity instead of resolving it. Back in India he feels as a visitor from the wilderness to the marts of the big city. He reflects as Sindi does in *The Foreigner*:

> I see a roomful of finely dressed men and women seated on downy sofas and while I am looking at them under my very nose, they turn into a kennel of dogs yawning (their large teeth showing) or snuggling against each other or holding whisky glasses in their furred paws. I sometimes wonder whether civilization is anything more than the making and spending of money. What else the civilized men do?[1]

The imagery of dogs with furred paws and large teeth betrays his dislike for the so-called elite and the character he thinks they bear. He admires the Swedish girl Tuula who treats money "a whole lot of paper" (177) and hates the world that "hangs on this peg of money." These constant pricks of conscience make Billy look strange. Gone are the staggering intelligence, the spectroscopic interests and the sense of humour which were part of his character and personality. His sensibilities get blunted, as if some part of his being has gone on strike. The Billy that Romi knows, is "finished, snuffed out like a candle left in the rain." (10)

Later, from the extracts of the letters that Billy has written to Tuula Lindgren, his Swedish girl-friend in America, we learn a great deal of the strangeness overtaking Billy. The raw beauty of primitive and tribal nature seems to have captivated his mind. His cynicism almost borders on insanity and now he begins to question his own being, his parentage and his relation to his wife and child. He wonders who they are or what accident of creation has brought them together. Life at a lower ebb of the remote tribals of the Central Provinces now haunts him. He is in a fit of frenzy to explore the earth, the river, the moonlight, the imperishable rocks, the touch and smell of the primeval night, upto the lees. He has undergone a deep metamorphosis. "Layer upon layer is peeled off him until nothing but his primitive self is left trembling in the moonlight." And Bimal Biswas, a graduate of Columbia, the only son of a Supreme Court Judge, husband of Meena Biswas, the father of a handsome child, seeks a perpetual refuge in the tribal wilderness, simply vanishes into the *saal* forests of the Maikala Hills. He believes he has greater responsibility to his soul than to his family.

Great commotion has followed the heels of Billy's disappearance as he has disappeared "totally" without leaving a trace. Various theories have been fabricated. A theory which is ultimately adopted by the C.I.D. is that Billy has been killed by the maneater who has been heard repeatedly in the vicinity of their camps the night before Billy's disappearance and hence the police closes Billy's case. The strange case of Billy Biswas--that is how it appears to the civilized world.

The officially accepted surmise that Billy Biswas is dead falls as under when Romi the narrator, who has become a Collector of the Central Provinces, meets Billy to his astonishment after ten years on his tour to a famine-stricken area. Billy is very much alive with a tribal belle Bilasia whose "enormous eyes pour out a sexuality that is nearly as primeval as the forest that surrounds them." If the forest and the hills have beckoned him earlier, Bilasia is now leading him by hand. Bilasia is the essence of that primitive force which has been calling him night after night, year after year.

Billy is thoroughly tribalized. He wears a loin-cloth, grows beard and is some kind of a demi-god to the local tribals. He emerges among them as an archetype of their collective consciousness:

> And so Billy Biswas, a refugee from civilization, sat in the shadow of a *saal* tree, a thousand miles away from home, and gradually underwent his final metamorphosis. (140-41)

When Billy enters the world of tribals and watches their drumming and dance, his unconsciousness craves to become a conscious part of their world:

> He squatted at the edge of a promontory and stared into the basin of a gorge five hundred feet below while the tumultuous drums chiselled away the edifice of his past. (141)

He has become the *mahaprasad*, the greatest friend of Dhunia, the village headman. Billy is described in mystical sweetness and classical tradition. To the tribal people of the hills, Billy is,

> like rain on parched lands, like balm on a wound. These hills have not seen the like of him since the last of our kings passed away. (160)

One is reminded of the Tamil devotional poet Manika Vāsagar's (late seventeenth century) description of Siva:

> Shall I call you honey on the branch,
> Or nectar from the sounding Sea?
> I know not what to say, Our Hara!
> Our precious balm, our King![2]

Romi, the only link from civilization that Billy keeps, turns out to be his betrayal. Romi tries to protect him from the recalling arms of civilization, but things get beyond his control when through Romi's wife the secret of Billy's reappearance is shared with Billy's father and wife who are determined to get him back. At the persistence of Billy's father through the interference of the Chief Secretary of the State, Rele, the police officer and his men combed the entire tribal area to restore Billy to the "civilized society" to which he owes his birth. But the effort to capture him only leads to the final catastrophe. Billy dies of bullet wounds and only his ashes reach the civilized world. His strange case is disposed of "in the manner that a humdrum society knows of disposing its rebels, its seers, its true lovers." While the civilized world destroys him, the tribal world seeks to perpetuate the memory of the mangod by offering him a shrine. The death of Billy "should not be taken as the death of an isolationist but as the triumph of his ideals and principles."[3]

It is a tale told with an excellent craftsmanship maintaining the contrast between the impulsive and seemingly eccentric behaviour and actions of Billy and the cool, collected account of Romi, the collector friend of Billy. The novel begins with a very human and natural association between these two Indian students in America. It is not with a view to make any value judgement nor to evolve any confrontation between the East and the West that the author has put them in an American setting. The purpose of the author is to convince the readers that a great primitive force--*urkraft* as the Swedish girl Tuula puts it--is so very strong in him that even an expensive schooling and exposure to a highly civilized and modern Western society cannot destroy or overcome that force which possesses him. Like an internal haemorrhage it has hit upon him and he tries to suppress it Romi notices several paradoxes in Billy in the wake of their friendship when Billy takes him to his room in Harlem in New York. As in *The Foreigner*, the author makes use of the opportunity to reflect on the American sub-culture:

> His apartment was appalling. It was on the second floor of a tenement house that housed at least a dozen other families. It was situated in what must have been one of the worse slums of New York City... The shutters hung loose; so did the mail boxes in the hall. Nearly all the glass in the front door had been knocked out... The stairs were cluttered with empty beer cans, newsprint, children, and an occasional condom. At night you could hear the rats scampering among the garbage drums. (9)

It is an appropriate choice of Billy what with his aversion to the civilized world and a strong streak of primitivism in him. Romi says that he is one of those rare men who has poise without pose. He talks without gestures. Another evidence of such primeval longing in Billy is seen in a "music session" he has at a party in his friend's apartment:

> Billy's session--for that was how it came to be known subsequently--lasted for nearly a quarter of an hour. I am certain it was nothing very skilful or sophisticated from the viewpoint of music. What it had, I think, was a mesmeric pull that held us by its sheer vitality. Little packages of sound detonated in the smoke-filled air in quick succession, falling in one rhythm or another, creating patterns of sound that deep down I knew were not merely that but carried a more fundamental message although what it was I, or Billy for that matter, could not have said. (21)

Thus, the recognition of a new region beyond the frontiers of ordinary human consciousness is here narrated with great ease, retaining in its tone, all the dry normalcy of the apartment atmosphere with Romi sitting on an empty crate of California oranges.

The story is made all the more interesting and convincing on account of Billy's brilliant, rational outlook and the author's artistic expression of this *urkraft* that triggers off that creative energy of Billy which prompts him to do what he does. Billy was only fourteen then. He goes along with his uncle's chauffeur to Bhubaneswar and visits Konark. They go to the tribal people. The chauffeur wants to enjoy life, but Billy sits there and sees the tribals dance, drink, sing and make love. Watching the tribal dance the young Billy feels that this is where he belongs. The ritual enactment of dancing ceremony becomes a symbolic test of the power of faith over the power of dehumanizing contemporary reality. Unlike Sindi, Billy listens to the voice of his soul and has the courage to go ahead discarding the world where

> Nobody remembered the old songs or the meaning of the festivals. All the sensuality was gone. So was the poetry. All that was left was loud-mouthed women and men in three-piece suits dreaming their little adulteries. (179)

He is not inactive as Raja Rao's hero musing over philosophical speculations. He makes no cowardly compromises like Sindi. He was a man of deep conviction capable of turning his vision into reality.

With an admirable dexterity of material and a controlling of the weight of the details in the first-person narrative, Joshi manages to explore the protagonist's psychic and psychological instincts. He turns to the hero's inner self, to the inner man in him to expose what he is inside as he had done in the case of Sindi Oberoi in *The Foreigner*, where Sindi is a lonely individual wanting to love and be loved but afraid of committing himself. In the same way as Sindi is misjudged by the Khemkas, Billy is also misunderstood by his father who thinks that man is "governed only by engineering and law and nothing else." Billy longs to "burst the spirit's sleep" and comprehend the magnetic pull of the Chandtola cliff. Billy's behaviour, that is his disappearance to the forest, poses a problem to his father and all others who know him even as it poses a problem to the reader. His behaviour is shrouded in mystery and he becomes an enigmatic figure. But this enigma can be resolved if one tries to interpret his behaviour in terms of certain psychological and anthropological facts at work. In fact it can be explained in terms of Jung's theory of the collective unconscious. In addition to the immediate consciousness, which is thoroughly personal in nature and which we believe to be only an empirical psyche, there exists a second psychic system of a collective, universal, and impersonal nature which is identical in all individuals. This collective unconscious does not develop individually but is inherited. It consists of pre-existent forms, the archetypes, which can only become conscious secondarily and which give a definite form to certain psychic contents. "But if we consider the tremendous powers that lie hidden in the mythological and religious spheres in man the aetiological significance of the archetype appears less fantastic."[4] He only expresses something which millions of people before him have believed. The phantom that Billy once saw and has described to Tuula is vividly objectified and visualized in Bilasia, the tribal girl with beauty and dignity. She is the untapped subterranean resource of psychic energy. Joshi depicts the beauty of Bilasia with an unforgettable lyrical fervour fusing myth and nature so remarkably:

> She had that untamed beauty that comes to flower only in our primitive people. It was as though nature were cocking a snook at the Meena Biswases of the world, informing them once again how little it cared for their self-proclaimed superiority. Looking at Bilasia one could well believe that these were the children of kings condemned to exile by those rapacious representatives of civilization who had ruled the thrones of Delhi and still continued to do so. Where else could be found that proud carriage, a figure so graceful, eyes whose brightness made your pulse quicken. Where else had I ever seen a grief so tragic that it might well have brought tears to the eyes of a stone-god. (143)

Billy was happy living with these persons who lived closer to the elements and ways of nature. Thus, in the character of Billy, Arun Joshi opens a new vista of Matthew Arnold's Scholar Gipsy.

Without such a choice his life may have turned out to be miserable. Thus, the subtle interplay of situation and character make Billy a complex individual. If Meena had possessed a rare degree of empathy or even a sufficient idea of suffering, things may have been different.

But her upbringing, her ambitions, twenty years of contact with a phoney society--all have ensured that she does not have it. He married only to avert hallucinations that some terrible thing may happen unless he does something drastic. In a close-knit Indian family the only thing he can think of is to get married. It is like taking out an "insurance" on his "normalcy." (182) But marriage does not solve his problem. Feeling insecure again, he tries to channellize his passions through the course of his romance with Rima Kaul which even borders on seduction. It was her sympathy that he abhorred. He comes to realize that his relationship with her is nothing but a degradation. It is a corruption of his being. His is "a quest for self-realization for a union with the missioning part of his soul."[5] Meena deadens his senses, Rima corrupts him. "In terms of psychoanalysis, Billy and Bilasia are two selves of the same personality." "For him Bilasia is 'Prakriti' and he is 'Purush' and the cosmic whole can be experienced in their union." It is not the gross sexual lust which makes him desert his wife and child for the amorous dalliance with Bilasia. He is impelled by the elemental human impulses which are almost primitive and are in consonance with the innate nature and what is done by him is nothing but the manifestation of those organic impulses:

> I had no idea it was going to happen. It was two days--and two nights--before I knew what I had done. By then it was too late. (111)

In his total repudiation of his earlier life-style, Billy tells Romi that, without such a choice, his life would have been disastrous.

It is true that as in *The Foreigner*, the narration does not move in a straight line but is pieced together very much like a jigsaw puzzle.[6] The author himself is aware of it when he says that if the narrative still sounds melodramatic in places, the reasons must be sought in the narrowness of our own range of experience rather than in anything that Billy says or does. (111) While narrating the psychic secrets of his hero, the author ungrips his control over the narrative letting the sweep of his imagination carry it forward with a full thrust.

"Renunciation has always been an Indian ideal of life."[7] Like all ideals it is a difficult condition, attainable only by a few. But in literature it is not impossible to create a credible individual. Hence, while the writer does not disregard the circumstantial reality--Billy Biswas's expensive schooling, education abroad--on another level the novel transcends the axes of time and space, probing into a fundamental metaphysical question. What happened to Billy is, perhaps, inevitable; as inevitable as the "star-constellations" in which he comes so absolutely to believe. If life's meaning lies not in the "glossy surfaces" of our pretensions but in those "dark mossy labyrinths" of the soul that languish forever, hidden from the dazzling light of the sun, then the narrator knows of no other man who seeks it more doggedly than himself. Again, having received a signal, he abandons himself so recklessly to its call.

The most important act of Billy in the novel is his disappearance from the civilized world and whatever he says or does earlier is but a movement in that direction. Billy's withdrawal from the world is in the nature of a reflex action, he withdraws in order to preserve himself from "those rapacious representatives of civilization." He fails to establish any communication with his wife and the life around him because of his distinct innate originality. As Jasbir Jain points out: "Long before his physical disappearance into the *saal* forests of the Maikala Hills, he had ceased to belong to the world."[8] His is not an escape from reality but an escape into reality, a rich inward life. This exit reminds one in a way of Prince Siddhartha's renunciation of wife and child in search of enlightenment. To Billy too, it is a movement from darkness to light. As Sindi in *The Foreigner* gets his revelation sitting on a "weathered stone," Billy gets it when he meets Bilasia. It is a movement which makes him feel that he

> has suddenly discovered that bit of himself that he has searched for all his life and without which his life is nothing more than the poor reflection of a million others. (142)

It is in this life that Billy finds fulfilment and identification and the essence of human existence. He craves to lose his identity, sacrifices it, surrenders it for the higher things of life. He leads a vigorous life in the dark jungles in contrast to his earlier restlessness. The jungles have an immense scope to nourish his primordial urges. It is no matter what trails of glory or shattered hearts he leaves behind in his turbulent wake. Hence, the problem of a gross misrepresentation of the natural order of life does not arise. It is a natural representation of an unnatural order of life.

The recognition of myth in a narrative gives punch to the reading experience. It can be said that as a nation the Indians are still closer to mythology and most of the Indian epics are nothing but the collective unconscious of the whole nation. P. Lal rightly says: "Without an absorption in the myths of the lands of one's forefathers, it isn't even possible to live a meaningful life."[9] In using myth as a structural parallel, one often notices a mythical situation underlying the whole novel or a part of it. As a digressional method we find a weaving of story within a story like the stories that we find in the *Panch Tantra*, *The Vishnu Purana, The Ramayana* and *The Mahabharata*.

The Strange Case of Billy Biswas is "a compelling novel about a strange quest drawing upon myth and folk-lore to reiterate its elemental concerns."[10] The sharing of a common mythology between the narrator and the audience is a general condition of the oral tradition of story-telling. It is interesting to note that the union of Billy and Bilasia can be taken as the human soul's longing for reunion with the divine as symbolized by Krishna, the union of "Jeevatma" with "Paramatma." Billy, like Sindi, is in search of a world of meaningful relatedness which he can find neither in white America nor in the upper-class Indian society. That was the beginning of his quest to understand himself and the nature of reality, something beyond oneself. Becoming a primitive is the first step, a means to an end and in the second stage he is still seeking something 'else.'

> "What is that?"
> He seemed to be thinking.
> "God?" I prompted.
> "There, there, old chap, that is too big a word."
> "Something like that?"
> "Yes, something like that." (189)

This again is not an escape from order and form into reckless freedom, for, interestingly enough, in his second phase as a tribal we see order and form of a different kind.

Localized myths, otherwise known as "sthala-puranas," are also used by Arun Joshi. Dhunia comes out with a folk-legend. The gist of the story can be examined as it has a direct bearing upon Billy. Thousands of years ago there lived a great king who built a temple for which he wanted to have the chief idol for the inner shrine made by himself. He went on working, and the idol was so beautiful that God decided to enter it. That night the brothers of the king who got scent of this divine benediction on their brother poisoned him and the queen, Devi, immolated herself prophesying that she would return when her husband returned to the forest. Dhunia identified Billy as the king. For the tribals he is a mythical king who is destined to return and on his return Chandtola, the peak, will glow again on moonlit nights. Billy's story parallels the king who attempts to sculpt the face of God, but is spoiled in the midway in the mad, bad, absurd world.

And it is here, while narrating the story of the king, Joshi introduces another recurring mythical concept in the novel: the concept of *matra*. According to the Indian tradition, men who transgress their "matra" (i.e., natural limits) are punished for it by a kind of Nemesis. Legends and fables may have this common underlying pattern--how men who overstep their "matra" are finally punished. If Billy knows that he is the king he will lose his powers. Dhunia says:

> those who must not will hear of it, and Billy Bhai will lose his powers. (159)

Strangely enough it is after the narrator mentioned this to Billy that things began to go wrong for him and it is ironical that Billy has to pay with his life when he steps out of the "stifling confines" (240) of the humdrum society to which he owes his birth. The news of his presence leaks out when he tries to restore the health of the narrator's ailing wife, through whom the secret of Billy's reappearance comes out. The pestering of Situ to get hold of the secret from Romi and her subsequent betrayal remind us of the Biblical characters Samson and Delilah.

Dhunia regards Billy as the best magician who has got his magic power from Devi Mata of the Chandtola abode. The efficacy of magic implies a belief in magic.[11] His chief functions, however, are those of a priest. So we are inclined to consider him as the archetypal hero, as the Saviour or Deliverer undertaking some long journey during which he must perform impossible tasks, battle with monsters, overcome insurmountable obstacles in order to save his subjects. Rama in *The Ramayana* belongs to this category. Billy who in *The Strange Case of Billy Biswas* takes up a long journey to understand himself and the nature of reality does a lot of miracles. He is a sort of mangod, an "avatara" to the tribals and this sort of belief is in tune with the Indian tradition:

> The East is trying to see God in man (hence the avataras or incarnations) while in the West the difference and distance between God and man is unbridgeable.[12]

Dhunia is reported to have narrated a number of miracles performed by Billy even though the credibility of some of them is questioned by Billy himself at the time of his conversation with the narrator. Billy drives away a tiger roaming in the jungles, he brings Dhunia's grandson who is as "dead as that fly" back to life, restores the health of Bilasia, cures the migraine of Situ and even predicts the rainfall. It seems odd that his regret over the appearance before Romi has proved to be true even though the latter is devoid of any ulterior motive to betray him. The superstitions prevalent among the elite society are also in keeping with the tribal beliefs. The "bad omen" of asking water by Romi when they are about to set out in search of Billy proves to forestall disaster, for the search ends in Billy's death.

Thus, apart from the allegorical function all myths are used with a view to bring out Billy's experience in line with that of "rishis" and other "refugees from civilization." Myths and legends form the underlying design holding together all the digressions, the tales within tales enriching the main structure of the novel. It may be because of the oversight of this mythical pattern that one of the critics disparages the novel as "not as powerful."[13] It is as powerful as many other Indian English novels.

The entire novel is an attempt to discuss and justify the primitive instincts of Billy Bimal Biswas. Since the narrator cannot write anything that he does not know, the narration turns out to be purely subjective and in the first person singular. It is not merely the events of his life that the narrator recounts but he also tries to find the truth hidden behind them. So, instead of a straightforward narration of events in their chronological order, the narrator leads us through the introspective memories, inmost thoughts and feelings, analysis of intimate human relations, personal letters and discussions. Several characters are made to have discussions with the narrator, including the hero himself. Most of the characters, except Bilasia, have been drawn simply for the expediency of the plot. The discussions with Rima Kaul who is so "head over heels in love" with Billy, Bilasia his paramour, "the nosy little fellow from Patna," and with "the drooling old advocate" all serve this purpose. The discussion with Dhunia, the tribal headman, is important because he explains in his own tribal dialect the nature of the psychological impact made by *Kala Pahar* on Billy Biswas which forms the foundation of the novel.

> You see what you can when you are awake, and what you cannot see when you are awake comes to you in dreams. It is all the same. (161)

It is in consonance with the belief and faith of the tribals. Here, one is reminded of the Biblical statement:

> Now faith is the substance of things hoped for, the evidence of things not seen. (Hebrews, 11:1)

As a technique, the letters that Billy has written to Tuula achieve the desired effect in throwing light on the inner recesses of his mind without making him verbalize such vulnerable thoughts even in private conversation. It is these thoughts that support Billy's option of the tribal world.

The words "strange" and "case" in the title have thematic significance. Billy's case is both strange and not so strange either. It is strange because in a world where everybody is crazy after civilization and its comforts, Billy, the America-educated engineer-anthropologist and a member of the sophisticated upper strata of the Delhi society, opts out of civilization for the primitive life. But in another sense it is not so strange either. For many people had felt frustrated with civilization in the past and had opted out. Not only that, in India the idea of people leaving civilization for a primitive life is not something new. Our "rishis" and sages in the past had renounced civilization for the primitive life as a way of realizing truth and God. In a sense this is what Billy also does. Again a sense of disillusion with a society whose superficial glamour covers up the scum beneath and impatience with the glib hypocrisy and poses of the so-called successful world are not anything uncommon. Maugham's Lawry Darrel has become an archetypal figure of such disillusioned young men who seek refuge in a simpler world. Disco-culture, drug-addiction and dipsomania are all symptoms of the disease. But whereas all these objectify a lack of direction, Billy's is a determined quest.

He is definitely a "strange case" for psychoanalysts and psychiatrists. As for the word "case," normally "case" means a psychological case. In fact Billy's case is a good psychological case-study. For his predicament is something psychological and his search is also after the psyche and reality. In the legal sense Billy's disappearance is treated as a case of killing by the man-eater and in the end Billy himself is hunted by the police as a killer. The title also suggests the civilized world's comment on Billy's behaviour which to the conformists looks "strange" indeed.

The following passage brings home to us the use of a style that reflects the rhythmic sensibilities of the Indian psyche:

> When the *Kala Pahar* calls you, Collector sahib, there is nothing you can do but go. The first time I heard his drumming I knew the Rock had called him. It is like a woman calling you. You become blind. . . . All you hear is its call. Day and night it calls you. Night and day. And you go like a fish hooked on a string, in spite of yourself, bound hand and foot. There is nothing you can do but go, when the *Kala Pahar* calls you. Yes, Collector sahib, the Black Rock is the Master of us all. (160)

The quick succession of the precise sentences here suggests the nature of the overpowering effect of the big Rock on Dhunia who fails to communicate something more for which human language is grossly inadequate.

Arun Joshi uses aphorisms such as "Boons are not given everyday, as though they were guavas" and "You speak what you think, and think what you speak."

The dialogue in the novel is crisp and carefully wrought. It strives for and occasionally rises to poetic heights without any damage to the quality of the prose style which has been adapted suitably to the theme and mood of the novel. Another important feature of the novel is the authenticity of the dialogues presented. The exchange at a party in America, the interview with Rima Kaul and the conversation between the narrator and Billy have the naturalness of the spoken dialect. The dialect of Dhunia has a "regional flavour which does not sound either transliterated or outlandish."[14] It is an emblem of accumulated human experiences condensed into myths.

We find magnificent use of humour and irony in the novel. The narrator's pedigree, with his great-grandfather's foolishness, and his "song-writer uncle" with all his fervour for the "film world" and "musical adventures" are humorously portrayed. It brings into focus the close family ties which one finds in the Indian society. Mrs. Biswas gives "tips" to the narrator on how to get along in the service avoiding quarrel with his superiors and also advises him never to let the police get an upper hand in any situation. It is one of these ironies of fate that this is precisely what he has managed to achieve by his visit to the Chief Secretary. Further, Romi in whom Billy has deep faith, indirectly rises against him.

The action in the novel has a definite movement. The narrator looks back at his life and events in America and India in juxtaposition. It is Billy's resolve to flee the civilized world and go back to a world where he will be free to obey his primitive instincts and impulses which lends force to the plot of the novel and again it is his death at the hands of the humdrum world that provides pathos to the story. This tragic event, though intensely pathetic, does not add any sentimentality to the novel except that Romi the Collector shows a deep concern for Billy. Billy is not a tragic hero who rises to noble heights from which he might fall nor does he have that necessary tragic flaw which might cause his downfall.[15] Though he is regarded as a mythical king by the tribal folks, the credibility of which is questioned by Billy himself, his death is a loss only to his immediate relatives. It is with Billy's clandestine appearance in Romi's presence that the second phase of the novel begins. From here on, the novel moves steadily and moves to a purposeful end. The impeccable epiphany at the beginning is maintained and carried over to a neat denouement. The thrust of the novel is embodied in the couplet cited on the opening page. It refers to the rituals of the tribals both at the births and also at the time of funerals.

Apart from the existential shrouds, the novel strives to assert much needed values. "An apocalyptic light spreads over the novel. The Promised Land gets lost in the Promised end."[16] In a way the novel speaks for a spiritual regeneration in contrast to the spiritual decay. Hence, the novel opens in New York's Harlem against the "white dissipation" around and shuttles in between Satpura Hills and New Delhi. These two geographic locations have been presented not so much to dramatize the yawning gap but to make the situation plain, to unveil what has been lost and to stress on the utter falsity of the refinement of the upper crust. In no way is it an encounter between these two worlds. This is the same thing that the novelist wants to assert in contrast between Meena and Bilasia, the essence of that primitive force.

Though Arun Joshi does not use symbols in any significant way in his novels, one can find in this novel a few events and happenings which are symbolic. For instance, when Romi, his uncle and Billy stand watching the kites one of the pair is irrevocably cut off from its moorings and with a tragic dignity it floats to the ground across the roots and lanes of the ancient city, ominously foreshadowing Billy's disappearance and finally his death. "Bongo drums" and "ghunghrus" stand for the erotic and the primeval instincts in Billy. Tuula's "ignition of match and lighting the cigarette while she speaks to the narrator is about something buried too deep (not ripened enough to ignite) to name itself."[17]

> We looked at each other in silence. Tuula lit a cigarette, then with the same match lighted the two candles that stood on our table, pale and vulnerable against the dark red table-cloth. She blew the match. (23)

The red table-cloth, the blowing of the match, the act of ignition and the leaves of tobacco consumed with fire, which originally burnt two candles with its singular purity suggest the signifiers which foreshadow the real life-force which Billy meets among tribals. These signifiers merge with one another to form a flame of human shape that melts into Bilasia in the tribal world. Dhunia with his tribal instincts can sense the extraordinary rhythm of Billy's drumming which is a powerful medium of communication for the tribals. The exploratory nature of Billy to understand himself is symbolized by the faceless idol that has been made by the king. Billy's last words, watching his close friend Romi approach him, is--"You bastards." It is a significant utterance which acquires multiple meanings in the context. Thrice he uses the word in the novel. "It is at the same time a direct abuse, an expression of anger at the betrayal of friendship and the meaningless assault of the civilized world on his creative privacy."[18] It is his final verdict on civilization which is nothing but bastardly to him and, perhaps to the novelist too. In *The Foreigner*, it is Sindi who infringes the society; it is now the society which is responsible for the tragedy of Billy.

As in the case of *The Foreigner*, this is an equally powerful story of the narrator's awakening awareness:

> As I grow old, I realize that the most futile cry of man is his impossible wish to be understood. The *attempt* to understand is probably even more futile. (7)

This does not necessarily mean that the protagonist is pushed into the background. In fact both the stories, the story of the narrator Romi, and the story of Biswas, run concurrently in the novel forming an interesting structure of parallelism and contrast. This contrast which is generated primarily by character and individual nature is maintained throughout in all the actions and events too. At the same time the two stories are linked to each other because most of the events in the life of the protagonist have a direct bearing on that of the narrator, whose prime purpose itself is to expose Billy Biswas. It is this aspect of the novel which makes Billy Biswas an important character in the novel and the view that Billy Biswas is only a shadowy figure[19] in the novel without any significant place in its structure is not quite correct. He does have a place in the novel which is as important and significant as that of the narrator, Romi, though the latter may appear to be dominating the action of the novel.

What may appear to be a mere report on the surface is saved by a mode of narrative, the tone of which has a combination of concern, disinterestedness, casualness but all under superb control. The novel is a dramatic presentation of the complex character of Billy who, though his values are profoundly human, is aspiring to get beyond this advertised world. Even this aspiration of his is blended naturally and spontaneously with his primitive instincts. The fact that Billy's reappearance is only accidental and that he has already lived like a tribal for ten years signifies the undramatic manner in which the most dramatic act of Billy is presented. In fact Arun Joshi does not depend for the success of his narrative art on devices of dramatization or use of symbols or images. Without recourse to any of these devices, he is able to produce a totality of effect which is dependent purely on the force of his narrative which again is objective and free from all sentimentality or subjectivity. For instance, Dhunia's interpretation of Billy's powers as a priest, his identity with the mythological king and the overpowering effect of *Kala Pahar* are narrated without any traces of sentimentality. In all such situations where there is a danger of sentimentality creeping in, the narrator overcomes it by introducing counter-statements which raise doubts about the credibility of the statements made by Dhunia. In other words, he is able to handle his narrative art in such a way that without being excessively sentimental or emotional or dramatic, he can make the situations credible and convincing. We see all the events and situations filtered through the consciousness of a narrator who is detached and objective and it is here that we find the technique of first-person narration proving helpful.

Thus, *The Strange Case of Billy Biswas* makes a complex and interesting piece of narrative structuring which is based on principles of parallelism and contrast. There are two narrative streams which not only run parallel to each other but also set each other off through contrast and ultimately run into each other. Into this complex narrative structure are interwoven myths and legends which add a new dimension to the meaning and significance of various events and characters. These myths and legends tend to add an allegorical dimension to the novel. There is of course no strict adherence to the chronological order in the novel because the narrator who is interested in the deeper meanings hidden behind every event explores them through dream and introspection and also through letters and discussions. To add to all this there is the use of symbols, images, aphorisms and patterns of irony and humour which deepen the meaning and significance of each event. What is, however, particularly striking about the narrative method followed in *The Strange Case of Billy Biswas* is that it combines detachment and objectivity on the part of the narrator with his involvement in and concern for all that happens in the novel. In short, the narrative methods control very effectively the action, the meaning and the character of the novel.

NOTES

1. Arun Joshi, *The Strange Case of Billy Biswas* (New Delhi: Hind Pocket Books, 1971), p. 96.
2. As quoted in Edwin Gerow, "Indian Poetics," *The Literature of India: An Introduction* (Chicago: The Univ. of Chicago, 1974), p. 136.
3. A.N. Dwivedi, *Studies in Contemporary Indian Fiction in English*, ed. A.N. Dwivedi (Allahabad: Kitab Mahal, 1987), p. 313.
4. Joseph Campbell, trans., *The Portable Jung* (New York: The Viking Press, 1978), p. 65.
5. Hari Mohan Prasad, *Arun Joshi* (New Delhi: Arnold-Heinemann, 1985), pp. 55, 58 and 60.
6. Murli Das Melwani, *Themes in Indo-Anglian Literature* (Bareilly: Prakash, 1977), p. 67.
   Madhusudan Prasad, "Arun Joshi" *Indian English Novelists* (New Delhi: Sterling, 1982), p. 58.
7. Meenakshi Mukherjee, *The Twice Born Fiction* (New Delhi: Arnold-Heinemann, 1971), p. 97.
8. Jasbir Jain, "Foreigners and Strangers: Arun Joshi's Heroes," *The Journal of Indian Writing in English*, 5, No. 1 (January 1977), p. 54.
9. P. Lal, "Myth and the Indian Writer in English: A Note," *Aspects of Indian Writing in English*, ed. M.K. Naik (Madras: The Macmillan, 1979), p. 17.
10. Mukherjee, p. 203.
11. Claude Levi-Strauss, trans., "The Sorcerer and His Magic," *Structural Anthropology* (1963; rpt. Penguin, 1972), p. 168.
12. Prabhakar Machwe, *Modernity and Contemporary Indian Literature* (Delhi: Chetna, 1978), p. 105

13. Shyamala A. Narayan, "Indian English Novel: Steady Growth," *Littcrit*, 5, No. 2 (December 1979), p. 26.
14. Melwani, p. 67.
15. Sudhakar R. Jamkhandi, "Arun Joshi: An Emerging Voice in Indian English Literature," *The Literary Endeavour*, 6, Nos. 1 to 4, ed. Adinarayana (Anantapur), p. 40.
16. D. Prempati, "*The Strange Case of Billy Biswas*: A Serious Response to a Big Challenge," *The Fictional World of Arun Joshi*, ed. R.K. Dhawan (New Delhi: Classical, 1986), p. 187.
17. Devider Mohan, "The Image of Fire in *The Strange Case of Billy Biswas*," *The Fictional World of Arun Joshi*, p. 199.
18. C.N. Srinath, "The Fiction of Arun Joshi," *The Literary Criterion*, 12, Nos. 2 & 3 (1976), p. 126.
19. Shyamala A. Narayan, p. 26.

The Short Stories of Arun Joshi: A Study

M.G. HEGDE

I

Arun Joshi's output as a short story writer is meagre; so far he has published only one selection of stories entitled *The Survivor*[1] which contains ten stories. Two other stories are published in different magazines. Some of the stories merit serious consideration.[2]

Arun Joshi has no "theory" of the short story. However he firmly believes that the short story is as effective a literary form as the novel is:

> Each has its own place. In my case it is the theme which determines whether it would be a short story or a novel. For example, I wrote a short story called "The Gherao" which was about students gheraoing a principal. Thematically I would not like to handle a novel about the academic world which I don't know about; so a short story.[3]

In fact "The Gherao" is the only story of Arun Joshi which is about the academic world. Most of his stories deal with the decaying upper upper-crust of the Indian society. Even when he writes about the lower class--say a servant, ("The Servant") or the peasant boys ("Harmik") or a poor young widow whose suppressed passions could find an outlet only in the institutionalized prostitution ("The Frontier Mail is Gone")--it is viewed from the point of view of an essentially aristocratic narrator. Thus we have a "case study" of the servant ("The Servant"), a business executive's account of Leela ("The Frontier Mail is Gone"), and a superficial presentation of the confusion of the two peasant boys in London while the glitter of London itself comes alive ("Harmik"). On the contrary, Arun Joshi allows a first-person narrative while writing about the affluent society. This explains the conviction of Arun Joshi to write only about the world he is really familiar with. The impelling credibility of his fiction thus stems from his very conviction.

Like his novels, Arun Joshi's short stories too satirize the glittering flimsiness of the Indian affluent society. Arun Joshi brings home the point that in a society in which all scruples are given up in favour of making money, neither a genuine human relationship nor an authentic existence is possible. Pseudo-Westernization, which has devitalized the individual by curbing his creativity, is yet another target of Joshi's satire. Sensitive protagonists of Arun Joshi's stories survive the modern Indian society by rebelling against it as in "The Survivor" or in "A Trip for Mr. Lele." Antiquated moral codes which do not take into account genuine human feelings are also indicated as in "The Frontier Mail is Gone."

Also, Arun Joshi's short stories show him to be singularly conscious of technique and experimentation. Not all these experiments achieve a uniform success. But the successful ones are those which force the readers to read between the lines, to see beyond the story. A good short story, as Hemingway put it, resembles an ice-berg: The one-ninth above the surface suggesting the eight-ninth below. Arun Joshi too seems to agree with this for somewhere in *The Last Labyrinth*, Som Bhaskar, the protagonist, muses: "Reality was so like an ice-berg. You never saw the whole of it."

II

That Arun Joshi forces the reader to see beyond the story can be illustrated by an analysis of "The Gherao" and "The Homecoming." "The Gherao" is an objective account of a shapeless, unpremeditated confrontation between the principal and the students of a college. From the point of view of form, it belongs to a class of the short story which can be called "the story of situation." Here Joshi perfectly catches the violence, hostility and incomprehension in the atmosphere; convincingly depicts the amorphousness and inexplicability of the student-mob; and successfully probes the disturbed and the injured sentiments of the gheraoed principal. Moreover, as the story develops, one finds it assuming an altogether new dimension and the combination of circumstances gives Joshi the privilege of witnessing, and making the readers see, in a tragically concentrated form, the encounter between the principal and the president of the Students Union Chiru Pandey, which, virtually, is a confrontation between the older generation and the younger generation. At one point in the story, the narrator becomes aware of this and remarks:

> For the moment, the fifty yards that separated us represented all the agony and the hopelessness that divide one generation from another. (21)

III

"The Homecoming" records the impressions of a young man just returned from the Eastern Front with a first-hand experience of war. He has seen "several hundred dead, gashed, charred, bloated, hacked, shot through with their hands behind the backs." (98) He has seen a hungry mob starving to death, and half of his men being killed in his very presence. His return to a world of affluence with its arty-arty girls and week-end parties, speeches and talks, poetry and flowers, movies and dances does not make much sense after what he has been through. He does not feel at home on his homecoming. Instead he is thoroughly disturbed: "He did not know how to fit it all together or whether it *could* be fit together. Ever." (104) The point of the story is not that war has ruined him for normal life; it is, paradoxically, that he finds the so-called "normal life" abnormal and unreal.

"The Homecoming" fashions the response of the readers by a careful juxtaposition of what the soldier has been through on the Front and what he sees around him on his homecoming. On their drive home from the station, his fiancee says that "she had been eating too much and would now have to diet." And in the place where he has come from, "he had not met a man, woman, or child, who had not been hungry; constantly hungry." (98) He was, as his mother has been, keen on his marriage until before the war. But now he wonders as to "the meaning of one man's marriage; one man's life." (99)

Evidently, Joshi has tried here the interspersed method of spacing out the two movements of narration. The ultimate purpose, it appears, is to make the reader conscious of vital disjoint in the ways of the world seen through what happens to the protagonist.

The story, then, operates at three levels; at the level of characterization it dramatizes the metaphysical anguish of the war-torn protagonist: "what life was all about. Who . . . could possibly be running the world." (99) At the level of plot--which derives its strength by a careful juxtaposition of the *thoughts* of a man who has actually participated in the war and the *talks* of the people who are placed in a comfortable distance from the war--it implies a stark contrast between the two attitudes to war; and at the tonal level it implies "the vast unbridgeable gap between life in its starkness and suffering, and the cushioned unreality of affluent life"[4]--the vital disjoint in the ways of the world. It is the third aspect of the story which has lent it a universal significance and tends to make the protagonist a representative figure.

From the point of view of narrative strategy, "The Homecoming" is a curious experiment. Though the story is narrated by the omniscient narrator, it is narrated from the vantage point of the protagonist "he." Nowhere in the whole narrative do we find a distinctly authorial comment. Thus the author or the narrative voice is only a passive and non-committal reporter. This unique device has yielded a marvellous result: while the vantage point of the protagonist has put a check on the possibility of idealization and rationalization on the part of the narrator, the narrative voice of the author has put a check on the possibility of sentimentalization on the part of the protagonist. Hence the subdued tone of the narrative and hence a "clinical objectivity" which is so typical of a Greek drama. It is because of this hybrid narrative strategy that Joshi has admirably succeeded in probing the nature of a predicament in an objective manner.

Secondly, as his direct intellectual or emotional or moral involvement is avoided, the narrative self of the author remains non-committal and the reader derives "the meaning" from what he sees and hears for himself from behind the arras, as it were, what the character does, or speaks, or thinks, and the story achieves that ideal so forcefully stated by J.W. Beach: "The story shall tell itself."[5]

IV

The title story of the collection, "The Survivor," which first appeared in between the publication of *The Apprentice* and *The Strange Case of Billy Biswas*,[6] treats one of the key motifs–corruption–in both these novels. The problem of Kewal Kapur, the protagonist of the story is that, like Billy, he is sick of "that fantastic racket that passes for the MODERN INDIAN SOCIETY." (96) His sickness is accentuated both by his job at the public relations department of a drug company in which all he has to do is to give a phoney reply "I remain yours faithfully, sir . . . or madam" to the complaints of the people, and by his wife who like Meena, Billy's wife, always talks of money. "Nobody in this world wants to hear the truth" (82) is the conclusion he arrives at by his experience.

The story thus is a severe indictment of mechanized existence and a sad commentary on the modern Indian affluent society. The story is told in retrospect by the protagonist, keeping the chronological order which fits the straightforward and dashing narrator--a man much given to calling a spade a spade. The style, rough and colloquial, is indeed a curious experiment in the context of Arun Joshi. One even hazards imagining that Arun Joshi is exploring the possibilities of a style for a sustained monologue when one considers that Joshi was then working on *The Apprentice*--the novel which gave him maximum trouble.

V

In "The Frontier Mail is Gone" Arun Joshi points at another malaise of modern Indian society. The story is set in a representative new industrial town–Faridabad–in which there are a few rich and many poor as is usual with our new industrial towns. The poor here have a bristling edge of discontent.

> They appear perpetually to be striving towards some new middle class possessions, burning themselves out in the process, without probably achieving very much more than others who proceed more peaceably to the inevitable end. (31)

One such unfortunate poor is Leela, the daughter of an old man who manned a level crossing at the entrance to Faridabad. The girl is sixteen and is already a widow. One fine morning Leela darts into a carriage of the Frontier Mail going to Bombay. She becomes a resident of Kamathipura, the red-light district of Bombay. The narrator concludes:

> If that is where she can meet men like me isn't that the only place we would ever dare to meet a girl like Leela? (43)

Leela too is a survivor in her own right. She is a survivor of traditional morality which pays no heed to human emotions. And her sad story is again a bitter commentary on the modern Indian society where human emotions are often dissolved in the smog of industrial existence and, what is more, in the name of morality.

VI

An element of abiding Indianness in idiom as well as sentiment with which Arun Joshi suffuses "The Only American from Our Village"[7] has lent it a haunting quality only to be found in Raja Rao's celebrated "Javani." Though the story unfolds from an omniscient point of view, soon that marvellously realized character *ashtamp farosh*'s breathless narration of events hushes the omniscient voice reminding one of the narrators of Raja Rao's early stories and *Kanthapura* and also the spell-binding intensity of the tribal headman Dhunia's narration in *The Strange Case of Billy Biswas*.

Dr. Khanna, the most outstanding immigrant physicist at the University of Wisconsin, comes to India, which he has left fifteen years earlier, on a four-week tour along with his family. At the fag end of his successful trip, after his final talk at a college in his former home-town, he encounters an old man. The old man introduces himself:

> I am the *ashtamp farosh* of the town . . . your father and I were close, like brothers, and I was not then the *ashtamp farosh* because I had property and I did not have to be an *ashtamp farosh* and I

> lived in style. Of course, all this does not interest you. I know that. (69-70)

The *ashtamp farosh* tells Dr. Khanna that Khanna's father Kundan Lal was very poor then and could not have continued his education but for the scholarships. But he made a mark as a brilliant student. And "If he had made a mark he did not let it get to his head." (70) Soon after his graduation, Kundal lal took up a job. He came back to his village only after retirement. He was proud of his son who had settled in America:

> He used to say you would be a big Government man when you come back. He would say you were coming back in one year, in two years, any time. Then you got married and he was quiet for many months. But he started talking again. He said you were the only American from our village. I asked him once what was so great about being the only American from our village. He said it was an honour. (70)

A more shattering blow is yet to come for Dr. Khanna. Unwittingly the *ashtamp farosh* remarks:

> "We had foot in the grave, all of us. What did we care for your achievements--what you did and what you did not do. I told him so one day. He was angry with me. (70)

The old man continues his narration dwelling in detail on Kundan Lal's expectations to get a return ticket to the US from his son; his disappointment and shame when he did not receive one; and finally on his illness. The *ashtamp farosh* tells how in spite of his illness Kundan Lal revisited the school where he studied and how while coming back he crossed the boiling sand of the *cho* with *dhak* leaves--as he used to do in his school days and had no money to buy shoes:

> He walked the whole half mile. The leaves fell off on the way. God himself could not have stopped him. He had fever by the time he got home. The next day he died. (72)

In spite of the perfect training in the new civilization, Dr. Khanna winces. Back in the US, he has generally come to be known as the man who does nothing but stare at his feet.

Evidently, wit and irony, humour and pathos have gone into the making of this poignant piece. It is also clear that Arun Joshi is consciously experimenting with the traditional art of story-telling, trying to adopt the tone, tempo and rhythm of a traditional Indian story–a breathless and seemingly endless narration of events that brooks no "buts" and "ifs" but flows interminably. However, though the psychological dimension of the story is very typical of Arun Joshi, as far as its style is concerned, the story stands out as an isolated experiment--not very representative of Arun Joshi.

VII

Since as a novelist Arun Joshi appears to be singularly preoccupied with an agonizing quest of his protagonists, with forging an aesthetic pattern, the variety of themes, technique and style of his stories strike the attention even on a cursory glance. Also, as the germ of all his novels could be traced back to one or the other of these stories it could be argued that Arun Joshi experiments with various narrative strategies on a smaller scale which eventually lead him to the finished triumph of his mature novels. It is in this sense that his stories have a significant place in the context of his artistic career. His stories have an important place in the context of Indian English short story in general too. For, no other Indian English writer has given such authentic vignettes of modern Indian industrial world with a consistent seriousness of purpose as Arun Joshi has done, the authenticity of which could only be compared to the vignettes of the pre-Independence rural life in Raja Rao's short stories. Arun Joshi has created an exhilarating variety of characters with, of course, varying degrees of success. The portrait gallery includes rich industrialists, travelling salesmen, Westernized intellectuals, poor peasant boys, young eve-teasers–the survivors as well as the victims of the modern Indian society. Irony and wit, satire and humour have gone into the making of these characters. Taken together, Arun Joshi's stories give a sure insight into the pseudo-Westernized affluent society of India where decadence has set in. His narrative strategies include first-person narrative, omniscient author narrative, multiple perspective narrative, and objective reportage. He experiments with style too which varies from the typical rhythm of English prose to that of English adapted to the rhythm of traditional Indian story-telling. In short, in spite of his brief corpus of short stories, with such finished models like "The Homecoming" and "The Only American from Our Village," Arun Joshi takes an honoured place among the best of Indian English short story writers.

NOTES

1. (New Delhi: Sterling, 1975).
2. M.G. Gopalakrishnan, "The Short Stories of Arun Joshi," *Arun Joshi--A Study of his Fiction*, ed. N. Radhakrishnan (Madurai: Scholar Critic, 1984), pp. 68-72.
3. "A Winner's Secrets: An Interview with Purabi Bannerji," *The Sunday Statesman*, Feb. 27, 1983, p. IV.
4. Meenakshi Mukherjee, ed., *Let's Go Home and Other Stories*, (Madras: Orient Longman, 1975), p. 126.
5. J.W. Beach, *The Twentieth Century Novel* (Ludhiana: Lyall, 1969), p. 16.
6. *The Illustrated Weekly of India*, Vol. XCIII, No. 27, 1972, pp. 29, 31, 33.
7. *Quest*, 94, April-May, 1975, pp. 69-72. Rep. *Contemporary Indian English Short Stories*, ed. Madhusudan Prasad (New Delhi: Sterling, 1984), pp. 64-70.

The Apprentice: Self as Labyrinth

V.V.N. RAJENDRA PRASAD

Arun Joshi's fiction explores the self and brings to a central focus the way in which the self tries to assess its involvement in the alienation from the family and society. For example, Sindi Oberoi in *The Foreigner* says,

> I worked in New York for a few more weeks, just enough to finish the project I had started. As it had happened after Babu's death the laboratory provided me a sanctuary where I could forget my conflicts, at least at the conscious level. But in the inner recesses of my mind the trial went on. Each day the judges met and examined the witnesses. My parents, my uncle, my lovers, Babu and June, their parents, and finally myself, one by one all were called by the invisible judges and asked to give their evidence. Under normal conditions this would have been painful but after the shock of June's death it came as a great therapeutic process. I felt as if some indefatigable surgeon was cleaning up my soul with the sharp edge of his scalpel.[1]

The above passage may be taken as a thematic statement of Arun Joshi's fiction. The exploration of the self is like "a great therapeutic process." By narrating his own experiences, Sindi Oberoi tells us how June, Babu, Mr Khemka, and his daughter, Sheila, contribute in their own way to his understanding and awareness of the problems of the self. What is more, the passage seems to convey many levels of awareness through which he passes. Mr Khemka's son, Babu, dies in a car accident in Boston. Sindi knows at the conscious level that he did not cause it. But an inexplicable fear haunts him. Perhaps it is this fear that converts the inner recesses of his mind into a court, where he is tried. But the oppressive nature of the trial takes a different shape, because of the shock created by the death of June, who is engaged to Babu but continues her association with Sindi. The image of the "indefatigable surgeon," reminding us of Eliot's "wounded surgeon,"[2] concretizes the therapeutic process and disinfects the self. Sindi comes to India and meets Mr Khemka, who offers him the post of a manager in his firm. Pursued by a tormenting sense of guilt and uncertainty, he feels, "I tried to understand why I was afraid. It was nothing physical. They couldn't put me in prison. I feared something much worse – the abominable hands groping and probing into my own soul, ripping dry scars open and dipping into old wounds." (50) The participles "groping," "probing," "ripping" and "dipping" suggest that evaluation of the self is a very painful process. Sindi seems to experience the reality of the process whenever he is alone. He tells us, "When I did go out I walked about the streets lost within myself unseeing and unheeding while the scalpel continued to move from chamber to chamber and tissue to tissue cutting out much that was rotting and disembowelling cells which had never been seen before. It was an awesome sight." (207) The words "chamber," "tissue," and "cells" suggest that the self is a sort of labyrinth, and to subject the self to groping and probing is to pass through a maze. Narrating his love-affair with Kathy, the painful consequence of his separation from her, and the sadness caused by the separation, he says, "Even after several years, somewhere in the *labyrinth* of my consciousness the wound still bled. I felt sad and perhaps showed it." (72, emphasis added)

The image of labyrinth signifies the nature and the function of the self. In this context, we may also note that the word "labyrinth" and its analogue occur quite frequently in Joshi's texts. The core of Joshi's fictional theme consists in viewing the self as a labyrinth, and any kind of assessment that the self makes of itself is a therapeutic process. *The Foreigner,* while developing the theme of the self/soul/labyrinth, brings to the fore the social framework within which the theme becomes meaningful.

The Apprentice elaborates the theme of corruption of the self in a society which is itself corrupt. Himmat Singh tells Ratan Rathor, "My soul was killed, you put yours to pawn. But souls that were pawned could perhaps be retrieved. . . . May be souls are like muscles, Ratan Rathor. May be to develop them one has first to put them in use."[3] The word "muscles" calls to mind the passage in *The Foreigner* in which Sindi confesses: "When I did go out I walked about the streets lost within myself unseeing and unheeding while the scalpel continued to move from chamber to chamber and tissue to tissue cutting out much that was rotting and disembowelling cells which had never been seen before. It was an awesome sight." (207) The process of retrieving souls is an "awesome" process, and Joshi makes use of "labyrinth" and its analogues to graph it.

The Apprentice is a fictional experiment – a confessional novel which employs psycho-narration. Ratan Rathor narrates the way in which he becomes a victim of corruption in a metropolitan society during the war between India and China. His audience is a student, who just listens; the narrator himself puts the questions and expresses the doubts that may arise in the listener's mind. The narrative runs like a monologue of Browning, in which there is an audience whose participation is just passive. The son of a freedom fighter who laid down his life for the sake of a cause, Ratan Rathor comes to Delhi during the later stages of the Second World War in search of a job. Through the good offices of a stenographer, he is appointed a temporary clerk in a department for war purchases. His first boss, the Superintendent, noticing his docility and implicit obedience, recommends him for confirmation. After his confirmation, Rathor becomes a careerist. He shamelessly pursues advancement in his career and agrees to marry the Superintendent's niece. Though all his colleagues call him a whore, he turns a deaf ear to their sarcastic comments and concentrates on getting ahead of others in pursuit of his ambition. As an officer in the military stores department, he clears spurious war material after taking a bribe from Himmat Singh, a notorious character. He has a friend, the Brigadier, who absconds from the front when the Indian army is suffering reversal and humiliation at the hands of the Chinese. After the ceasefire, the military authorities suspect that a shady deal was responsible for sending useless war material to the front. Not only has it caused loss of life and disaster, but it also humiliates the country. Ratan Rathor is very much aware of this. The intelligence branch of the army suspects Ratan Rathor and authorizes an S.P. to interrogate him in a prison cell. But Himmat Singh, using his influence, gets Ratan Rathor released from police custody. Meanwhile another serious situation develops. The military authorities institute a court-martial to try Ratan Rathor's friend, the Brigadier, for deserting the army. The S.P. once again contacts Rathor and tells him that if he confesses his guilt, it may help the Brigadier escape court-martial. When he makes a decision to confess, Rathor learns that the Brigadier has killed himself. Immediately Rathor goes to Himmat Singh in order to wreak vengeance, but Himmat Singh tells him that the Secretary has double-crossed him. He takes him to the Secretary but by then Rathor's determination to wreak vengeance on his betrayers loses its hold on him.

The above summary of the novel demonstrates the kind of society in which Ratan Rathor lives and pursues his ambition. The narrative is punctuated with words like "sham," "bogus," "whore," "humiliation," "fake," and other similar words. Rathor's father calls career-making "bourgeois filth." (33) The word "filth" occurs too often to go unnoticed. For example, Himmat Singh "was born in filth and in filth he had grown." (144) There is a close correspondence between the pursuit of career-making we notice in Ratan Rathor and in Himmat Singh. Starting his career as a shoe-shine boy, Himmat Singh becomes a pimp, a petty thief, a waiter and finally involves himself in a minor black market racket. As the narrator puts it, "With the success of his rackets he was now face to face with the men who had had his foot broken, who had, perhaps, made a whore of his mother. Those men had angered him. And then they had made him laugh. . . . He had taken first to women, then to drink and finally to drugs." (145) The ubiquitous nature of corruption is such that not only persons like Himmat Singh, Rathor, the Secretary, and the Minister, but the *pujari* in the temple which Ratan Rathor frequents is also not free from it. When his son's payment is stopped, he approaches Rathor for help. The *pujari*'s son is a contractor and builds three hundred quarters for slum-dwellers in a record time. The new engineer refuses to pass the bills because he notices too much sand in the mortar. Even though Rathor tells him that his department is different, the *pujari* persists in his request, and as Rathor puts it, "He said he would not mind if he spent some money to get all that done. Everyone had the right to a cut. He said he understood that. He could suitably meet the desires of all concerned, the clerks, the officers, of the engineer concerned, even, here he asked me to forgive his impudence, even mine. MINE. MINE. He said he was a poor man and could hardly afford bribes but he did not mind it in a case like that. After all, he said, we all had to live. And that boy was his only son. He said he would give me any reasonable cut that I demanded." (124) The *pujari*'s problem and the means he employs to solve it characterize a society in which all values are inseparably tied to the craft of making money. As it usually happens, the more the money, the greater the frustration that accompanies it. The narrator, in spite of his awareness, fails to get out of the corruption racket. He finds his daughter and his wife always showing some sort of discontent. Even though he doesn't need money, he takes a bribe. As he reflects,

> First of all, I did not need the money. I am quite sure of that. I needed it no more than sitting here, after two cups of tea, I need a third. I may drink it because others do, or because it is offered free, but I need it for neither survival nor happiness. In this poor land I can be called comfortable, even well-off. I have a car, a flat, a concrete roof, running water. I have a refrigerator. My wife is not swimming in sarees but she does not even use what she has. My daughter has all the money she needs; for college, clothes, and the cinema. We eat as much as a human being can possibly eat. Our health is looked after by the government. There are delays no doubt but with a bit of telephoning – I have a telephone which is not common – one always gets it. I have insurance. I have twenty thousand in the bank which is not a fortune but will tide you over a rainy day. Besides, I would have pension when I retire which should be enough for me and my wife. My daughter, God willing, should be married by then.
>
> So, you see, I did not need the money. If I had ever needed money it was when I had been offered it the first time – by the contractor – and I had refused. (61)

The passage, while revealing the tormenting and tortuous self-examination of the self when it is sorting out its own problems, unmistakably suggests some of the civilized values that obtain in a metropolis. The self-analysis makes the narrator discover that along with money one involves oneself in other new distractions like women and power, and becomes crazy about "brand-new enjoyment." (78)) As he reflects, "I was expected to behave. Instead, I had merely walked into a brothel hounded by a strange disturbance. All that I could think of was my money and the fact that I was not enjoying life or what I imagined enjoying life meant. The more money I accumulated, the more I was dissatisfied and the more I was determined to 'enjoy' life. And all the time I thought of *death*." (89, emphasis added) The word "death" obliquely suggests that a distracted life is death of the self. This may look like a philosophical commonplace, but a close look at *The Apprentice* reveals that there are ways of coming out of death, or what the narrator calls "the crookedness of the world; the crookedness of oneself." (148) As we have noticed earlier, retrieving souls that are pawned is an awesome process. The narrator-protagonist becomes an apprentice in order to learn the method of retrieving his soul. Without entering the temple, he wipes the shoes of the congregation. He tells himself, "Be good. Be decent. Be of use. Then I beg forgiveness. Of a large host: my father, my mother, the Brigadier, the unknown dead of the war, of those whom I harmed, with deliberation and with cunning, of all those who have been the victim of my cleverness, those whom I could have helped and did not." (148-49) The process of activating the self in this solemn mood of penitence and expiation (which we noticed in the protagonist of *The Foreigner*, Sindi Oberoi) is amplified and given a symbolic resonance in *The Strange Case of Billy Biswas* and in *The Apprentice*. In *The Last Labyrinth*, this is very convincingly dramatized in Anuradha's decision to give up her relationship with Som Bhaskar.

Arun Joshi's themes have contemporary relevance and socio-cultural significance. *The Apprentice*, for example, is a creative comment on the crisis of character with which we have been familiar for a long time. But what we should not forget in reading the novel is its claim to be considered a novel, not a sociological study of the roots and causes of corruption. This observation applies with equal force to the other novels as well. *The Strange Case of Billy Biswas* is not about the manners and customs of the primitive tribes in Jhansi District but about Billy's sensitive response to certain unusual psychic phenomena and his whole-hearted pursuit. They feel that "Billy had probably done something undesirable on a momentary impulse (I think she had something sexual in mind), something even more degrading than his affair with Rima Kaul, and did not have the courage to face his family. He might even have done it under duress. All along he had wanted to go back to them but was not sure how he would be received." (206) But the narrator and the reader know the psychic compulsion behind the leap of Biswas into an unknown and nebulous terrain. Explaining to the narrator the peculiar situation, Billy says, "It was as though a master mind had arranged the whole thing to give me a preview of what awaited me if I continued to defy its call. Poor Rima had crystallized for me the alternatives, although I did not realize this until I sat outside my tent that fateful night. I had two clear choices: I could either follow this call, this vision, whatever the cost, or be condemned to total decay. I suppose most men are faced with similar questions sometime or the other."[4] (189-90) The choice to make a leap so that the self may be retrieved from decay is brilliantly exemplified in Anuradha in *The Last Labyrinth*, when she takes the painful decision of snapping her links with Som Bhaskar so that he may live. These crucial decisions may plunge the self into an unknown terrain where the self, the family and society acquire new meaning. The new meaning emerges as a therapeutic process, a sort of cleansing. The self becomes an apprentice to itself, so that it may explore the labyrinth which is itself. As Ratan Rathor frankly confesses, "Then there is another thing that my father used to say, whatever you do touches someone somewhere." (149) In fine, Arun Joshi's novels dramatize the truth embodied in Rathor's confession by forging an aesthetic pattern in which we come across dreams, stories within stories, characters experiencing hallucinations, and visions verbalized and reconstructed.

NOTES

1. Arun Joshi, *The Foreigner* (Delhi: Hind, 1972), p. 207.
2. T.S. Eliot, "East Coker," p. 147.
3. Arun Joshi, *The Apprentice* (New Delhi: Orient Paperbacks, 1974), p. 146.
4. Arun Joshi, *The Strange Case of Billy Biswas* (Delhi: Hind, 1971).

The Apprentice: An Existential Study

V. GOPAL REDDY

Arun Joshi's *The Apprentice*[1] rendered in a confessional form is a telling commentary on the decaying values of a degenerating civilization. It is the story of a young man who out of sheer exhaustion of joblessness and privation is forced to shed the honesty and the old-world morality of his father to become an "apprentice" to the corrupt civilization. One is alienated in this "phoney" world unless one accepts and adjusts to "the guilt" of the modern society in order to belong.

Ratan Rathor, the protagonist of the novel, after his initial hesitation yields completely to the corruption of modern society and thrives on it. It takes almost a lifetime to reject the "petrified and frozen" world of civilization for he is the child of a double inheritance: the patriotic and courageous world of his father and the worldly wisdom of his mother who tell him:

> It was not patriotism but money . . . that brought respect and bought security. Money made friends. Money succeeded where all else failed. There were many laws . . . but money was law unto itself. (20)

Modern man may either try and adjust to the "others," to society, to the system, abdicating his true self, or he may strive to keep and develop his individuality and thus alienate himself from society.[2] We find both these types of alienation in Ratan Rathor. Ratan begins his life with high ambitions and ideals to be honest, true to his self and, like his father, make a mark in the world. But he finds himself a misfit in the modern world. He had to abdicate his true self to fit in the corrupt society and eke out a living. He is alienated from his true self in the process.

In his feverish pursuit of careerism, Ratan submits himself to all sorts of corruption that the modern world offers. His corrupt deal at the end costs the life of the Brigadier, his closest friend. Ratan feels a vicarious responsibility for the Brigadier's death. His sense of individuality comes into conflict with his life of hypocrisy. With deep remorse, he realizes the futility of his life and decides to be of some use to others. He takes up the menial work of a shoeshiner on the stairway of a Delhi temple to purge his impure heart. At the same time a rich limousine awaits him to take him to his office.

Unlike Billy Biswas who opts out of the modern world in a bid to seek his communion with the primitive world, Ratan lives in the modern world and yet untouched by its impurities and seeks fulfilment in serving others in the humblest form as in the symbolic act of shoe-shining. *The Apprentice* exemplifies that the theme of alienation in Joshi has been growing right from his first novel, as it moves from alienation to community.

While Sindi in *The Foreigner* depends on his philosophy of non-involvement, Ratan in *The Apprentice* holds on to his careerism. Sindi slowly learns that real detachment lies in involvement. In the same manner, Ratan's sense of alienation makes him understand that a combination of humanism and religion can be the saving grace of mankind steeped in corruption.

It has been argued that the novel commends the value of humility and self-purification. In this sense the novel is a study of the loss and the retrieval of one's soul. The cause of alienation and inner emptiness of Ratan is neither the rootlessness of Sindi nor the unusual urge of Billy. The compelling force of civilized society shatters the idealism of the young like Ratan and compels them to turn cynical and even hypocritical.

According to Srinath, *The Apprentice* "is the tale of conscience-torn man with a curious mixture of idealism and docility, a vague sense of values, a helpless self-deceptive effort to flout them for the sake of a career – in short, with a deep awareness of the conflict between life and living.[3] The sadness of the story is that while the society was responsible for shattering Ratan's personality with its confusion of values and caused alienation, it has however failed to help him retrieve his lost integrity of the self.

One may unmistakably find in *The Apprentice* the impact of Camus's *The Fall*.[4] Jean-Baptiste Clamence, a successful Paris barrister in *The Fall*, appeared to himself and to others as the very epitome of good citizenship and decent behaviour in the beginning. But suddenly he sees through the deep-seated hypocrisy of his existence to the condescension which motivates his action. He turns to debauchery, and finally settles in the fog-bound wilderness of Amsterdam where, as a self-styled "judge penitent," he describes his fall to a chance acquaintance. The monologue in *The Apprentice* as in *The Fall* holds a disquieting mirror up to modern morality.

II

Ratan Rathor started his life as every young man full of ideals and illusions does. His childhood friendship with the Brigadier is beyond his imagination. Ratan recollects his father's reverence for Gāndhiji whom he called a "man of suffering" and under whose inspiration he gave up his lucrative legal practice to join the freedom struggle. He toyed at times with the idea of following his father who wanted to be respected and to be of use. He wanted to join Subhash Bose's army. The very idea elated him and he believed that he was ready to sacrifice all without promise of reward or success. He identifies himself with the people suffering for the cause of the motherland:

> Every now and then someone I knew was imprisoned, maimed, or killed and for days afterwards I felt burdened as though in some way I had been responsible for the killing. (21)

Ratan however discovers soon that the honour of being the son of a freedom fighter is of no practical value whatsoever in the world. His father, dying a martyr to the cause of the country's freedom, left behind an ailing, starving and cynical wife and a patriotic and penniless son. The people, for whom his father has squandered a lifetime, forget him within a year. He moves out of his village and goes in search of a job in the metropolis of Delhi. He leaves his home hoping to be worthy of his father and his ideals.

As long as Ratan remembered his father he retained his moral core, which gradually got tainted in the competitive urban environment. Embittered with a bleak future, without influential connections, Ratan undergoes a humiliating experience as he is rejected and jeered at while hunting for a job. All his education and intelligence do not help him. Then he learns to keep up appearances by discarding even ordinary decency and friendship. Thus he completely alienates himself from his true self and his ideals. Ratan himself describes his own aberrations with a sense of self-awareness and objectivity:

> I had become, at the age of twenty-one, a hypocrite and a liar; in short, a sham. I had been insecure before and full of strange fears. But I had never undertook such sustained, if harmless, deception, for once I had lied about having a job I had to lie about numerous other things.... I had become a master faker. (28)

Ratan narrowly escapes the starvation-death through the generosity of his equally miserable roommates in an inn. A chance introduction by one of them secures him a job of temporary clerk in the department of war purchases. From that day the "practical" Ratan never looks back. He even surprises himself by ignoring those who saved him from death. He becomes obsessed with wealth, influence and security. He stops at nothing:

> I was a different cut: educated, intelligent, cultured, and it was my right that I should rise in life, to levels higher than the others aspired for. (32)

Although Ratan is well-settled in life, he cannot feel a sense of satisfaction because he holds his career dear and sacrifices the principles that have guided him all the while. In spite of all the material comforts available to him, discontentment has become a way of life for Ratan. He finds himself deeply lost in the corrupt atmosphere. For the sake of confirmation and promotion, Ratan is forced to marry a girl related to the Superintendent, though he is not particularly interested.

It does not take much time for him to realize that the world runs on deals. In fact his own marriage is a deal for his career:

> If men forgot how to make deals the world would come to a stop. It would lose its propelling power. Men would not know what to do with themselves. They would lose interest. It is not the atom or the sun or God or sex that lies at the heart of the Universe: it is deals. DEALS.... They are simply there, like air. (51)

In the process of these strange bargains with the world, Ratan becomes a hypocrite. His hypocrisy fetches him a car, a bungalow, and a good place in society at the cost of his peace of mind. Thus his conscience degenerates totally and suffers a "crisis of character." In short he becomes a whore in the pursuit of his career and ends up by accepting a bribe when he least needs money. At every stage he puts up an initial resistance only to discover the futility of his effort like so many others of his kind in the contemporary society. He leads a frustrated and exhausted family life. The more money he accumulates, the more dissatisfied he is. A strange fear of death haunts him all the time. He feels restless.

When the Brigadier was on the brink of madness in a military hospital, Ratan felt that some priceless essence that he had known and recognized for forty years had vanished. It was the second time in his life that he had felt the pain of another as his own, the first being the time when his father was shot:

> And standing there by the glass window I felt as though it was not the Brigadier but I who was rocking through some dark dungeons of the world. (103)

At first Ratan is mentally resolved to save his friend. He writes his confession, but modifies it instantly and tries to justify his act by convincing himself of his "innocence" and finally pockets the confession letter for ever. Now his main concern and objective is how to get out of the mess he has made. Ratan was surprised to find that the Secretary of his Department and the Minister concerned came to his rescue and got him released quite magically. Ratan later found that these persons at the highest level were the agents behind the act of bribery, and he was simply an instrument. The Brigadier could not, however, wait for his confession and killed himself.

Ratan realizes that there is no end to human vanity, or, for that matter, to human stupidity. The dead Brigadier's vision trailed him wherever he went. Ratan is filled with an endless torment of fear. He realizes the gravity of his sin. At last his alert consciousness alienates him from the degenerated society:

> Twenty years and nothing gained. An empty lifetime. What had I learned? Pushing files? Manoeuvring? At forty-five all that I knew was to manoeuvre. A trickster, that was what I had let life make of me. Did I know the meaning of honour, friendship? Did I ever know it? Would I ever know it again? (139)

Ratan realizes that his life has been a great waste. He is not sure what precisely corrupted the atmosphere of the society. He feels the need of doing something for changing the prevailing situation. But he is full of doubts about the way to rid the society of this pestilence.

Ratan finally realizes that one cannot live for oneself because no human act is performed in isolation and without consequence. Therefore each act should be performed with a sense of responsibility. Hence out of an acute sense of alienation and a quest to understand the meaning of life, Ratan undergoes the sternest apprenticeship in the world. Symbolically he starts at the lowest – dusting the shoes of the congregation outside the temple every morning on his way to the office. Thus he would like to expiate his sins of cowardice, dishonesty and even indirect murder. He learns the lesson of humility. He seeks his fulfilment in this symbolic act. He feels that the only sustaining basis for action is to be of use to others, "without vanity and without expectations and also without cleverness." (149) He earnestly pleads with the young that there is nothing wrong to make a second start: "one must try and not lose heart, not yield, at any cost, to despair." (149) Ratan, standing at the doorstep of the temple that offers a deserted look, "frozen, petrified, like our civilization itself," (150) hopes that the young can turn the tide.

The realization by the young is possible only when they have integrity. This integrity is tested in the fires of existential choice. Ratan has lost his self and felt the anguish of loss. His existential decision to recover the lost self through an act of peritence reveals the need to realize and prize one's integrity.

NOTES

1. Arun Joshi, *The Apprentice* (Delhi: Orient Paperbacks, 1974).
2. Ignace Fuerlicht, *Alienation: From the Past to the Future* (Connecticut: Greenwood Press, 1978), p. 41.
3. C.N. Srinath, "The Fiction of Arun Joshi," *The Literary Criterion*, XII, 2-3 (1976), p. 127.
4. See Murali Das Melwani, *Themes in Indo-Anglian Literature* (Bareilly: Prakash, 1977), p. 68.

The Language of the Dreams in *The Last Labyrinth*

REKHA RANI

Dreams in general are an important instance of free-functioning of the mind. Arun Joshi has used them adroitly not only to project the mind of Som Bhaskar, but also to set it against the logical and rational restraints of moral and social conventions. Basically a man is a rational creature. Being a part of its social structure. Som does not find himself at home in these religio-social norms. He feels uprooted because he wants scientific evidence for everything. Frustrated within himself, he finds this world alien. For him this world has no value, no meaning or truth. He is not able to find the cause of the "First Cause," i.e. where and when the life began and where it would lead to. For him this life becomes an eternal journey from nothingness to nothingness leading to an existential dilemma.

The unhampered working of his inner mind--what he feels above love, life, death or what he wants to have in his life--is explored through the dreams which haunt him again and again. The dreams are a sort of revolt against the logical and rational control of Som's world.

For Freud the dream is "parole" which can be understood only against the background of the unique and private "langue" which is the dreamer's past and present and the events of his personal history and chances. We can see Som involved in two worlds. Beyond the world of his wife and children, there is a wider world (world of Aftab, Anuradha and Gargi) which is disturbing him. His fear of death and Aftab, his urge to possess Anuradha, the image of his mother in Gargi are some of the recurrent features of his dreams. The dreams full of pain and disgust are, to him, "a kind of punishment, something like the fatigue that soldiers are sentenced to."[1]

The dreams are structured very systematically in the novel. The first and the last part of the novel contain two dreams in each and the middle one consists of only one dream. In the former division the dreams are short and simple but in the latter the dream is simple and longer one. "I dreamt" is the indicator of what follows in all of his dreams described in details except the dream occurring in the middle part of the novel. Despite the use of the past tense, the immediacy of the dream is enhanced by a sentence preceding the dream carrying the essential requirement of a dream, i.e. sleep: "I feel asleep." The dreams with introducing markers like "I dreamt" are narrated by Som for himself in order to evaluate his own condition. The longest and the most disturbing dream makes use of the present tense. It is narrated directly to Dr. K. and to his wife. In spite of the place given to this particular dream it is foregrounded.

In describing the dreams, Arun Joshi has broken the conventions of the modes of artistic organization by using free-associations, violated syntax, non-logical and non-chronological order and juxtaposition of seemingly unrelated images. The dreams are intended for some symbolic interpretation related to the thematic aspect of the novel. Strange murky shapes appearing in Som's dreams stand for abstract ideas, concepts of life, love, death, which are not clear to him. The use of adjectives such as "murky" and "tangled web" makes them appear confused and mysterious. "Fire" and "sun" imply hope for brightness, light in his dark, misty life and also with the help of their light he is trying to understand the confused reality behind those shapes. Shoeless Anuradha passing through the burning desert is representative of her strength to survive in this world full of sorrows and suffering. With no firm support but with unflagging faith, she transcends the physical pain and suffering and commits herself to the cause of the human welfare and happiness. The dream consisting of a wedding ceremony brings to the surface Som's desire to possess Anuradha.

The dream which involves the death theme is an index to Som's fear of death. It consists of the structural imagery that stands for the short and narrow life succeeded by a certain death. Tall, deserted houses stand for hollow, empty materialism. The emptiness of outer surroundings is symbolic of the inner emptiness of modern human beings. The phrase "black gashes for windows" indicate the collapse of moral values based on religion which has been the true spirit of human culture. Everyone is aware of the cruel fact of life, i.e. death, but too much fear of it does not let one admit it in advance. Som is so much afraid of death that he cannot think who is under the shroud. The moonlight giving a purple look stands for a natural light of faith, a faith in values which shuns the darkness of doubts and establishes light. The street turning into the Blue Room of the haveli suggests the ruthlessness of men of fortune in their pursuit of material and physical indulgence. The reference to Azizun's songs is used to emphasize the futility of life, viz. how men are pushed into despair, from despair to decadence and thence into madness and death. The reference to Azizun's songs reflects the loneliness of life around which all of us are built.

Som's recurrent dream of flying in the sky gives an outlet to his deep desire of rising high in his life: "It is something about flying." The beginning of the dream reflects his confused mental state. Constantly haunted by this dream, he finds himself baffled, and is not clear about his direction to move about. He tries to remember that he was going somewhere – so the phrase "something about." But the content of the dream gives us the idea of his going towards the highest point of rise in life indicated by the mountain. Snow-covered peak is symbolic of brightness, peace and calm on the top. The media he adopts to reach the mountain peak is "the plane," a symbol of materialism. It is not the materialism which troubles him more, rather it is the money, status and more and more shares which he wants to hold. His need of something, somebody, somewhere in which the two worlds--the world of matter and the world of spirit--combined is reflected in this sequence. He wants to have faith in God, moral values, calm and quiet life along with more and more money enjoying this materialistic society. His sitting in the front while in the plane symbolizes his yearning for his place on the top, ahead of all. Clouds, mist, fog and rain stand not only for obstructions in his journey but also demand struggle, survival instincts on his part in the presence of suffering in order to arrive at the goal. Despite the darkness of suffering, trouble etc. one goes on his way and once he gets on the top he would shine like anything and would have peace, calm and everything that he wants. The glow of enlightenment spreads all around and shuns away darkness. When he reaches the mountain, its height, its huge size frighten him and he with his plane crashes down in the mountain. All this symbolizes his confrontation with the God. Though he is afraid of the great Entity yet he is ready to confront Him in order to see the proof of his existence.

The dreams are projected mainly through visual images. The abstract ideas of life, of struggle, of light, darkness, the inevitability of death are visualized in the images of metaphors, viz. "suns," "skies," "desert," "labyrinth," "Blue Room," "shroud," "cowrie" etc. Once an auditory image also occurs in one of his dreams, that is, singing of Azizun. He can't see Azizun in the dream but can hear her voice. The imagery is used as a clue to suffering. In addition to this, we see the use of "kinesthetic" imagery in "ran up flights of stairs," "pounding of feet," "slaughter of goats," "flying bird," "kill a dog" etc. in the dream which contains the death theme.

The dreams containing the images of Anuradha, Gargi and Aftab are either the fulfilment of a wish to possess Anuradha (which however remains an unfulfilled desire) or are the realization of an apprehension realized through the dream consisting of death theme. Sometimes the dream reverses the desired solution; the appearance of the haveli in his dream signifies his wish to go to it and meet Anuradha, a wish against which he is fighting inwardly. The dream of his flying high over the mountain is concerned with future which is surmised in advance through the language used. This dream epitomizes both the fulfilment of his wish as well as the reversal of it signalled by going up and up followed by his falling down.

The dream in which the images of his mother and Krishna occur reproduces simply the reminiscence of his past. In his dream he sweeps away the wooden Krishna from the table as he used to do in his mother's prayer room. The instance of Gargi's taking the place of his mother can be taken as his seeing the image of his mother in Gargi, the symbol of that affection and care which he used to get from his mother. That is why he is more at ease with Gargi than with anyone else in the novel. He has great regard for her and she has a calming effect upon him. The dream in totality recalls the illness of his mother and with that the cause of her death which he thinks is "Krishna." The image of labyrinth stands for the haveli as well as some other mysterious place. But the context takes the first interpretation. Damp caverns and low ceilings stand for the stuffiness and the dense structure of the haveli.

The presentation of the dreams can be divided into two parts: Som's description, and the direct speech of those who appear in his dreams. Descriptive language with visual and auditory imagery represents things, actions and even abstract ideas making the whole dream pictorial. From Anuradha the train of thoughts proceeds to Gargi and then to his mother and then Krishna, thus showing ·them one by one like a picture. The use of conversation between the characters within the descriptive language of the dream evokes the pictorial quality and also produces the illusion of reality as if the reader himself/herself is having that dream. The speech of the characters is used as it is, by the use of punctuation mark, viz. inverted commas. The contracted verb forms and negative forms such as "that's," "can't," "isn't," "don't," "I'll" etc. strengthen the informality of the conversation. The progressive aspect of the verbs like "men carrying knives in hand," "running behind," "foot step following," "his sweeping away the Gods from the table" etc. makes the descriptions vividly moving. It captures the reader's attention maintaining the illusion of reality.

Besides the pictorial quality of the language of the dream, Arun Joshi has also made use of the hallucinatory, disconnected and surrealistic language. In his dreams Som moves freely. Within a moment he reaches from Bombay to Benaras, from Gargi to his Mother. The alley gets changes into the Blue Room in his dream world. Aftab's ancestors who are in no way concerned with Som do appear to him. Various unrelated images are juxtaposed: light and darkness, life and death, suffering and wedding.

The simple lexis is an indication of simple style with less use of abstract terms. The abstract ideas are presented through the concrete images. Various lexical words belonging to the same set of collection stress on thematic aspect taken up in one's dreams: (a) fire, brilliant burning sun, desert, volcano; (b) alley, houses, windows, Blue Room; (c) flying, plane, pilots, wipers, space crafts, speed, cockpit; (d) mountain, snow-covered peak; (e) sky, clouds, mist, fog, rain; (f) wedding, lamps, light. The lexical simplicity is reinforced by a degree of naive simplicity of the syntax. The sentences are short and simple with a number of compound or complex sentences. Where Joshi could construct a long sentence by using the subordinating conjunction, he chunks it up into various clauses which on the surface seem to be independent as carrying no subordinate marker. But the context indicates the subordination, so the purpose behind this division is to attract the attention towards each part and also to give syntactic simplicity. Co-ordination which itself is a mark of a simple sentence structure, is indicated by the punctuation mark, i.e. full stop rather than by "and" or by semicolon, hence the graphological deviation. Grammatical deviation can be seen in the use of the plural form of the abstract nouns as in "fires of sun." Also sun and sky are made plural by adding plural morpheme /z/ to them. The purpose is metaphorical. "Suns" is not the ball of fire in the sky but the light spread all around. Similarly "skies" is not the sky above our head but the vastness of the universe. The pun can be seen in the use of the verb "lay" in "I lay on top of her" meaning both the lying down as well as having sex. The context makes both the meanings equally relevant hence the pun can be called "equivoque." But linguistically, the latter meaning seems to be more appropriate in the sense that it strikes as a deviant use of the present tense against the background of the past tense used in all the sentences of this particular dream.

Symbolically used, dreams act as reflective insiders where God, man, love, death sprawl before him. His inherited culture and values, his desires and yearnings in his life crying for fulfilment otherwise are given an expression in the form of the dreams. The language of the dreams becomes the language of the inner Som. Each dream looks like a shattered mirror in which he looks deformed and distorted. Thus the content and the language ascribed to the dreams help in enhancing the theme of conflict in Som's mind.

NOTE

1. Arun Joshi, *The Last Labyrinth* (Orient Paperbacks, 1981), p. 204.

A Stylistic Insight into *The Last Labyrinth*

ANUP BENIWAL

Arun Joshi is concerned with the search for the core of life which he has tried to convey through the external symbols like "haveli," "Benaras," "Bombay" etc. The passage chosen here (the text is given at the end) gives the details of the setting of Lal Haveli, the central motif of the novel. The description is so vivid and direct that a clear picture of the whole building can be reconstructed. Details are unfolded not in a systematic way that one part of the haveli is described after another but as the narrator sees it and thus making the description pictorial and natural. In a way, the complex arcane architecture of the haveli becomes an index indicating the confused self of Som Bhaskar. Let us see how this descriptive accuracy and vividness is achieved.

Lexical Features

The vocabulary used here is very simple--vocabulary of common experience, of day-to-day use except for a few rare words like: gazebo, mezzanine, adrenaline. These lexical items are used not only to enrich the language but for the purpose of the emphasis. When it is a mere description of the structure of the haveli, the vocabulary and the expression are simple but the moment the narrator starts evaluating the structure, complexity in vocabulary and expression jacks up. "Peepul," "haveli," "Aftab," "Som" are Indian but even a foreigner can understand them by the context in which these are used. Repetition of the "haveli" clubbed with such words as "rooms," "passage," "verandah," "garden" is indicative of the fact that it is some house or building which is being described by the narrator. Moreover, once "the house" is also used in the passage which can be taken as a co-reference to the haveli.

Nouns

The concrete nouns belonging to different semantic fields--nature, architecture--dominate the descriptive vocabulary. *Nature*: garden, the grass, the peepul, trees, shrubs, a bush of nettles, roots, a branch, vines, flowers. *Architecture*: the haveli, narrow facade, a room, a verandah, balconies, cornices, patios, doors, spire, the house, passages, terraces, courtyards, wall, sarcophagus.

But where Joshi has to emphasize the abstractness of a noun he uses the concrete nouns headed by the abstract nouns: noises of the city, a passive view of a spire, a variety of balconies. Very few abstract nouns like "sensuality," "intensity" occur in evaluative vocabulary. Som starts with the description of the garden. But the description of the nature consisting of the garden, grass, peepul which gives the image of greenery is not something of a very green, alive nature but that of an old and decayed nature. "A grinning, pink-faced monkey" is used as a sign bringing life against the drab background of decrepit nature. The presence of Aftab and the narrator also, if taken on mere human plane, add to the lively aspect of the surroundings.

Adjectives

The nominal group structures are modified by a variety of adjectives: attributive as well as predicative. Visual adjectives attributing to colour, shape etc. occur with referential adjectives as shown in the examples given below:

Attributive visual adjectives	*Predicative visual adjectives*
long	the peepul was very "old"
narrow	the place was "bigger"
green	terraces covered with "moss"
marble	the flowers were "coloured"
coloured	
a monstrous	
a grinning pink-faced	

The adjectives in predicative position are marked out by the use of inverted commas.

Referential adjectives
empty mezzanine
decrepit and decadent surroundings

Perceptual adjectives such as "strange, intense sensuality" usually are abstract. Adjectives giving a grim picture are placed against the all colourful adjectives in the table given here:

brooding	airy
desolate	bright
broken	coloured
decrepit	green
decadent	mottled

Adjectives are used in a zig-zag manner: premodified adjectives are followed by postmodified adjectives in the next sentence. Nouns having double adjectives are usually postmodified. "A grinning, pink-faced" (here premodified) is deviant against the background of postmodified double adjectives in the passage. The force behind this deviation is the emphasis on the sign of life amidst the dead surroundings. By the use of colour adjectives, Arun Joshi brings greenery and hope where there is decreptitude. "Strange," "intense," "secret" express the strangeness which the mind of the narrator tries to comprehend. Adjectives not only modify the nouns/pronouns but these themselves are preceded by a determiner that in turn is modified by a predeterminer. This is illustrated in the diagrams below:

(i)

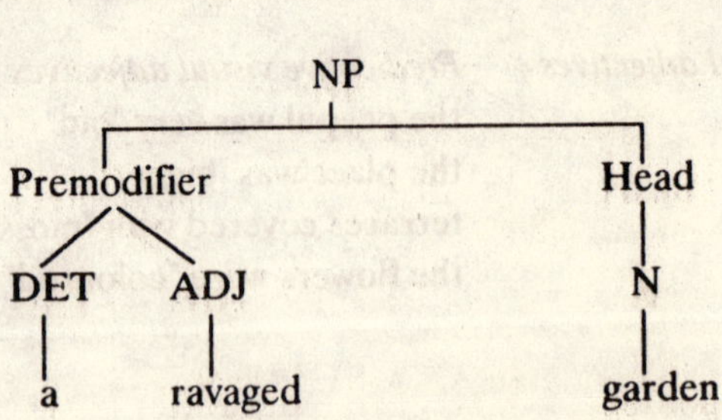

(ii)

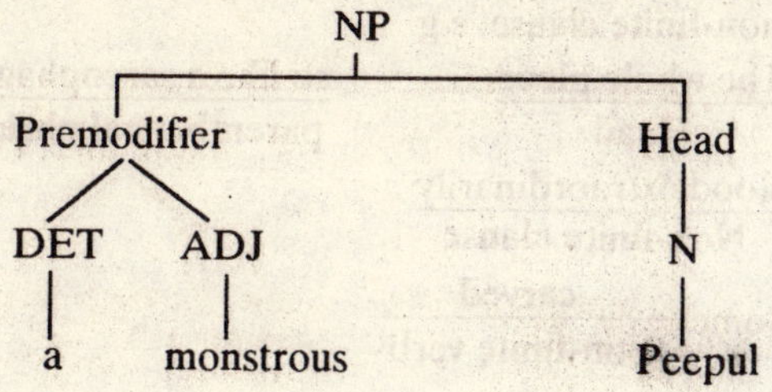

(iii)

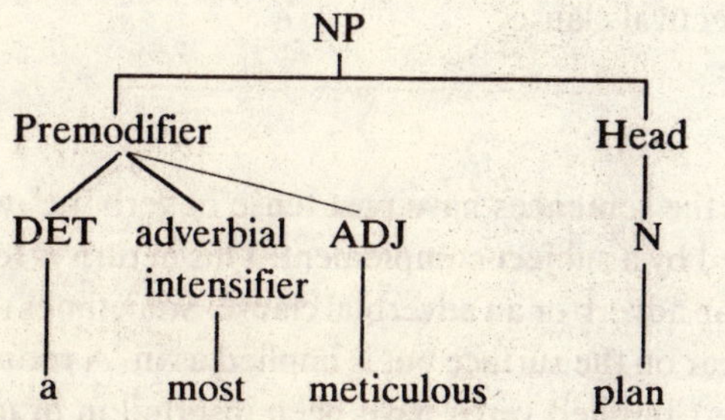

DET = Determiner
ADJ = Adjective
N = Noun

Postmodification is of various types as

(a) in the form of prepositional phrase, e.g.

(i) idiosyncracies (N) of the differentbuilders (PP (postmodifier))

(ii) Doors (N) of all shapes and colour (PP (postmodifer))

(iii) Others (N) in all shapes and colour (PP (postmodifier))
(cross-referring to rooms)

(b) in the form of adverbial clause, e.g.

(i) Others (N) where sunlight never enters (AC)
(cross referring to rooms)

(c) in the form of non-finite clause, e.g.

(i) The whole piece (Head) so like a sarcophagus (parenthetical phrase) stood extraordinarily (Non-finite clause)

(ii) Some carved (Non-finite verb)

PP = prepositional phrase
AC = adjectival clause

Verbs

Almost half of the sentences have past tense of verb "be" which is intensively followed by a subject complement. This in turn is followed by an adjective or an adverb or an adverbial clause. Sometimes the verb "be" does not appear on the surface but is implied as in "A room here," "A verandah there." Implied verbs have been inserted in brackets: a room (was) here, a verandah (was) there, some (were) carved, others (were) painted in ornate, fading enamel.

The verbs which are stative generally have implications of physical movements, position or posture. Some of the examples of this kind are: hung, spot, caught, stood, consummated. The following verbs indicate the act of perception: explain, realized, became aware, overwhelm.

Adverbs

Adverbs resembling each other occur successively one after another sentence.

Time adverbials

Suddenly	then
occasionally	now
(ending with the same morpheme/li:/)	(similarity in the repetition of the sound/n/)

Adverbial phrase of place
on it
out of it
on one side
on another
at the bottom
against the mottled wall

We see that a particular preposition indicating the place and direction is dominating the adverbial construction. Also the prepositional phrase of time "over a long period" acts as an adverbial phrase. The frequent use of the adverbials of place emphasize the pictorial description of the haveli. The adverbials of time put focus on the condition of the haveli and thus compare it with its earlier position. Some of the adverbial phrases and clauses are found in initial position while the others are in their final position. Once or twice the middle position is also seen just for the sake of keeping the balance.

Adverbial phrase in initial position
equally suddenly, . . .
occasionally, . . .
on it . . .
at the bottom . . .

Middle position
until, . . .
. . . from the ventilators . . .

Final position
. . . over a long period
. . . from its branches
. . . here
. . . out of it
. . . against the evening sky
. . . on one side of the
. . . where sunlight never entered

Sentence Structure

Different varieties of sentence structure occur in the description of the haveli. One can see the simple major clauses with minor clauses, interrogative sentences, sentences starting with adverbial clauses, sentences with co-ordinate clauses, and sentences starting with "and" and "now." Descriptive passages start with simple and short sentences. Few of these are so short that they contain just subject + adverb, e.g. "A room here" or subject + modifier, e.g. "Doors of all shapes and colour." Or only modifier, e.g. "Much bigger," which refers back to the noun "the place" in the preceding sentence. Most dominant simple sentence patterns are as given below:

(a) S + be + SC
- (i) The grass was patchy and brown.
- (ii) The peepul was very old.

In most of the simple sentences, their functioning as the subject of the verb "be" is used to draw attention to the fact stated, i.e. the existence of the haveli. Here are few examples:

- (i) There were rooms, bright and airy
- (ii) There were terraces covered with moss
- (iii) There was a chunk of green marble

(b) S + V + PP
- (i) Noises of the city rushed in with the opening of a door.

(c) S + V + O + adverbial
- (i) Bits of plaster fell on us as we went past.

When the narrator comes to evaluate the description, the sentences become longer and hence complex, e.g. "Standing in an empty mezzanine with a stream of coloured lights pouring in from the ventilators, its primal intensity nearly overwhelmed me." The sentences are elaborated by co-ordination and subordination. In the sentence "there were rooms with windows of stained glass that was fashionable fifty years earlier," rooms are modified by the adverbial in the form of the prepositional phrase, viz. "with windows of stained glass" which in turn is defined by the relative clause starting with pronoun "that" which refers back to the "stained glass." Co-ordination in the description of the haveli is marked by the use of co-ordinate punctuation mark, i.e. semicolon. The last portion of the illustrative extract in which the narrator tries to perceive the complex haveli starts with longer sentences and slope down to the shorter ones. So he ends up the description the way he had started.

Elsewhere in the novel (pp. 28-29), the thought of the haveli comes to his mind. The language of his thought process has a tentative impression about it. That he is undergoing a thought process is reflected in his self-questioning, i.e. "Did Lal Haveli ever exist?" That half of the sentences are interrogative strengthens Som's dilemma and doubts about the mysterious haveli. In addition to this, interrogative sentences appear as structurally deviant sentences against the use of simple declarative sentences. "Could it be a fragment of an overheated imagination, a vapour . . . of the midnight moon?" As we know that Lal Haveli is important in the context of the novel so it is quite possible that to draw the attention of the reader to it, Joshi started off the very idea of the haveli in this manner. The thought of the haveli takes him to Benaras and through the ghats of Ganges he is in the haveli with Anuradha and Aftab.

The present extract shows Som with Aftab who takes him on the round to show the haveli. Here the visual quality of the Joshi's narrative is noticeable as shown by the analysis of the nouns, verbs, adjectives and adverbs and various kinds of sentence structures. The reader is made to see only what the characters themselves see and hear without the intruding authorial voice at any time. The pictorial quality is sustained throughout the novel wherever there is description. In the extract taken here, the visual quality is accompanied by the sound just once as "noise of the city rushed in."

This organized arrangement of the visual images results in a narrative closely akin to a film script, a script that includes concrete and precise directions of camera angles, frames etc. The long shot of the camera takes the reader to Aftab and to the narrator standing in the middle of the garden. In the garden, the camera shifts from patchy and brown grass to peepul to the long roots and then to the monkey hanging from a branch. One sees the monkey's close-up: grinning and pink-faced. Som is standing and his thought process is going on. The camera moves along with Som and Aftab to get an impression of the haveli as they move through it: a room and then a verandah. A shot is followed by Som's evaluation of the haveli. Then the camera moves from balconies to cornices to patios to doors glancing at the shape and the colour. A sudden voice is heard in the background; then a spire and camera shows Aftab and Som moving with the plaster falling from the roof. They are climbing up the stairs and immediately are shown coming down. Again the camera pans through the passages to mossy terraces to courtyards where the focus is on the vines. The process continues and finally the camera comes back to Som showing him thinking and interpreting the structure. Throughout, the atmosphere is of quietness and silence.

The shorter sentences, at the end of the extract taken here for the analysis, conclude the description. The sentence construction with initials of "and," "now," "then" relates the narrator's evaluation and perception to his earlier description. The descriptive language shows him seeing the haveli and evaluative language shows him trying to understand its complexity. Clauses within clauses are symbolic of labyrinth after labyrinth. The complex interiors of the haveli are reflected in the complexity of the structures of the sentences.

Definite article "the" is used as a co-referring device. It is accompanied by a noun identifying a previous reference. "The" in "The peepul" co-refers to the monstrous peepul; "the" in "the house" to haveli. Monkey, the only living animal brought to the scene amidst the dead surroundings, is introduced by an indefinite article. This makes it stand out as a new and unfamiliar against the natural and structural background.

Arun Joshi creates a visually perceptible haveli mostly without overt metaphoric illusions. Only at one or two places does one come across metaphors or similes. Lal haveli in itself is used as a metaphor. Here the haveli has been compared to a "fragment of an overheated imagination." The tenor is concrete and the vehicle is abstract as if he is trying to feel the sense of the existence of Lal haveli. The world "overheated" has concealed in itself a metaphor. Imagination is much heated which means that imagination goes so high that the heat evaporates the imagination and turns it into vapours and he is not able to see it. So he is made doubtful about the existence of the haveli. The haveli is compared to a cloud also. Here a very simple kind of simile is used. As a cloud crosses the face of the moon in the midnight, the vapour which is the fragment of imagination crosses the haveli and for the time being covers it. Lal haveli has been identified with a maze also. One thing noticeable is that the haveli has been compared with abstract things like fragment of imagination and a maze.

The excessive use of the words like "as," "as if," "like" though used for comparison (simile) also carries the impression of tentativeness about them. So the similes are used not only as similes but also as an index of all his overheated imagination. This finds ample manifestation in the following examples: For sarcophagus he has used "the whole piece." Though it is sarcophagus only, still he says that the whole piece is like a sarcophagus. So "like" indicates not the use of the simile or comparison. To him it is not only a constructed piece of marble and cement but a seal to the mystery of the haveli because he is not able to infer the meaning of the couplet inscribed on it. The analysis shows how the elegant variation at different levels--lexis, grammar, figures of speech--helps the reader to build up a coherent and consistent picture of the haveli.

Text

After tea, Aftab led me into the middle of a ravaged garden. The grass was patchy and brown. Except for a monstrous peepul, it had neither trees nor shrubs nor even a bush of nettles. The peepul was very old. Long roots hung from its branches. A grinning, pink-faced monkey hung from a branch.

"Let me take you around the haveli," Aftab said.

The place was bigger than its narrow facade would have led one to believe. Much bigger. It must have been built over a long period. A room here. A verandah there. You could spot the idiosyncracies of the different builders. They were eccentricities more than differences of style. A variety of balconies and cornices and patios. Doors of all shapes and colour; some carved, others painted in ornate, fading enamel. There were rooms, bright and airy as a gazebo; others where sunlight never entered. Aftab explained nothing nor did I bother to seek explanations. Noises of the city rushed in with the opening of a door; equally suddenly, they were choked off. Occasionally, I caught a passive view of a spire against the evening sky. Bits of plaster fell on us as we went past.

The house was built either with no plan or with a most meticulous plan, though directed at an elusive objective. We climbed and came down meaningless flights of stairs. Passages twisted and turned, ran through uninhabited rooms. There were terraces covered with moss, and courtyards so airless that no one could ever have sat in them. Vines had been planted in what might have been toilets at one time. There were rooms with windows of stained glass that was fashionable fifty years earlier. The rooms contained little furniture.

There was a chunk of green marble against a mottled wall. On it was carved a tall vase. Long-stemmed flowers spilled out of it. The flowers were coloured with bits of glass. There was a parrot on one side of the vase and a horse on the other. At the bottom, a verse in the Arabic script was engraved. The whole piece, so like a sarcophagus, stood extraordinary sharp amidst the dead surroundings.

We went through another set of rooms and corridors and, then, at the end of a passage, we came upon the same sarcophagus of green marble. And now the artifacts started to repeat themselves, until, I realized, that it was a maze that we were moving through. Perhaps, the entire haveli had been built as a maze. What an idea! Passing once again by the marble sarcophagus I wanted to ask Aftab what it was the couplet said. I did not. It was as if the couplet was the seal to a mystery that would be destroyed if I were told its meaning.

And then, as though on the rebound, I became aware of the strange, intense sensuality that, like adrenalin the decrepit and decadent surroundings had released in my blood. Standing in an empty mezzanine with a stream of coloured lights pouring in from the ventilators, its primal intensity nearly overwhelmed me. Heaven knew what acts men and women had consummated in the seclusion of these secret chambers. In this place anything could happen. Aftab was looking at me. The spasm passed. We moved on. Coming out on some other front, we stood on a platform.

"It is all run down now, this haveli, but its labyrinth remains."

The City and the River as a Political Novel

BRAHMA DUTTA SHARMA

In his political novel *The City ana the River*, Arun Joshi presents the malpractices in which people wielding political power indulge and the ways in which people respond to them. Taxonomically speaking, the malpractices presented here are of two kinds: the malpractices resorted to in order to gain and retain power and the malpractices resorted to in order to eliminate dissent. The responses of the victims range from total surrender to uncompromising resistance.

So far as the malpractices resorted to in order to acquire and retain political power presented here are concerned, the first of these is the practice of manipulating people and incidents in order to lift oneself to the apex by giving the impression that one is very popular and that it is the people who want one to have power. The Grand Master, the ruler in the novel, is the person who employs such tactics: he has a Rallies Master to organize rallies in his support to give the impression that he is loved by his subjects and he makes the Master of Trade propose in the meeting of the "Supreme Council" that he be made king, and argue that it is in the interest of the people, rather than that of the Grand Master, that the Grand Master is made King. The following words of the Master of Trade:

> I shall briefly put forward certain criteria that the king of the city should meet. First, as already decided, he must be a wearer of the sacred thread. Second, he must come from a family which has already demonstrated its willingness to make sacrifice for this city. Third, he must command the affection of our masses and the trust of the armed forces and the business class. Fourth, he should be above the petty squabbles of the bazaar. . . . Now gentlemen, the

> only person who meets these criteria is our beloved Grand Master. I propose, therefore, that he be requested to accept the onerous burdens of the king's high office.[1]

make the fact evident. Here the Grand Master stage-manages what he himself wants to achieve.

Another malpractice in which a person wielding political power indulges, as presented in *The City and the River*, is that he tries to ensure that he is succeeded by his descendant. In *The City and the River*, the Rallies Master is made to organize rallies also for the Grand Master's son so that people may gather the impression that he too has endeared himself to the masses, as the Rallies Master tells the journalist: "And now, journalist, I must gather rallies not only for the Grand Master but his son as well. The city must now face its final humiliation and I must be an instrument to it."(76) The Astrologer is the Grand Master's tool in the novel and advances attractive arguments in order to justify the perpetuation of the rule of a family when he argues:

> The sacred and mysterious has shown us the light and we have unanimously concluded that the Grand Master must immediately request his son to help him maintain the *Dharma Rajya* that he has established. We know what we are asking. We know we are asking for great sacrifice. No sacrifice is greater than the sacrifice of a young son. But we know we are asking this sacrifice from a family that has for a hundred years sacrificed its men, its women, its children, its wealth, its very all for the sake of this city. They have suffered endless privation just so that this city might prosper. Such is the family that we are asking this sacrifice of and we have no doubt that the Grand Master will listen to our pleadings. This city needs his son and he must give him to us. (101)

Here the narrator is satirizing the efforts to give power to a man under the pretension that he is obliging the country by agreeing to get power. The attack is overt in the following remark of the Minister for Trade: "At one go every tradition of the city is abandoned. But even that does not satisfy the Grand Master. He must crown the Son as well, make him an heir apparent above the heads of all of us, put him on the

Advisory Council, and, in days to come, train him for a thousand mischief." (111)

Another political malpractice in the novel is the ruler's making people regard himself as the nation. In the novel the Astrologer identifies the Grand Master with the river, that are the symbols of the ruler and the nation respectively, when he says to the Headman: "Do not bring the Great Yogeshwara into this, Headman. All I ask is that you also swear to the Grand Master. He and the great river are one." (164) His words remind us of the assertion that Louis XIV of France made, viz. that he himself was the state.

Another malpractice presented here is one of keeping oneself in the seat of power with the help of guns and thus using the army and the police, which are expected to protect the state from external and internal aggressions, in order to protect oneself from even the dissenters. The logic that is advanced in order to justify the mischievous approach lies embodied in the following arguments of the commissioner to the Professor:

> "If you ask me, the New Era is not enough. What we need is a violent clean-up."
>
> "But the people too might become violent?"
>
> "The people do not have the guns. Only we can afford guns, not that we should use them (for anything other than securing justice for the poor."
>
> "But the whole city is poor," the Professor pointed out.
>
> "That is why we need more guns. This might sound absurd but the fact is that the poorer a city is the more guns its government needs." (82)

There also comes a time when the police use guns to eliminate opposition, nay even people who are staging a peaceful sit-in. The narrator reports: "Then all exits were barred from the outside and all lights were switched off. For the next two minutes the machine guns sprayed the pitch dark hall with bullets. . . . At the end of the two minutes the lights were switched on and the gunners were given another two minutes to finish their job." (184-85)

The novelist also shows the ruler indulging in the malpractice of giving ministerial posts to persons for political reasons rather than for their talents and capabilities. For instance, the post of the Education Adviser has been given in the novel to a person who has won the support of students and teachers, whose support the Grand Master wants to win, and talent or capability is not taken into consideration at all. The boy tells the Professor: "When the Grand Master inaugurated the New Era the Astrologer advised him to appoint the Education Adviser to the Council. That was the only way of keeping his shock-brigades from joining hands with the boatmen." (35-36) Giving posts for political reasons is likely to encourage politics rather than bring efficiency in administration.

The narrator in the novel also mentions an occurrence which evidences that according to the novelist public funds are misused by some rulers to gratify the needs, the wishes or even the whims of their near and dear ones, rather than meet the needs of the people. In this novel, the road called the Avenue Great River is straightened because the Grand Master's wife wants it to be so for no reason other than one of having a nicer view as she says: "How much nicer would the view be if there were a straight road running from here to the river." (37) Even though this involves making people living there lose their homes and hearths. It is sheer tyranny to deprive people of their homes and hearths only to make the view look nicer to the ruler's wife! Views do matter, no doubt, but they do not matter more than homes and hearths.

That efforts are made by rulers to cajole people to continue tolerating poverty in the name of leading a life of spiritualism has been shown in the novel when the people who have been deprived of their homes and hearths are exhorted to accept poverty on the ground that they belong to a country the civilization of which is spiritual rather than material, as if spiritual civilization fails to provide people even homes and hearths! The narrator reports: "The Astrologer issued an order next day authorizing the homeless to carry on living on the spots where they had their homes as though their homes were still there. The Asthough attitude, his orders said, was fundamental to spiritual civilization like ours, where even kings had preferred the purity of the forest to the suffocation of palaces. No doubt there would be initial inconvenience but, in the long run, all was bound to work out the best."

(37) Here spiritualism is being used as a narcotic to keep people homeless and reminds one of the religion which, as Karl Marx put it, was made to work as opium.

Another political malpractice hinted at in the novel is the authorities's manipulating the prices and the trade of commodities in order to earn money for the state or for oneself. It is this malpractice that has been hinted at in the following piece of conversation between Pinstripe and the Minister for Trade:

> Pinstripe went on: "In the light of the approaching Festival of the River cooking oil can bring in excellent revenues. Prices can be pushed very high if the produce of the Gold Mines is cornered."
> "I shall do what I can do." (64)

A government needs money, no doubt, but its role is different from that of a trader.

Yet another political malpractice presented here is the ruler's declaring that people's demands will be accepted even when he has no intention to implement the decree and, thus, cheating people. The malpractice has been employed when the Grand Master instructs the Astrologer to issue a decree but not to think of implementing it. The fact comes to light when we read

> "Yes, Astrologer, let us decree that all prisoners shall be told their crimes, or, set free"
> "Issuing a decree, Astrologer, does not mean its immediate implementation." (167-68)

The ruler who makes announcements of this kind is a cheat rather than a statesman.

The malpractices employed by a ruler in order to eliminate dissent, as presented in the novel, are again various. One of them is using coercion in order to frighten people into loyalty. In this novel, a large number of boatmen are sent to prison only because they refuse to declare that they are loyal to the Grand Master. The narrator reports: "a decree from the palace announced the beginning of a new era to be known as 'The Era of Ultimate Greatness.' It enjoined the people to beware of the enemy within and the enemy without and reminded them of the Astrologer's Three Beatitudes. The new era was inaugurated with the arrest of a boatman and a clown. The boatman's wife had borne an illegal child. The clown was arrested because he had been heard to laugh when the old boatman was being put in chains." (23) The narrator is laughing at the ways of this ruler as there is no point in arresting a boatman for his wife's having borne an illegal child as it is his wife who deserves to be arrested for having cuckolded her husband rather than he. Likewise, a clown is there only to make people laugh and so there is no point in arresting a clown for laughing. Moreover, laughing is an innocent exercise and one indulging in it does not deserve any punishment. The Commissioner tells his subordinates: "the boatmen have spurned the Astrologer's three Truths, that they have ridiculed him, calling him a pompous fool; and have, indeed, burnt his effigies along the banks of the river." (24) It is evident that the boatmen are arrested not because they have committed any crime but because they have refused to take the oath of allegiance to the Grand Master and have raised a voice of dissent against the Grand Master's hypocritical announcement of the beginning of "the Era of Ultimate Greatness."

Another such malpractice presented here is one of restricting the freedom of the press and not letting any independent newspaper flourish. It is this state of affairs that prevails in the Grand Master's "City" in the novel. The fact has been brought to light by the Little Star who informs the Professor: "There are two newspapers in this city. One of them is owned by a trust of which the Astrologer is the head. the other is owned by a girl. The girl is five years old and cannot manage a newspaper. It is managed for her by the Master of Rallies. The Master of Rallies also controls the satellite. The satellite controls the radio and the video. The Master of Rallies controls the satellite on the Grand Master's behalf because the satellite is the private property of the Grand Master." (88) It is almost impossible for people trying to find facts through newspapers and radio to find them in a country where such a situation is prevailing. Here people can know only the establishment's version of facts. Since most people are too credulous to distrust the press and the radio, they are misled into accepting the establishment's version and taking fiction as facts. In the novel, the Grand Master and his men are successful in spreading the fiction that Master Bhoma has hatched a conspiracy to unseat the Grand Master.

The press is further restricted in the novel by forcing newsmen not to use their papers against persons in power. It is this malpractice that is being presented when the Rallies Master tells Vasu: "unless his underground daily, *The Rumblings* ceased publication or changed its tune before the Festival of the River, which was only a month away, he would be expelled from the journalists' guild and the businessmen and the little girl who owned the newspaper would be instructed not to give him employment." (74)

Another malpractice adopted to discourage dissent is that of harassing the dissenters and causing them inconveniences in one form or another. It is this malpractice that has been highlighted in the novel when the Grand Master gets the boatman's musical instruments destroyed only because he himself has an "antipathy to music."(48)

Yet another such malpractice is that of cresting a phobia of external and internal threats. It is this malpractice which the Astrologer is using when he is trying to argue the latter into silence and says: "It seems to me, Headman, you have come here only to counter me word for word. Nor does it mean anything to you that there are enemies within and without, that the very existence of the city is in danger." (21) He uses it even in his public speech when he says: "In the darkness of the night there has come a new wave of deadly assassins. Daggers in hand, they have crept out of their holes. They stalk the night, determined to strike at the very root of our lives, at the very heart of the man whose heartbeat is the heartbeat of the city itself." (99)

A barbarous malpractice adopted here in order to suppress dissent is one of disabling the dissenters. This malpractice has taken the form of blinding the Headman, the lady chief of the boatmen. The incident has been reported by the narrator in the following words: "During the night the guards pierced the Headman's eyes with long pointed needles and poured acid into the perforations." (164)

Still another political malpractice to discourage dissent presented here is that of the ruler's trying to restrict the growth of the population of the section of the people who are not loyal to him. The Grand Master tries to freeze the population of the boatmen, as they are politically so conscious that "[a]t the slightest excuse they raise rebellious standards." (15-16) When he issues the orders: "Let their numbers be frozen by law . . . the force of arms if necessary. Nothing else will suffice." (16) The novelist rejects the very thinking behind the philosophy of population-control when he says through the Headman: "You think an ant is born on this earth without God's will? If it is His will that there should be only one child to a mother then surely it shall come to pass. There is no need for the Grand Master or you to pass a law." (19-20) The Headman gives one more argument against the policy of population control: "Is it not true, Astrologer, that the city's granaries are full? And is it not a fact that out of the mud-people the city shall always extract work equal to what it feeds them, even as it is done to the animals?" (20) One may have reservations while agreeing to accept these arguments, but one cannot justify efforts to restrict the growth of one single section of society. However, the system of giving power to one who is supported by the majority of the citizens is very likely to encourage the rulers to try to speed up the growth of their men and to restrict the population of the dissenters and sooner or later the group manipulating the growth of the population of the country or even of the world, irrespective of principles, is likely to come to power and hold it.

One more political malpractice to discourage dissent adopted here is that of laying the blade for every unhappy incident at the dissenters's door irrespective of facts. The wrong-doer blames the victims even for his own repressive measures and, thus, tries to direct the edge of people's anger towards the dissenters. The fact comes to light when one finds the Grand Master blaming every boatman for his having been using the police and the army against the latter: "He forces us to beat him with sticks and fire bullets and lasers into him. He forces us to call out the army."(58) The novelist is ironical here and is laughing at the wrong-doer's blaming the victim for the wrongs heaped on the latter.

The responses of the ruled, as presented in *The City and the River*, range from total surrender to armed struggle. They can be grouped into two broad categories namely those of non-resistance and resistance. The path of surrender falls in the first category and that of struggle of any kind active or passive, physical or intellectual, literary or non-literary can be included in the second category. The path the common people other than the boatmen choose to adopt is that of non-resistance as they do not know what the announcement by the Astrologer implies as the narrator says: "The Astrologer's speech left the people pleased, because they liked big words, but confused. . . . As was their custom, when they did not understand something, the people of the city decided to ignore the speech, to make believe that it had never been made." (18) The narrator's observation that "they did not understand" signifies that in his view those who do not understand the political implications of political steps can do nothing but surrender. Even the boatmen once resolve to surrender and the narrator reports: "When the marigolds pierced the top of the mango grove the boatmen decided to capitulate and take the Astrologer's oath and put their thumb impressions on affidavits of the same." (144) Since this resolution is not transformed into action, it is surrender in resolution and so a temporary adoption of the path of non-resistance. The path that Bhumiputra, the Grand-father, the Professor, Shani, and Shailaja's brother adopt is one of resistance and all of them in one way or the other resist the steps the Grand Master is taking in order to gain more power.

The resistance of the victims presented in the novel is broadly of two kinds: passive and active. Those who do nothing to counter the measures of the Grand Master but at the same time refuse to surrender can be called passive resisters and those who do anything physical or intellectual to counter those measures can be called active resisters. The Grand-father's resistance is an illustration of passive resistance as he does nothing to counter the moves of those wielding power but only keeps Bhumiputra at his rose-farm and puts a few obstructions in the way of the Police Commissioner and the Son when they come to arrest Bhumiputra as a result of which he gets his house destroyed and loses his life along with Bhumiputra.

The active resistance presented in the novel is again of two kinds: physical and intellectual. The resistance of those who take up arms against the oppressor is physical active resistance while the resistance of those who simply educate people and explain to them what is wrong with the Grand Master's policies is intellectual active resistance. For instance, the resistance of the boatmen who take up arms to fight oppression and defend their way of living is physical active resistance. So is Shani's as he too takes up arms against the forces of the Grand Master. But the resistance of Bhumiputra who tells people the symbolic story of the naked king is intellectual active resistance. Even when Bhumiputra drafts a petition and sends the Grand Master a charter of four demands, namely: "One, immediate withdrawal of the Astrologer's oath. Two, return of all the vanished ones. Three, a public trial of all those responsible for the Professor's death and the Headman's blinding. Four, the legalizing of the illegal children as well as the restoration of future children." (187) So is the Headman's resistance when she is trying to persuade the Astrologer to let boatmen live in their own ways: "The boatmen, Astrologer, are children of the great river, and only of the great river. You must have known this when you made that speech. How can we become children of the Grand Master or of anyone else? Your speech upset the boatmen." (19)

The intellectual active resistance presented in the novel is again of two kinds: non-literary and literary. The intellectual active resistance in which the speaker puts his arguments in a straightforward manner is non-literary but the one in which the speaker puts his arguments through their objective correlative "or in an aesthetically appealing manner, is literary. For instance, the resistance of the Professor when he sets up a lottery stall and starts speaking to the crowds to convince them "that Bhoma is innocent" (122) is non-literary, while the resistance of Shailaja's brother who tries to communicate to the crowds through a story that Bhoma is innocent is literary. Of these two, the novelist seems to favour the second one as he shows that the Professor's speeches fail to create the desired effect on the audience while he lauds the way of Shailaja's brother when he says: "With practice the Professor noted, Shailaja's brother's style of narration had undergone a change. He recited the story of the naked king as though it were a ballad out of the city's hoary past and he an ancient bard who had emerged from out of the depths of the Great River to remind the city of a long forgotten truth. By the end of the second day he had begun to sound like the Astrologer when he recited verses in the ancient tongue that no one understood. But everyone understood the young man and listened to him in silence." (129) Since this form of resistance is the most effective one, it can be safely concluded that the novelist stands for it more than for any other form.

The novel embodies the view that one who misuses political power cannot escape undergoing punishment for it even if he succeeds in eliminating all his opponents. In the novel, punishment comes to the offender from nature. Even though none of the men rising against the

Grand Master succeeds in removing him as the Headman is blinded and later, deserted by her own followers, Bhoma's telling people that the king is naked comes to a stop when he comes to stay with the Grand-father and, later on, dies when the Son demolishes the Grand-father's house in an attempt to arrest him, the Professor dies as a result of his fast unto death in prison, and Shailaja's brother immolates himself, there comes in the river a flood in the face of which the king finds himself helpless:

> The waters now reached the top of the fourth hill on which the offices of the new Grand Master stood. A wave went up encircling the base of the building. The touch of chrome and glass seemed to cause a special reaction in the foaming waters because all of a sudden the river was not a river any more. Under the all pervasive glow of the searchlights it turned into an ancient city, like the sea that had first condensed on the whirling planet a billion years ago. Waves nearly as high as the building rose in quick succession and threw a lock around the shining structure. The inmates of the palace shuddered in horror as the new Grand Master's building broke in the middle and floor by floor, frame by frame, fell into the sea. One last wave uprooted the foundations and sent them flying into the sky. The waters swept over the top of the hill and cascaded on to the other side in a loud waterfall. (157-58)

One feels that when human beings have failed, Nature is using water, one of the elements, to punish the guilty. The fact signifies that Arun Joshi posits his faith in, what has come to be known as, the Divine justice.

Now comes the question whether the novel provides a solution to the problem as to what kind of political system is safe for the people. Since the novelist is exposing how a democratic set up can be misused and replaced by dictatorship, it is evident that he stands for neither dictatorship nor democracy. The course of incidents included in the novel signifies that the novelist likes to have a political system in which the ruler does not oppress people, as when the Professor is lying on his death-bed he has a hope: "There will be no Grand Masters. There will be a new world, a new race of men will be born." (167) Besides this, none of the virtuous characters in the novel says categorically as to what kind of political system is better than a democratic system. That signifies that Arun Joshi does not suggest any alternate political system but wishes to have one in which there is no oppression.

The novel has a few weaknesses. One of them is the prophecy in accordance with which incidents occur. The prophecy in question reads as follows:

> Who knows, who can read the signs,
> The workings of immortal time?
> A king I see upon a throne,
> In astronomer's grove the boatmen mourn,
> A thing of darkness growing dark,
> On city walls the shadow's mark.
> The river, I see, from a teacher rise.
> The hermit, the parrot, the teacher die.
> Under a rain the waters burn,
> To his kingdom at last the king returns. (26)

This prophecy is an embodiment of the view that the incidents which are occurring in the city of the novel are occurring because they are destined to occur. But if the incidents are destined to occur, the persons who appear to be making them occur cannot be held responsible for them and so deserve neither rewards nor punishments for them. For example, the Grand Master could have been charged with having declared himself king and, thus, having realized his ambition at the cost of people's civil liberties, cannot be charged with that in the light of the prophecy as the prophet has already written "A king I see upon a throne" and that signifies that the Grand Master is destined to come to the throne as the king of the city. This makes the Grand Master a simple instrument in the hands of destiny and frees him from the blame of any kind. When one has read,

> Finally the Astrologer said, "Grand Master, the time has come to let you know that there exists a prophecy that speeks of the coming of a king. Your dream is the herald that we have been waiting for."

one begins to feel that the Grand Master is a helpless tool in the hands of fate and has been chosen by Fate to declare himself king and so when one comes to the Minister's distorting facts and misguiding his listeners to agree to having a king in the land in the following words,

> As far as peace and stability are concerned, our history clearly indicates that we have been stable only when ruled by a strong yet benevolent king. Nation states and such things have never been understood by the average citizen. He always reserved his allegiance for the monarch. At the same time of course, the monarch took full responsibility for the citizens' material and spiritual needs. In short, gentlemen, what this city needs above all is a monarch, a king. And unless we first provide it with one the disturbances will continue, army or no army. (210)

the whole force of satire behind the speech is lost. If the city is destined to have a king, neither the Grand Master nor the Minister is to blame for his coming into existence and if it is so, there is no point in punishing him for what he has done.

Since it is a part of the prophecy that "A thing of darkness growing dark,/On city walls the shadow's mark," (216) it is evident that the king is destined to become more and more tyrannical and when one comes to the description,

> While the brigadier was soothing his old friends, taking advantage of his absence the "police bastard" had ordered a commando to let Bhoma have a taste of his rifle butt. As the rifle hit his cheek the mathematics teacher felt half a dozen teeth fall onto his tongue. The second blow fell on his ear and his eardrum exploded into his skull. His eyes bulged at the pain but he did not utter a sound. As though a tap had been opened, blood gushed out of his ear and nose. (245)

one cannot lay blame at the door of the authorities as one knows that they are destined to grow dark and the "shadow's mark" is destined to reach the walls of the city.[2]

Likewise, since the prophecy includes the prediction: "The hermit, the parrot, the teacher die," (216) the sacrificial sufferings of the persons opposing the king's tyrannical ways fail to become pathetic because one knows that they are instruments in the hands of fate and are destined to die.

One deserves punishment for a misdeed only if one has chosen to do it of one's absolutely free will. Likewise, one deserves admiration for a noble deed only if one has chosen to do it of one's absolutely free will. If an incident has already been prophesied, it is evident that one is doing a deed as an instrument rather than of one's own free will with the result that none of the characters deserves either blame or praise.

Another weakness of the novel is the novelist's showing that what the Grand Master does is not peculiar to him alone but is a phenomenon that occurs again and again when the Great Yogeshwara tells his disciple: "In the new city is another Professor, another Bhumiputra, another tribe of boatmen. There is also another Council and another set of Councillors. The men have other names but the forces they embody remain unchanged. And into all this when you go you will, perhaps, be known as another Hermit of the Mountain. And it is possible you will have a disciple whose name will be Little Star. To someone this replay, this repetition of things, might appear as a charade, a joke. But, then, whoever said the good Lord did not have humour," (262) one gets the impression that the fault lies not with a person but with the chair because if the fault had been with a particular person, there would have been no repetition. In other words, this reminds one of the popular saying that power corrupts everybody. And if everybody occupying the position of the Grand Master behaves like this Grand Master, the Grand Master, who makes himself king in the novel, cannot be regarded as guilty. And if he is not guilty and all that he does has to occur whoever comes to the chair of the Grand Master, there is no point in blaming him for it. A hero or protagonist has to have free will and is to be presented as facing misfortunes on account of having chosen a wrong path rather than the right one. Unless this is done the hero cannot be charged with having done any wrong.

One may say that the Great Yogeshwara's words, "It is ruled by another Grand Master, which, of course, need not always happen," (262) signify that the novelist does not regard it as inevitable for one to behave like the Grand Master of the novel and so he does give a Grand Master freedom of will and freedom to choose to behave like this Grand Master or otherwise. However, this single line is not in concord with the rest of the passage quoted above, as in every other sentence of the passage he is stressing the fact of repetition. Even the following remark of the Great Yogeshwara to the Nameless-One, "The main thing is to prevent this endless repetition, this periodic disintegration. But to achieve that we need purity," (262) implies that but for the cases of purity, the repetition is inevitable and this implication too implies that most Grand Masters are likely to behave like this Grand Master. One naturally comes to the conclusion that the fault lies with the post rather than the person holding it. However, the strength of the novel lies in passages such as this:

> fear was the greatest ally of the kings and grand masters of the world, for without fear to freeze the hearts and the limbs of their subjects many a throne would have been toppled and many a crown blow off with the breath from the oppressed.
>
> And I saw that where man had thrown off his blanket of fear there alone truth had triumphed and great civilizations flourished and man had taken another step towards God. . . .
>
> This city, this world, all this is the manifestation of the One, and not the shadow of the Grand Master's ego, as the Grand Master might imagine. And it is he, the One without a second, who, secretly supports and guides all that you see, and what you do not see; and what you might have seen through the Professor's telescopes. . . .
>
> There is the upward path that leads to freedom and there is the downward path that, for the moment at least, must lead to perdition. The city is free to choose either. (155-56)

Such utterances as this bring order where disorder has been prevailing.

Another such passage is the following one: "So let not fear sow confusion in your heart. Whatever happens the Lord will not forsake you, nor will work be fruitless. Of this you can be certain." (157) Such utterances as these give people hope and enlightenment and the readers of English literature are not likely to let them die.

NOTES

1. Arun Joshi, *The City and the River* (New Delhi: Vision, 1990), p. 213.
2. Even the Grand Master's dream in which "a vast host of naked men" form a circle like a noose around the Grand Master and the circle tightens "until he could feel their breath of a volcano from out of the depths of the surrounding sea" and he shouts at them, "This hill is mine," (14-15) signifies that the conflict between him and the boatmen is destined to be there, irrespective of what he does.

Archetypal Patterns in *The City and the River*

USHA BANDE

> "Do you hear music, my son?" asked the Great Yogeshwara.
> "Yes, father. And the dancing of a god."
> "That is good. I shall tell you now a tale and in my telling, perhaps, you will know who you are. Listen, this is how it goes."

> "As a first step it will be enough if our people are taught a lesson. Let the fear of the palace – and its laws – be first drummed into them. Let us, I suggest, declare a new era. Let the new era discipline our people and provide new food for their thoughts. Let it lift the darkness from the land and prepare for the glorious dawn of which your dream is a harbinger."

The above two extracts quoted from Arun Joshi's novel *The City and the River*[1] reveal two facts: first, that it is a political satire and second, that it follows the mythical narrational pattern of a story within a story told by an old wise teacher, a *Guru*, to his keen disciple, preparing him for a quest and a mission. Within this thematic and structural framework the apparently simple tale of a city and a river unfolds itself, gaining multi-dimensional meanings; and a discerning reader can read it at many levels: as an exposition of the psychology of the masses, the ruling classes and their sychophant coteries; as an existential commentary on the absurdity of human situation; as a parable of the river and of Time: as a treatise on the question of man's allegiance "to God or to man." (262) While these thematic contents tend to draw the attention of reviewers and scholars, the structural patterns slide into background as being reductive.

However, a close study of the novel reveals the mythic perspective by which it becomes a unifying and integrating literary experience. I, therefore, propose to explore the archetype and their relevance to the structural pattern of the work. In dealing with these, I shall identify archetypal symbols, myths and legends and trace the "collective unconscious" which, despite national and cultural leanings of the novel, help to give it universal appeal. The purpose of this analysis is not to be reductive but to study the use of archetypes as technique and to show the insight of the author in perceiving links between the present situation in the past which gives continuity to human experience.

I

The novel has a Prologue, and Epilogue and nine chapters. The Prologue recounts the last day of the Nameless-One with the Great Yogeshwara, his teacher. On the day of his initiation, the Great Yogeshwara celebrates his pupil's thirtieth birthday by telling him who he (the Nameless-One) is, and after a 250-page eventful account of the city and its final doom, the Great Yogeshwara commissions the Nameless-One, in the Epilogue, to go and prevent the "endless repetition" and "the periodic disintegration" (262)) of the city and its people. The nine chapters enclosed within the beginning and the end contain the story of the Grand Master, his dream and the prophecy. The Grand Master, in order to fulfil his dream of becoming a king, lets his coteries adopt ruthless measures to crush the masses, stifle all dissenting voices and compromise all ethical norms. A corrupt regime where sycophancy, inefficiency, selfishness and nepotism thrive, is revealed to the readers. Finally, power-struggle and in-fighting leads to complete annihilation and the city is doomed.

Nearer home, the events portrayed here have obvious links with the Emergency time in India; at human and universal level, however, it is an exposition of human folly and the futility of human aspirations devoid of moral codes. The novel lashes out at corruption in public life, selfishness of the rulers and the political shenanigans of the cronies. It is interesting to note that the author achieves his goal of delivering his message without giving us psychologically realized characters. One of the charges levelled against the novel by reviewers pertains to Arun Joshi's failure in developing characters. It is felt that characters do not develop spontaneously and that they lack psychological depth. I, however, feel that the author is more interested in depicting archetypes than individuals so as to give mythic proportion to his work. That is probably the reason why the city and the river develop as archetypal symbols.

Apart from the city and the river, the novel makes use of other archetypes such as the old wise man, the great mother, the demonic, apocalyptic and analogical imagery, and quest-motifs which run through the story. We shall now see how the novelist makes use of his archetypal material for a structural pattern to convince the readers of the authenticity of his story woven around a situation without convincing individual characters. We shall also see how the quest-motif moves to give a feeling to the reader that he, instead of the characters in the novel, has accomplished the quest.

II

The sequence of the novel is chronologically arranged. The Prologue and the Epilogue join the beginning and the end. The story ends where it begins and begins where it ends. The entire drama of the rise and fall of the city reminds one of T.S. Eliot's lines: "In my beginning is my end. In succession/Houses rise and fall, crumble, are extended,/Are removed, destroyed, restored." In the beginning of the novel, the city is there "spread along the bank of the river." (12) It has grown over the years, it sees ups and downs, and is ruined by human stupidity. But, that is not an end. On its ruins a new city grows, it has its Grand Master and others. The Great Yogeshwara explains this phenomenon to the Nameless-One, which speaks of human continuity, thus:

> On the ruins of that city, as always happens, a new city has risen. It is ruled by another Grand Master, which, of course, need not always happen. In the new city is another Professor, another Bhumiputra, another tribe of boatmen. There is another Council

> and another set of Councillors. The men have other names but the forces they embody remain unchanged. And into all this when you go you will, perhaps, be known as another Hermit of the Mountain. And it is possible you will have a disciple whose name will be Little Star. (262)

This continuity gives a circular movement to the novel. Moreover, by joining the Prologue to Epilogue, the author ensures a cyclical motion. There is also the prophecy which runs all through the story and on which the action depends. The prophecy, stated as an epigraph and then repeated at the end, embodies linear as well as circular movements.

According to Northrop Frye, the Biblical circular movement forms the universal structure of the human mind. In Indian mythology also, the cycle of life-death-reincarnation implies the cycle from creation to the end and again to the new beginning. This is the apocalyptic rhythm which supplies us with "two epic frameworks: the epic of return and the epic of wrath."[2] Both these cyclical movements are symbolic of the cycle of pre-existence, life-in-death and resurrection. The re-appearance of the Nameless-One signifies a period of future hope for humanity, that the Messiah has the power to come through the esoteric regions which vouchsafe human continuity.

Human continuity is also communicated to the reader through various archetypal symbols. The Hermit is the "old wise man" who is the saviour of the human race. His timely action saves the "illegal" child to be rafted across to the Great Yogeshwara. The child is the chosen one. He is made to pour "Ahuti" in the Hermit's "*Yajna,*" thus purifying himself by fire. The *Yajna* also erases the blasphemy of the Astrologer. After this symbolic act of purification by fire, the Hermit plans the child's future course and reveals the regions beyond the Seven Hills to the crowd. The glow of the peak dazzles the people. This shows the Hermit's own purification by the fire of the *Yajna*; he hears the celestial music and gets ready to face the ordeal by water. The great waters engulf him. That the Nameless-One should be the future Hermit is an indication of psychological rebirth of the Hermit. Symbolically, it is his march toward development of personality.

Other archetypal symbols working in the novel are those of the Great Yogeshwara, the Nameless-One, and the hierarchy of pupils. The Great Yogeshwara is the "Puran Purusha," and his pupil, the Nameless-One, is symbolic of Manu on the raft, on the day of the Great Deluge--*Pralaya*--saving the Vedas (signified by the little box containing the prophecy). From another angle, the Great Yogeshwara is Lord Krishna telling his pupil the gospel of "duty" and revealing to him the mystery of existence and of the cosmos. This is particularly obvious when the Great Yogeshwara gives him "a heady elixir" and when he drains the elixir, the Nameless-One feels "as vast as the sky and as tall as the mountain," and hears a "music," (11) a melody coming from beyond the stars. It is only after this revelation that the pupil appears to be ready for his initiation.

The Nameless-One is also a Christ-figure. He is an "illegal" child but he is the chosen one. He is sent with a mission to purify the city of its "egoism, selfishness and stupidity." (263) Both, the Great Yogeshwara and the Nameless-One are "instruments . . . of the great God . . . who is the Master of the Universe." (264) All these archetypal symbols, though different in their origin and appeal, become communicable images and unify the literary experience. The scheme of things, as narrated by the Great Yogeshwara, is ageless – the Nameless-One is the Hermit of the future city, he will have Little Star as his pupil, there will be a Professor whose student will be Bhumiputra and there will be a parrot. The first three in the lineage, the Great Yogeshwara, the Nameless-One and the Little Star stand for divine activity; the Professor and Bhoma represent the human spirit; and the parrot signifies the spirit of nature. Together they suggest the moral neutrality of the world of nature as also the mystery of the world which eludes human understanding. This mystery is glimpsed but never seen. It forms a rapport between the divine and the human world which illustrates the movement from innocence to experience.

Running parallel to these archetypes is the symbol of the great mother – the river. It is interesting to note that the novel does not have a memorable female figure, least of all a mother-figure. The "headman" of the boat people is a woman, but she does not have the feminine touch. Shailaja is referred to at several places but she fails to be a palpable presence. Only the river is the moving, loving, protecting force to whom the boatmen owe full allegiance. For them the river "is a symbol of the divine mother. Of God himself." (22) The boatmen are her "children" and they are ready to die for her. On her part, the great river speaks to its children when they are in trouble. The Professor often hears her. He instinctively turns to her for help. The Professor appears almost a *Bhishma*-figure seeking help from his mother, Ganga, in the *Mahabharata.* The Hermit performs his *Yajn*a to purify the "mother, the great river." (249) The river is the protecting mother, but in her most terrible aspect she can be destructive. She sustains the city and destroys it when it becomes too overbearing. That, however, does not mean that she is life-negating. In fact, she is life-enhancing. On her bosom the child is borne to the Great Yogeshwara so that he is trained and sent to yet another city as its saviour. Taken as an Indian archetype, the river is mother *Ganga*. As a universal archetype, she is the "water of life."[3] The river is the life-line of the city. Like blood circulating in the human body, it circulates through the city. Questers turn to it to venture forth on its current.

Questers seek forth, in the novel, for several reasons. Bhoma goes out in search of peace of mind after the disturbing events. The boatmen go far off on the waters for their livelihood. The Hermit of the Mountain seeks knowledge in isolation and he comes back to save the child for the benefit of the human race. The real quester, however, is the Nameless-One. The raft carries him as an illegal child and brings him back as an illumined one. The Nameless-One seeks knowledge during his discipleship with the Great Yogeshwara and comes back in the same raft to restore peace and order amid chaos. He is thus a Messianic-figure whose mysterious birth is followed by an epiphany and who is trained to face setbacks, betrayals and the final sacrifice.

Apocalyptic, demonic and analogical symbolism also runs through the novel ensuring structural richness. The title itself delineates the world of water and the world of buildings. The city is the living presence and so is the river. The city makes its own "horoscope" and has its egoism and stupidity for which it suffers. It has its buildings, gardens, avenues and Seven Hills – features that make it a throbbing reality. When identified with apocalyptic symbolism, the city is the city of God because as Northrop Frye maintains, the apocalyptic world presents the categories of reality in the form of human desire, "as indicated by the form they assume under the work of human civilization."[4] But, when the city is associated with its buildings and other man-made things, the apocalyptic imagery is displaced to make it an earthly place. The city is a human world where the Grand Master and his people are engaged in their human activities. This human world has two dialectically opposing forces operating within: the apocalyptic and the demonic. Apocalyptic imagery is appropriate for its mythical structure. The grandfather's rose garden, for example, is a state of innocence: it is destroyed by the Satanic forces of the Grand Master's son. The Seven Hills are symbolic of both mythic heights from where a ruler is supposed to rule, and of the demonic regime which sinister forces bring on human beings to inflict suffering on them. The city has its dungeons, known as Gold Mines. Here, men are interned and destroyed. This reminds one of Dante's *Inferno*, which is symbolic of the hell man creates on earth to torture others. The Grand Master, his men and his demonic machinery create a "sinister" world. They demand sacrifices, punish the rebels, enforce obedience and destroy life. Theirs is a demonic world in which "society is held together by a kind of molecular tension of egos."[5] Here, one "individual pole is the tyrant-leader, inscrutable, ruthless, melancholy and with an insatiable will, who commands loyalty . . . the other pole is the *Pharmakos* or sacrificed victim who has to be killed to strengthen the others." In its demonic image, the city becomes the city of destruction, a great ruin of pride.

The City and the River works on three district levels: mythic, primitive and modern. The mythic elements are represented by the Great Yogeshwara, the Nameless-One, the Hermit, the Little Star, and the river; the primitive forces are signified by the boatmen, their rites and rituals; the modern components are illustrated by the weapons, the lasers and other engines of war which are, in fact, ultra-modern. These three factors unite the structure of the novel. Mythical parallels, woven with the lived reality, raise certain controversial issues and give the work an existential depth. Arun Joshi creates the measured rhythms of myths, legends and archetypes to make his work realistic despite the absence of psychologically-realized characters. As a realistic fiction, the novel becomes an indictment of social and political chicanery; at the archetypal level, its rhetoric builds up the tempo of quest. By the time a reader finishes the story, he achieves a sense of having completed a quest. It is a universal human quest for purity through the sacrifice of ego. The question is not of individual success or failure but of collective efforts for the common good.

NOTES

1. Arun Joshi, *The City and the River* (New Delhi: Vision, 1990)
2. Northrop Frye, *Anatomy of Criticism* (Princeton: Princeton Univ. Press, 1957), p. 317.
3. *Ibid.*, p. 146.
4. *Ibid.*, p. 141.
5. *Ibid.*, p. 147.
6. *Ibid.*, p. 148.

Towards Authenticity: A Study of *The City and the River*

SUBHASH CHANDRA

Ostensibly, *The City and the River* marks a departure from the existing oeuvre of Arun Joshi, inasmuch as it delineates the political shenanigans indulged in by the rulers of the city. There are unambiguous parallels between the Emergency regime in India and the one portrayed in the novel. These are consolidation of power by the Grand Master (the Head of the City) to the extent of anointing himself as the King with unlimited powers, coronation of his son as the heir apparent, presence of a coterie of self-seeking, aggrandizing (but basically hostile) sycophants who pay scraping homage to the Grand Master and who constantly misguide him, the political clout wielded by the Astrologer who guides and decides the destinies of the elite and the common folks alike, the Triple Way or the Three Beatitudes enunciated by the Astrologer to the boatmen, compulsive family planning and, above all, the very close similarity between what the Emergency was projected as (an era of progress and prosperity) and the Era of Ultimate Greatness promulgated by the Grandmaster, thereby arrogating for the administration more drocanion powers than hitherto possessed by it. The Era of Ultimate Greatness is heralded by the arrest of a boatman's wife for having born an illegal child (more than two children in a family was considered a legal offence) and the arrest of a clown on a flimsy ground. Using the strategies of allegory, irony and satire, Joshi dexterously weaves a tale which is a mixture of fantasy and stark realism with a view to communicating the horrors and terror that are unleashed on a society, when a handful of individuals become overly ambitious and selfish. Cruelty and corruption, violence and destruction, hypocrisy and lies come to dominate the political and administrative fabric of society in which people's lives turn into fodder for the cannons of the rulers's aggrandizing competitiveness. The political vision incorporates the message that once the rulers resort to tyranny for their own ends, suspicion and distrust mark the relations amongst themselves and each plots to destroy the other in order to go up the ladder of power--even the Grand Master's position has eyes rivetted on it.

The contention of this paper, however, is that *The City and the River* does not constitute a departure from Joshi's penchant for exploring the existential predicament of man in his works. There exists almost a complete unanimity amongst Joshi's critics about this aspect of his fiction. Stressing the distinctiveness of Joshi's novels from those of Mulk Raj Anand, R.K. Narayan, Raja Rao, Bhabani Bhattacharya, Kamala Markandaya, Nayantara Sahgal, Manohar Malgonkar and Chaman Nahal, Madhusudan Prasad observes that "They [Joshi's novels] are singularized by certain existentialist problems and the resultant anger, agony, psychic quest and the like."[1] Inna Walter, commenting on *The Last Labyrinth*, says that "Arun Joshi plunges deeper into the depths of the eternal queries that have perplexed man's consciousness from time immemorial."[2] "Most of Arun Joshi's heroes are alienated beings,"[3] observes Ramesh K. Srivastava. One could agree with R.K. Dhawan who believes that "Joshi's 'fictional world' is a revelation of a world where man is confronted by the self and the questions of his existence."[4] *The City and the River* focusses on the aspect of authenticity (one of the most significant elements of existentialism) in the lives of individuals who are caught in the flux of the complicated business of living. Herein lies the difference between Joshi's earlier works and *The City and the River*.

The political scenario becomes both the backdrop and an active agent in the drama that unfolds as the novel progresses, making the question of authenticity acquire significance in the lives of both the people and the city. Absurdity, anarchy, meaninglessness, emptiness, alienation and despair are some of the characteristic features of the existential philosophy, but the most important element which stresses the sanctity of the subjective individuality is the authenticity of the self. Enmeshed in the debilitating and circumscribing ambience, constantly aware of the inevitability and finality of death, the existentialist gets neither incapacitated by the enveloping dread of death, nor does he take refuge in what Sartre terms Bad Faith. He creates his own values which determine the structure of his life, rejecting with conviction the "theory of psychological determinism," and leading an authentic existence which Sartre regards as "the new and absolute virtue in existentialism."

II

The social stratification of the City is signified by the altitude at which the different classes live. The Grand Master, the Ministers (who also act as his Councillors), whose social superiority is matched by the geographical height, live and administer the City from the Seven Hills (which are the highest in the City) varying in height according to the status of the Ministers, with the Grand Master living on the highest hill. The middle class people live on a comparatively lower ground in pink brick buildings. The lowly poor, including the boatmen, inhabit the area along the river bank which is the lowest in altitude. The level of authenticity varies in inverse proportion to the social position of the different categories of inhabitants. When the Era of Ultimate Greatness is declared by the Grand Master, apparently for the welfare and prosperity of the City (but actually to consolidate his own position and to pave the way for the realization of his dream of becoming the King), the elite Ministers, and Councillors practise Bad Faith. Their collusion with the Grand Master in propounding and practising the principles of The Era of Ultimate Greatness is conscious and willing. They are aware of the wrongness of what they are doing, but they still go on faithfully (in fact, more energetically than necessary) implementing all that is handed out to them by the Grand Master. The Minister of Trade, the Education Adviser, the Master of Rallies, the Astrologer, the Commissioner of Police, the Commander of the Army, General Starch, represent the group of people lacking in authenticity; they fail to probe the nature of their "freedom"--freedom to become "for-itself" or "in-itself." Valorizing freedom, Sartre asserts that man may choose to be "nothing" like a "table" or may choose "to reach above the stars."[5] The middle classes, living in the colony of brick houses, adjust to the circumstances (though they are not shown to compete with one another to please the rulers), and do not protest, and to this extent they, too, lack authenticity. Marjorie Grene, for instance, has this to say about authenticity: "The concept of authenticity is not a concept of adjustment--in fact with respect to the current ideal of the well-adjusted member of society it is truly and deeply a heresy."[6] Among the bureaucrats, there are some who slowly come to confront the reality of their situation, begin to chafe under the burden of Bad Faith, and eventually break down. Dharma's father, a high official in the administration, and Dharma himself, a police officer, have nervous breakdowns on account of the realization of the loss of their authenticity. Dharma's father becomes a complete wreck and begins to vegetate, while Dharma, after his breakdown, begins to imagine himself a boatman and dresses himself accordingly (perhaps to atone for the excesses he has committed in his official capacity).

It is only the poor boatmen, living in the mud huts along the river bank, who have the courage to lead an authentic existence, and are prepared to pay whatever price is involved in doing so. Commenting upon the honesty and courage of the boatmen, the Grand Master's father had once cautioned him: "They are not as simple as they seem. . . . They consider themselves to be the children of the river, and to the river, and river alone do they hold allegiance. They believe, unfortunately, with their hearts, and *for their beliefs they are willing to die. And don't let their poverty mislead you into believing that they can be bought*."[7] These boatmen refuse to work for anyone except for themselves. The Grand Master on his tours finds them ignoring him which is rather irritating to him because while others readily salute him, the boatmen "simply stare out of dark unblinking eyes as though he were a stranger." (14)

Inherent in the question of authenticity is the element of liberty or freedom. Is man free from fear of the threats that constantly lurk in the environment, or is he seeking out strategies of survival by compromising his freedom? Is man in bondage of the dread of death, which is the irrevocable certainty, or does he understand the nature of existence and, as Heidegger puts it, he comes to the inner realization that his "own past must take shape and significance in relation to" his "inevitable last tomorrow."[8] For Heidegger, "genuine existence is existence which dares to face death."[9] The boatmen assiduously safeguard their authenticity in Heideggerian sense inasmuch as they mock the threats and dangers hurled on them by the Grand Master and his coterie. They openly refuse to kow-tow to the Astrologer and boldly defy him, refusing to take the oath of allegiance to the Grand Master. Of course, they have to pay a heavy price for their recalcitrance, and their resistance. Their Headman (who is a woman) is the symbol and repository of strength, courage, honesty and commitment to freedom. In her hoary wisdom, she understands the phoniness of the Astrologer's speech to the boatmen. She challenges the intentions of the Grand Master whose mouthpiece the Astrologer is and insists that the welfare of the boatmen is merely a facade, hiding the fact of repression to be practised on the poor. They (the poor) are required to practise family planning and more than one child to a mother and more than two children to a family are declared illegitimate in the name of shortage of foodgrains. But the Headman queries: "Is it not true Astrologer, that the city's granaries are full? And is it not a fact that out of the mud-people the city shall always extract work equal to what it feeds them even as it is done to the animals, even though that cannot be said of the brick-people or of their children?" (20) There is, in fact, no shortage of food, but only that the mud-people are poor and cannot afford to buy the stuff which is easily available to the brick people and the ruling elite. The boatmen follow the path shown by their Headman and defy the Triple Way intended to fortify the position of the Grand Master and bind the people to the repressive laws unleashed in the wake of The Era of Ultimate Greatness.

The Era of Ultimate Greatness turns into the Era of gloom and suppression for the boatmen. The Commissioner of Police swings into action at the instance of the Astrologer and the nightly activity of arresting the defiant boatmen, who had refused to take the oath of allegiance to the Grand Master, is launched. Every night a few boatmen vanish; they are transported to the Gold Mines--the dark, dingy, suffocating underground jail where a long detention causes a slow but steady decay of body and mind and where "the idea of the self [is] suitably dissolved." (161) A representative case of the authenticity of the mud-people is the old man, Patanjali. He is arrested as a substitute of Bhumiputra (Master Bhoma) because he is not available for arrest.

The rule of the New Era is: if the actual person evades arrest, then his immediate neighbour would be picked up. Patanjali's boldness is revealed when he is told by Dharma, the arresting police officer, that he has only to apologize and he would be set free. Patanjali replies: "But why should I apologize? I have done no wrong. Rather the Grand Master should apologize for making such absurd rules."(26) The other boatmen follow in his footsteps. They are picked up by the police, incarcerated in the ghoulish Gold Mines, fired upon and killed, but they do not buckle under. The boatmen prove the authenticity of their selves in Sartrean terms. As Sartre says: "For the secret of a man is not his Oedipus complex or his inferiority complex: it is the limit of his own liberty, his capacity for resisting fortune and death."[10] Their liberty flows from their resistance, and therefore they remain free in their incarceration.

Bhumiputra again is a mud-hut man who stands for all those who are opposed to the dictatorial, self-serving regime of the Grand Master and his cohorts. Having gone underground for some time, he gives jitters and justification to the ruling elite to perpetuate repression on people in the name of a conspiracy (of which Bhoma is alleged to be the lynchpin) against the City. Bhoma is engaged in relating to the boatmen and others the parable of the naked king (the famous parable of the king walking publicly with no clothes) which through subtle ramifications conveys the moral nakedness or bankruptcy of the Grand Master who bears down on the City and its inhabitants with a heavy hand. Bhoma largely succeeds in enlightening the people about the tyrannical nature of the Grand Master's rule and rousing them to open revolt, though eventually he along with others is mowed down in an operation commanded by the King's (erstwhile Grand Master's) son. There are some brick-people, too, who are concerned about the authenticity of their selves. There is the Professor, interested in astronomy, (whose pupil Bhoma had been) who gives up everything, including his life, to search Bhoma, who is suspected to have been picked up by the police in one of their secret, nightly swoops. The Professor persists in making enquiries, writing out representations and meeting the higher echelons of power to find out the whereabouts of Bhoma. When in spite of the warnings to desist from doing so he continues with his search, he is consigned to the Gold Mines, where he languishes to death. The Grandfather, Dharma's father's father, who symbolically nurtures exotic, unique roses on his farm in a city otherwise blighted and barren, is yet another person who dares to oppose the will of the powerful rulers. It is the Grandfather who courageously keeps Bhoma at his farm, risking his own life and liberty. Ultimately he, along with Dharma, Shailaja and Bhoma, dies in the extensive attack launched by the armed forces in conjunction with the police.

III

The question of authenticity against castrating and corrupting influences operating in society has dominated the modern and post-modern literatures all over the wold. The self which came to be threatened with the rise of industrialism and commercialism, together with corporate capitalism in Western Europe made the aspect of authentic existence an important issue. The Angry Young Men (novelists of protest and rebellion) in England, and Black Humour and Absurd Movements in America underline the need to protect the authenticity of the self against the determining categories symbolized by power of the state, the military bureaucracy, and constricting social institutions. Arun Joshi, therefore, in his novel, *The City and the River*, is dealing with the universal predicament of the modern man, beseiged as he is by debilitating forces.

The novelist deftly evokes the devilish and barren nature of the City through a description of the Palace which houses the administrative offices, as well. The palace lawns were all "brown and yellow. No trees. No flowers. Not a patch of green," (31) and even though there was "so much water," yet there was "no grass or flowers." (36) All this is reminiscent of Eliot's *The Waste Land* which contains similar imagery to emphasize the nature of the modern existence. The all-pervasive violence that overshadows the world of the novel is forecast in the cruelty of the karate practice in which the Education Adviser's son (the chief of the students's force) kills his adversary. He gloats over it to the Professor: "I broke his neck. He is dead," and when the Professor, who has gone to seek help for searching Bhoma, expresses disbelief, the son adds proudly and nonchalantly: "Absolutely. The third man I have killed this month." (32) The throne of the Grand Master has legs which significantly taper into "the paws of a lion." Also, it is the "crimson" colour which covers the throne and its canopy. The dark deed of arresting the innocent citizens is perpetrated in the blackness of night. And when the cruelty and violence unleashed on the citizens reaches climax, a storm rises, the sky turns black, the river swells and, turning into an irrepressible ocean, sweeps away all–the powerful rulers and everybody and everything else.

A brooding somberness constitutes the core of the novelist's vision. The boatmen and a few others choose to preserve the authenticity of their selves, but it is at the cost of their lives. And eventually, the city containing both the victims and the victimizer gets wiped out, obliterating the distinction between the two. However, there is a subtle infusion from affirmation and hope in the prophecy the Great Yogeshwara makes about the emergence of another city with another Grand Master and his (the Great Yogeshwara's) sending his disciple, the Nameless-One, to teach people to fight for their freedom and authenticity. The oppression goes on, but so does the fight against it.

NOTES

1. Madhusudan Prasad, "Arun Joshi," *Indian English Novelists: An Anthology of Critical Essays*, ed. Madhusudan Prasad (New Delhi: Sterling, 1982), p. 51.
2. Inna Walter, "Arun Joshi's Vision of Life, Love, God and Death in *The Last Labyrinth*," *Studies in Indian Fiction in English*, ed. G.S. Balarama Gupta (Gulbarga: JIWE Publications, 1987), p. 46.
3. Ramesh K. Srivastava, *Six Indian Novelists in English* (Amritsar: Guru Nanak Dev University, 1987), p. 312.
4. R.K. Dhawan, ed., *The Fictional World of Arun Joshi* (New Delhi: Classical, 1986), p. 18.
5. Walter Kaufmann, ed. and trans., *Existentialism: From Doestoevsky to Sartre* (New York: New American Library, 1975), p. 47.
6. Marjorie Grene, "Authenticity: An Existential Virtue," *Ethics*, Vol. LXII, No. 4 (July 1952), p. 270.

7. Arun Joshi, *The City and the River* (New Delhi: Vision, 1990), p. 14. Emphasis added.
8. Marjorie Grene, p. 266.
9. Idem.
10. Quoted in Marjorie Grene, p. 274.

The City and the River: A Critical Review

ANUP BENIWAL

The City and The River, Arun Joshi's latest novel, is both a continuation of and departure from his earlier fictional endeavours. In his earlier works, Arun Joshi was mainly preoccupied with the existential predicament of his protagonists in an apparently indifferent and hostile world. This predilection of Arun Joshi still persists in *The City and the River* but now his canvas has widened and the crisis of an individual has been replaced by the socio-political and existential crisis of the "City" and by implication of the whole humanity. In this novel, Arun Joshi still raises his favourite questions about faith, commitment and identity. But these questions are now being analyzed from the standpoint of politics--an area hitherto untouched by him. Like a master craftsman, Arun Joshi with his keen insight and mature understanding of his subject matter dexterously weaves a graphic and poignant tale of modern day politics, thus raising the novel to a level of politico-allegorical satire.

The main plot of the novel is structured around an all-too-obvious premise of power struggle and behind-the-scene manipulations and intrigues on the part of the ruler in collaboration with his coterie to keep not only the ruled but also the secondary centres of power under his rule, and the consequent repercussions this policy has on the human beings at large.

However, this simple tale is imbued with universal and eternal significance. The whole action which unfolds itself in a "Nowhere and hence Everywhere City" is narrated through the Great Ageless Yogeshwara to the Nameless-One--the two symbolic figures--as a recurring myth of regeneration and decay, while initiating him into his life-mission.

This "City"--ruled by a line of hereditary Grand Masters from the "Seven Hills"--is located on the bank of the "River," and is inhabited by "The mud-people" and "the brick-people." Ostensibly under the pretext of ushering in a welfare state but in reality impelled by his own over-bearing ego, ambition and selfishness and compulsions of an ancient prophecy, the Grand Master in connivance with the Astrologer issues a decree whereby the allegiance of the people to "The Three Beatitudes" is made compulsory. Seeing through the Grand Master's design, the boatmen led by their head, the professor and eventually Bhumiputra refuse to fall in line with the Seven Hills. This refusal precipitates and accentuates the central conflict of the novel--the conflict between the City and the River, between the Grand Master and the boatmen; between manipulative ideology and instinctive faith; between the urge to dominate and the urge to assert one's identity and between allegiance to man and allegiance to God.

This conflict develops through a series of symbolic and ironic incidents--incidents that are chilling, repelling, bewildering, incredulous but always thought-provoking. The whole narrative is wrapped in an ambience where sophisticated scientific gadgetry co-exists with magical feats, where fact merges with fantasy and where the time present merges with the time past to project its legacy ominously into the time future. Finally the whole thing is dissolved into a mighty deluge. But this cyclic march of humanity continues. A new city springs up on the ruins of the old. The River flows on and the Seven Hills continue to rule.

The novel, however, ends on an optimistic note and certainly enlarges the vision of the reader by making him aware of the causes of this eternal conflict and suggesting panacea in the form of Great Yogeshwara's advice to the Namelss-One.

The novel though an enriching experience is not without its drawbacks. The characters do not develop spontaneously and lack psychological depth. The narrative moves with slow pace in the beginning and strains reader's patience and intelligence but eventually it gains momentum.

Nevertheless, the novel is a powerful and pungent comment on the political scenario that was, that has been and that shall be. This novel surely claims a pride of place among the political novels of the day.

Contributors

Joy Abraham, S. Battery, Kerala

Usha Bande, H.P. University

Anup Beniwal, M.D. University

Subhash Chandra, University of Delhi

R.K. Dhawan, University of Delhi

Thakur Guruprasad, Garhwal University

M.G. Hegde, Kumta

O.P. Mathur, B.H.U., Varanasi

Mahendra Kumar Mohanty, Salipur

R.S. Pathak, H.S. Gour University

Usha Pathania, H.P. University

V.V.N. Rajendra Prasad, S.K. University

D. Prempati, University of Delhi

K. Radha, Kerala University

G. Rai, Gorakhpur University

Rekha Rani, M.L.N. College, Radaur

V. Gopal Reddy, Kakatiya University

Brahma Dutta Sharma, Kumaun University

Susheel Kumar Sharma, G.B. Pant University

Index